Discoveries from the Fortepiano

Discoveries from the Fortepiano

A Manual for Beginning and Seasoned Performers

Donna Louise Gunn

OXFORD
UNIVERSITY PRESS

OXFORD

UNIVERSITY PRESS

Oxford University Press is a department of the University of
Oxford. It furthers the University's objective of excellence in research,
scholarship, and education by publishing worldwide.

Oxford   New York

Oxford is a registered trademark of Oxford University Press
in the UK and certain other countries.

Published in the United States of America by
Oxford University Press
198 Madison Avenue, New York, NY 10016

Library of Congress Cataloging-in-Publication Data
Gunn, Donna Louise, 1960–
Discoveries from the fortepiano : a manual for beginning
and seasoned performers / Donna Louise Gunn.
pages cm
Includes bibliographical references and index.
ISBN 978–0–19–939663–4 (hardcover : alk. paper)—
ISBN 978–0–19–939664–1 (pbk. : alk. paper)
1. Piano—Instruction and study.   I. Title.
MT220.B13 2015
786.2′193—dc23
2014039836

1 3 5 7 9 8 6 4 2
Printed in the United States of America
on acid-free paper

To Claire and Brad:
beacons of "unfettered joy in discovery"

CONTENTS

FOREWORD

Each period of keyboard history has been accompanied by treatises and guidelines to performance. Bach's son, Carl Philipp Emanuel, wrote his exhaustive *Versuch über die wahre Art das Clavier zu spielen* in an attempt to inform keyboard performers on issues of ornamentation, articulation, fingering, and figured bass realization. Similarly, several such treatises were written in the late eighteenth century to facilitate an understanding of performance principles on the new fortepiano, most notably the *Klavierschule* by Daniel Gottlob Türk.

These documents were written to articulate the correct interpretation of the keyboard music of their time. In the twenty-first century, ours is a more complex problem. We play on a modern grand piano, yet the keyboard music by Bach was played on an organ, a harpsichord, or a clavichord. Our instruments are considerably different from the fortepiano of Mozart's time, and we are confronted with a multitude of questions about the performance of that music. What did it really sound like? How was the construction and touch different from our pianos? Can we replicate that sound on a modern instrument? Should we even try to do so? We hold vague generalizations about classical performance practices: less pedal, limited dynamic range, more transparent texture. But most piano teachers and students have not had opportunity to practice and perform on a fine fortepiano, so our impressions of that sound and touch approximate guess-work. We are deprived of the thrill that comes from playing a fortepiano and hearing the delicate nuances that the instrument can provide.

Discoveries from the Fortepiano by fortepianist Donna Gunn is the product of years of reading and research, practice, attending seminars, and instruction with world-famous fortepianists. She is steeped in a practical understanding of the instrument and the intimate relationship between the sound of the fortepiano and the music written for that instrument. Gunn is both a performer and a teacher, and she has accumulated vast experience in conveying those principles of performance practice to students, teachers, and performers who play the piano. Now we benefit from those years of research, performance, and teaching in the form of this thorough study of the keyboard music of the Classical Era.

Discoveries from the Fortepiano is written for those of us who are interested in increasing our knowledge of the piano music of Mozart's time. Gunn leads us gently and progressively through the considerations we must make as we attempt to improve our understanding and performance skills of this important era of keyboard history. Here we have a guide to which we will return frequently for a review of the principles she so carefully outlines.

William S. Newman, noted scholar on the history of the sonata and Beethoven specialist, advised pianists that our obligation is to study the sources, understand the context, and then make informed decisions about the performance of these Classical Era piano compositions. Gunn follows in that tradition. In this examination of Classical Era performance practices, she informs us through numerous citations from musicians of the time about proper approaches to rhythmic interpretation, tempo considerations, ornamentation, pedal, fingering, articulation, and phrasing. Like Newman, instead of demanding a strict protocol of performance, the author offers numerous options and invites exploration. Through her guidance the reader learns to listen carefully, consider various possibilities, and draw personal conclusions.

When contemporary pianists and piano teachers read a book on eighteenth-century performance practices, we may become overwhelmed with the plethora of information on the approach to the various elements that comprise that style. However, it is refreshing to realize that eighteenth-century pedagogues placed their highest priority on expressive interpretation. *Affekt* is the word that appears most frequently in this text: projecting the music with its intended emotional content. Gunn maintains this focus throughout her book and measures every consideration of interpretation against the criterion of *Affekt:* do your choices convey the intended emotion?

Discoveries from the Fortepiano is aptly named, for through Gunn's thoughtful guidance, we discover. The focus of this book is limited to the performance of late-eighteenth-century keyboard music. It is because of this concentration that we learn most effectively. At the end of each chapter, Gunn provides the reader with "The Lesson." The same short quote from a Mozart dance provides the musical example of "The Lesson." Gunn poses questions about the performance of that dance on the basis of the chapter's discussion: for instance, how to phrase, how to articulate, possible ornamentation, fingering, and changes of sound stimulated by the changing texture. Like all good teachers, she helps us turn principles of understanding into practical application.

We discover, and we learn!

Marvin Blickenstaff

PREFACE

While attending one of the lectures from the Norman and Jane Geske Lectureship in the History of the Arts series at the University of Nebraska–Lincoln several years ago, I had the opportunity to hear guest speaker Bart van Oort present his topic, "To Speak or Sing: Mozart and Beethoven on the Fortepiano." For decades I had been aware of but not completely invested *in* historical performance practice. I was intrigued. From van Oort's one-hour presentation and accompanying booklet, many questions surrounding eighteenth-century repertoire that had plagued me for years were answered. A fantastic "ah ha" erupted in my mind. I immediately went to work, applying the concepts to my playing.

After much research, study at the fortepiano, and experimentation on the modern piano, I began to better comprehend this "new" language and its implications to me as a modern pianist. I also came to understand the cause of the frustration so many feel today—attempting to use twenty-first-century norms on eighteenth-century repertoire to limited satisfaction. Another "ah ha" moment and a transformative seed was planted.

Although there exist many primary tutors and treatises that outline eighteenth-century performance practice and several excellent interpretive resources to explain the sources, I found nothing to bring together the historical information to succinctly and simply make sense of the language. Means to apply the language to modern pianos were even more limited, and pedagogical guidance was almost nonexistent.

Thus, the impetus behind this book: to provide tools (rather than rules) to achieve a sound aesthetic—eighteenth-century style—in good taste. It is my desire to take the unaware or disheartened musician and offer tools to unearth personal discoveries that are based on historical content in context. It is my hope that the ideas presented in these pages will compel the reader to discover relevant historical information that will impact personal understanding of eighteenth-century style, facilitate comprehension of how the language was interpreted, and provide the means to make application and create new meaning on the modern piano. For it has been my experience as a performing artist and master teacher that we hunger for knowledge. We play meaningfully and joyfully when the language is understood and is our own.

The voice chosen for this book is conversational and pedagogical. The intention is to present a passionate exchange of ideas from one seeker to another. Most of the text is in present tense, ever-reminding us that we are called to a new *living* language. A language that may be passed on to the next generation of seekers through the Lesson section of each chapter.

Turn the page to encounter your *Discoveries from the Fortepiano.*

ACKNOWLEDGMENTS

To all who have contributed, may you feel my gratitude for your part in my discoveries, which may now lead others to speak a centuries-old language with authenticity and new life. Although it is impossible to mention everyone specifically, I wish to take notice and thank Music Teachers National Association, Nebraska Music Teachers Association, and the Piano Technicians Guild for funding portions of my research; the University of Nebraska–Lincoln Music Library and Lincoln City Libraries–Polley Music Library for their extensive primary source and scholarly interpretive holdings; and the University of Nebraska–Lincoln Glenn Korff School of Music for access to their Belt-Walter fortepiano.

Special recognition is expressed to all the outstanding musicians along the way—particularly Malcolm Bilson, Audun Ravnan, and Bart van Oort—from whom I have learned much. I have been awakened to new truths and challenged to formulate my own authenticity. The combination of these varied experiences have culminated in new discoveries; some planned and some that burst forth surprisingly.

I extend deep appreciation to Dr. Ann Chang, Artist-In-Residence at the University of Nebraska–Lincoln and Artistic Director at the Lied Center for Performing Arts, and Jill Timmons, Oxford University Press Author and Principal/Founder of Artsmentor, LLC (a music performance consulting firm), for graciously reading the first draft of this book as well as continually offering guidance, wisdom, and selfless support.

Heartfelt gratitude to Oxford University Press (OUP) for its commitment to scholarly pedagogical work. Suzanne Ryan's dedication to expanding the vision of music holdings at OUP benefits us all. Todd Waldman's creative vision in the incubation stage of this book was inspiring. He saw something much bigger than I could have imagined on my own. Lisbeth Redfield and Suzanne Ryan's expertise, advice, and encouragement throughout the process made this book possible.

Finally, I thank my parents for the gift of music, my family and friends for their unending support, and the countless students from whom I have been blessed to learn and with whom I have had the joy of including in my discoveries.

ABOUT THE COMPANION WEBSITE

www.oup.com/us/discoveriesfromthefortepiano

Oxford has created a website to accompany *Discoveries from the Fortepiano*. Material that cannot be made available in a book, namely, in-depth discussion beyond the scope of print, diagrams, and tables to illustrate topics, and instructive recordings of examples to bring the written language to auditory life, is provided here. The reader is encouraged to consult this resource in conjunction with the chapters. Examples available online are indicated in the text with Oxford's symbol ⊙.

Discoveries from the Fortepiano

CHAPTER 1

✺

Urgency—Why Bother?

*Our strong desire for knowledge and musical honesty
makes us go back to the fortepiano.*

As conscientious twenty-first-century musicians, we desire to carry
the composer's message. To the best of our ability, we strive to understand the instrument on which we perform and the score from which
we play. Focusing our attention on these goals alone may very well bring
artistic playing and professional success. So, if we are playing artistically
and with success, why would we bother to turn to the fortepiano, eighteenth-century music notational language, and eighteenth-century performance practice? The question is best answered with a question. Does
artistic playing alone ensure that the composer's message is being considered in each performance?

This is the urgency of this book: to uncover the composer's message
through exploration of the eighteenth-century Viennese five-octave fortepiano, music notational language, and performance practice. For if we
look back, we may then move forward in an informed manner to make
performance choices regarding this style on our modern instrument. It is
a transformative process that brings genuineness to the composer's message while at the same time renders an artistic and successful interpretation that is truly our own.

LOOKING BACK TO MOVE AHEAD

An open-minded historical approach opens doors to great advances. For example, medicine today relies on the benefits of a treatment first employed in Egypt approximately 2,500 years ago: leeches. Currently, leeches are an invaluable tool in plastic and reconstructive surgery. Modern medicine provides miraculous technology in its ability to reattach fingers, hands, toes, legs, ears, noses, and the like. But doctors must use the centuries-old method of leech therapy to restore proper blood flow. The benefits from this treatment cannot be duplicated with modern medicine. Hence, looking back informs and facilitates moving ahead.[1]

Present-day biotherapy (using living animals to aid in medical treatment) is another example of the benefits of looking back for advancements today. Take the lowly maggot. Maggots were used until the advent of antibiotics in 1935. Yet in some cases, antibiotic therapy is unsuccessful, so doctors employ the old treatment: maggots. Today, maggot therapy is practiced in conjunction with modern medicine to treat tens of thousands of patients suffering from ulcers, gangrene, skin cancer, and burns.[2]

Just as modern medicine looks to the past to create a better tomorrow, modern musicians have the chance to look back to the eighteenth century to create historically informed yet new performances today. If we are genuinely interested in uncovering the depth and richness of the style, we are forced to return to the instrument, the language, and the performance practice: three key elements. If we are to make great advances in our art, we must tap into the incredibly rich historical goldmine, heavy-laden with relevant nuggets: knowledge of the instruments on which eighteenth-century repertoire was played, comprehension of eighteenth-century music notational language that was written to express the desired musical sound, and contextual understanding of how period musicians practiced their art and spoke the language on their instruments. As a result, we will more clearly discern the composer's message and be better equipped to apply it to our artistry today. Dart supports looking back to move ahead:

> The keyboard-player, no matter what his instrument, should do all he can to meet an early composer on his own ground by discovering the lines along which he thought and the way in which he planned and played his music; for there is no other way of bridging the broken years between "then" and "now."[3]

From this vantage point, we may then become equipped to make discerning choices and create informed performances on modern instruments. Dart encourages this type of informed decision making:

> Performances must also be stylish; they must be illuminated by the fullest possible knowledge of the special points of phrasing, ornamentation and tempo that were associated with the music when it was first heard. The performer has every right to decide for himself that some of these special points are best forgotten; but he must at least be aware that they once existed, and that they were at some time considered to be an essential feature of a pleasing performance. Otherwise he risks throwing out the good with the bad, and the baby with the bathwater.[4]

BUT IT'S ALWAYS BEEN THAT WAY!

Perhaps the idea of looking back in this way is completely new, uncharted territory. An utterly untapped well-spring. This is simply an ingredient of the human condition: to naively assume the way things are is the way they have always been. For decades, I have had the pleasure of working with very young pianists. I am always amused at their reactions when they learn that I grew up without television, the internet, or a personal computer, and that the telephone was attached permanently to the wall with a cord connected to the receiver. By the look on their faces, I can tell they believe I must be hundreds of years old! But then, more importantly, I gratefully detect that they are developing an awareness that life has not always been as it is today.

Regretfully, many people carry this *naiveté* right into adulthood. After September 11, 2001, in the United States, patriotic pro-Christian–anti-Muslim sentiment was at a very tense, confrontational high. Shortly thereafter, in 2002, a court case was heard in the United States Court of Appeals for the Ninth Circuit, challenging the constitutionality of the use of "under God" in the American Pledge of Allegiance. Many Americans were aghast and in uproar: "How could this traditional pledge be challenged?! It has *always* been that way!" Yet a look at the historical facts sheds new light on the topic. From the Pledge's inception in 1892 until 1954, there was no mention of God. It wasn't until the advent of the Cold War that President Eisenhower urged Congress in 1954 to legislate the inclusion of the phrase "under God."[5] Likewise, "in God we trust" did not appear on U.S. coins until 1864 and was not made mandatory until 1908. In 1955, again during the Cold War, legislation required printing "in God we trust" on all coins and paper currency of the United States.[6] Accurate historical information impacts our entire worldview and informs our decisions moving forward. So it is with historically informed eighteenth-century truths.

When presenting workshops and seminars on eighteenth-century performance practice as applied to modern playing, I find most participants only vaguely aware of the existence of different pianos between Bartolomeo Cristofori's 1709 *"gravicembalo col piano e forte"* and the "modern" 1867 Steinway. For the most part, participants have just never given it much thought, assuming the piano "has always been that way." With the passage of time, instruments change, traditions change, and our belief of "what always was" is marred—much more than we realize. Listen to various recordings over time of Beethoven's *Moonlight* sonata to see how the tradition of playing it in cut time has mutated into much slower performances in common time. This one simple exercise brings to light that it *hasn't* always been that way!

This book will describe historical concepts in plain words, and create a pool of accurate, trustworthy information from which you may draw and further develop musicianship. In his treatise *Versuch*, C. P. E. Bach acknowledges the importance of this type of pedagogical thoroughness:

> [There may be some] divers truths [unwritten, understood principles] made necessary because of the matters on hand demand it,. . .and finally, because I feel certain principles cannot be stated too often. And perhaps, some will find themselves embarrassed by these truths, although I wrote them without the slightest intention of malice.[7]

There need be no embarrassment for any lack of awareness or understanding. For in your discoveries, you will become informed about from where we have come, who we are today, and how we might proceed tomorrow on the modern piano. If this is the category in which you belong, hold on to your hat! You are about to embark on an exciting musical journey!

I WANT TO GET IT "RIGHT"

"The first edition of [Beethoven's] Opus 2 was produced in at least eight different states."[8]

No matter how deeply we dig and how thoroughly we examine the information we uncover, we must remember that historical accuracy is an illusion. We can never know exactly how the music sounded or how it was

performed. There are no live recordings of eighteenth-century performances, the extant instruments are hundreds of years old, reproductions
of instruments are made without the benefit of input from original instrument makers, and the treatises tell only "part of the story." How, then, do
we strive for authenticity?

What does it mean to be authentic, anyway? That there is only *one*
right way to perform a work? The *New American Oxford Dictionary* defines
authentic thus:

> Made or done in the traditional or original way, or in a way that faithfully
> resembles an original; based on facts, accurate or reliable.[9]

So "getting it right" requires striving for faithfulness to the traditional
or original eighteenth-century performance standard. Which then raises
the next question: did eighteenth-century composers subscribe to the
belief in one specific way to perform their scores, as many believe today?
Is there only one way to be faithful? The *New Grove Dictionary of Music
and Musicians* provides insight. "There is no evidence that any composer
before, at the earliest, the late eighteenth century was concerned that
the holograph [an original in the composer's hand] should be followed
exactly."[10] From the various recordings in Peres da Costa's book, *Off the
Record*, substantial evidence corroborates that this view permeated clear
into the twentieth century.

Furthermore, what do we do when there are multiple versions of the
"authentic" score? Look at a first edition, an autograph, or a manuscript of
the same work. Composers changed their minds, yet all of these scores are
authentic. Which one is "right"? Listen to different live recordings of the
same work artists play over the course of time. Are they not different? Do
we not evolve and change over time? Do *you* think musically the same way
today as you did five or ten years ago? Why then bother?

Because, as Haynes articulates in *The End of Early Music*, getting it
"right" is not the point.

> More than anything else, Authenticity seems to be a statement of intent.
> Totally accurate historical performance is probably impossible to achieve. To
> know it has been achieved is certainly impossible. But that isn't the goal. What
> produces interesting results is the *attempt* to be historically accurate, that is,
> authentic.[11]

No, we are not looking to merely dig up and perform a dead language.
Like any archeological dig, the point is to learn about the culture behind

the artifacts (the scores and surrounding literature) so we may be better informed about how the music was understood and performed. If we are willing to learn from the past we may then create a new, ever-emerging present.

As Taruskin promises, this approach brings fresh ideas:

> Experiments based on historical research serve the purpose for performers to: open their minds and ears to new experiences, and enable them to transcend their habitual, and therefore, unconsidered, ways of hearing and thinking about the music. . . . The object is not to duplicate the sounds of the past, for if that were our aim we should never know whether we had succeeded. What we are aiming at, rather, is the startling shock of newness, of immediacy, the sense of rightness that occurs when after countless frustrating experiments we feel as though we have achieved the identification of performance style with the demands of the music.[12]

Yet what the composer meant was and *is* vitally important. In 1739, eighteenth-century music theorist Mattheson commented on the subject:

> Those who have never discovered how the composer himself wished to have the worked performed will hardly be able to play it well. Indeed, they will often rob the thing of its true vigour and grace, so much so, in fact, that the composer, should he himself be among the listeners, would find it difficult to recognize his own work.[13]

We have a responsibility to know as much as we can about what was said so we can make intelligent decisions regarding what we will consciously attend to or dismiss. Before we proceed any further, some long-held fallacies and faulty logic must be set straight.

FALLACIES AND FAULTY LOGIC

Fallacy #1: The modern piano is a product of evolution and is superior to previous pianos.

Perchance you are aware of historical pianos but have come to believe that modern pianos are a result of an evolutionary process and therefore superior. To presume the latest invention or advancement an improvement over the previous—*better* than the way it was—is a superiority complex of sorts, a form of contempt prior to investigation. A hard nut to crack. Examine the faulty logic and look at the facts for truth.

The faulty logic assumes superiority based on the each piano's chrono-logical place in keyboard history and presumes each progression is supe-rior to its predecessor. Throughout history, there have been many keyboard instruments, each with matchless traits, strengths, and limitations. Think of the crisp, clear, bright, and brilliant tone of the harpsichord that is lim-ited by lack of gradual volume change. Or the exquisitely beautiful, subtle, sensitive shading that is possible on the clavichord but can be heard only in the most intimate of settings. The modern piano has its own distinctive traits, such as its the glowing, luxurious melody that blossoms as the sound unfolds and a strong, projecting tone that enables it to be heard over the sizeable modern orchestra in a 2,000-seat concert hall, yet needs time to allow these traits to develop and be heard. The eighteenth-century Viennese five-octave fortepiano is no different. It is the consummate instrument for articulating feelings, or *affekt*, with superb clarity, yet struggles for a con-nected legato line. Fortepianist Bart van Oort observes thus:

> Composers from the Classical and early Romantic periods wrote music that not only sings, but pleas, argues, entreats, languishes, persuades, sighs, gnashes its teeth, shouts for joy, whispers . . . in short, music that must also speak.[14]

Historical pianos are neither better nor worse than the modern piano. They are simply different. As Haynes explains, "There is no 'better or prog-ress.' Instrument making does not operate that way. You gain something only by giving up something else. 'Better' really means 'best adapted' to the demands of the music."[15]

Fallacy #2: Eighteenth-century composers would have preferred today's mod-ern piano. That is to say, composers would have been happier with today's instrument.

This fallacy implies that eighteenth-century composers *weren't* pleased with how their compositions were expressed on the instruments avail-able to them—"this really is not good music, but in 200 years, on a 'bet-ter piano' it will be phenomenal!" It implies envisioning a future "better instrument," which is akin to supposing Chopin and Liszt were hoping for and imagining their music improved if only it could be performed on an electric keyboard. Dart takes the fallacy all the way.

> Pushed to its logical limits, this point of view leads to great absurdities. To assume all early composers whatsoever would have preferred to use the instru-ments of our own time, (some hundred years or more after in their graves), [is] a point of view that makes us appear impossibly conceited and arrogant.[16]

The facts blatantly point out the incongruity. Mozart wrote three let-ters in which he was *highly* complimentary of Stein's fortepiano. He wished to own one, but the cost was prohibitive.[17] He did, however, own a Walter fortepiano, one of the most popular instruments of his day. (His Walter piano is on display at his home in Salzburg.) The Viennese five-octave for-tepiano was an ideal instrument for the performing venues of the time, as a complementary instrument for accompaniment, and for ensemble work with contemporary instruments of the day. It wasn't until the advent of public concerts in the late eighteenth century, when halls became larger, that bigger instruments were developed. The change was not due to dis-satisfaction from composers.

In a letter from Beethoven to piano builder Johann Andreas Streicher (November 19, 1796), Beethoven comments, "I received the day before yesterday your fortepiano, which is really an excellent instrument."[18] Whether or not this was a ploy to favor himself with Streicher for complimentary instruments, as was a typical maneuver, Rosenblum states that "no evidence has been found that Beethoven ever specifically requested additional notes of any builder."[19] Over the course of Beethoven's life, he is known to have owned fourteen pianos, eleven of which were Viennese; four of those were from the Stein/Streicher families. In addi-tion, Beethoven was quite aware of the variety of constructions and was introduced to (and owned) an Erard (French) and a Broadwood (English) piano. Beethoven's correspondence indicates that he was well acquainted with the capabilities of each instrument and encouraged developments from all makers with whom he came into contact. His creative output is indicative of his masterly use of each instrument available, not an imag-ined instrument of the future. Newman emphasizes the need to honor composers and trust their judgment.

> We strive to approximate the composers' intentions as an act of truth and fidelity. We assume they understood what they and their contemporaries wanted, we respect and prefer their judgment, and we acknowledge their right to set their own ground rules.[20]

Willingness to accept instruments of the eighteenth century as valid, legit-imate, and suitable machines that were embraced by period composers opens untold avenues for understanding the music that was written for them.

Fallacy #3: We must play exactly what is written to honor the composer's intentions.

Eighteenth-century music notational language contains similar signs and symbols to twentieth- and twenty-first-century notation but carries, in some instances, quite dissimilar meanings. Lamentably, many modern musicians apply modern meaning to eighteenth-century music notational language, entirely missing the chief aim of honoring the style. *Much* will be said about this as the book progresses.

Holding onto this falsehood, performing Classical Era music with exacting twenty-first-century adherence to the score, produces a distant, dry, and transparent sound. But willingness to question, debate, and learn this "new" centuries-old language provides unimagined creative possibilities, with new surprises at every turn! Classical Era music is *not* a language of obvious, simple, clear-cut notes and rhythms, but one in which the luxuriously emotional character, or *affekt*, is deeply at the core of the style. In his *Violinschule*, Leopold Mozart clearly lays out the first step in honoring intentions:

> Before one begins to play, one must very likely consider and peruse the composition. One must seek out the **character** [emphasis mine], the tempo and the kind of motion required by the piece. . . .[21]

The Tasks at Hand

As we move forward, you may find more spurious information set straight. And so it is with great urgency that we proceed to create new art—to learn from the past to inform the future. You will become equipped to responsibly carry the composer's message as you strive to achieve the following goals:

- Understand the *instrument* for which the music was intended.
- Comprehend the *language* that was used when the music was written.
- Understand how the language was expressed through historically informed *performance practice*.

In order to achieve these goals, you will be immersed in primary sources from the eighteenth century and scholarly interpretative literature. The main thrust of this book is pedagogical in nature. Its intention is like Türk's: "Clarity, simple wording, accuracy, brevity and certainty are, as is known, the most necessary requirements of instructional prose. I have always sought to fulfill these requirements whenever possible."[22]

If this book were to conclude with these topics alone, it would serve as a purposeful, pedagogically sound, succinct synthesis of eighteenth-century performance practice. Yet it ventures further into action:

• Apply *relevant, applicable meaning for today's musician on today's instrument* to render a historically informed performance that interprets the intended message and creates newly transformed twenty-first-century art.

This stimulating journey you are about to undertake will guide you to better understand eighteenth-century repertoire and allow the understanding to inform your playing on the modern piano, thus making something brand new out of that which is old and cherished. That is why we bother. Proceed with urgency!

TERMINOLOGY AND "MAIN PLAYERS"

Before uncovering the "truths" we *do* know, a common understanding of terms and main players that are referred to throughout the book will prove helpful.

Terms

Affekt: The character, mood, emotion, and meaning behind the written score. A basic element to eighteenth-century performance.

Authenticity: The intention to bring historical perspective and understanding to a given work; to honor past traditions.

Eighteenth-century music notational language: The system of written signs and symbols used in the eighteenth century to describe a musical performance. This language system is both complete and imprecise, complete yet malleable. It requires understanding the interaction between the complete notational signs and symbols, the influence of *affekt,* and execution norms within accepted understood period performance-practice parameters.

Eighteenth-century style/Classical Era style: The sum of the parts of eighteenth-century performance practice, including *affekt,* notational language, performance practices (both notated and understood unnotated practices), period instruments, and cultural context that make up the whole; its gestalt.

Fortepiano: The Viennese five-octave piano used predominantly circa 1750–1800.

Performance practice: The appropriate parameters in execution that are applied to notation, including the "understood" conventions.

Eighteenth-century performance practice/period practice: Commonly understood conventions regarding how music notation was executed, including those conventions not indicated in the score but inherently understood in the temporal arts circa 1750–1800. This practice includes ambiguities that allow for more than one *right way* (within accepted parameters) to execute notation from a complete eighteenth-century score and consequently allow each performance to be a new creation.

Language: In a broad sense, from *New Oxford American Dictionary*, "any nonverbal method of expression or communication."[23] For this book, more specifically, a written representation of a thought or an aural sound.

Modern performance practice: Commonly understood conventions from post–World War II to the present, with an emphasis on absolute adherence to the score.

Period composer/musician: Composers and musicians from the eighteenth century, circa 1750–1800. Specific pertinent figures are named in the next section.

Urtext: German term that literally means "original text."[24] A music score that, through scholarly research, provides informed options for use in making educated performing decisions.

Main Players (Past)

Carl Philipp Emmanuel Bach (1714–1788): The second surviving son of Johann Sebastian Bach and Maria Barbara (J. S. Bach's first wife). He is considered the most important composer in Protestant Germany during the second half of the eighteenth century. He was admired and recognized particularly as a teacher and keyboard composer. For over sixty years, he was a prolific composer who wrote over 1,000 separate works, including many keyboard pieces.[25] *The New Grove Dictionary of Music and Musicians* states, "His teaching inspired the writing of his *Versuch über die wahre Art das Clavier zu spielen (Essay on the True Art of Playing Keyboard Instruments)* [referred to throughout this book as *Versuch*], the most important eighteenth-century German-language treatise on the subject."[26] *Versuch* was a well-respected tutor that was influential with period composers, including Haydn and Beethoven. Beethoven used it in his teaching. Although *Versuch* was intended primarily as a clavichord tutor,[27]

Bach was very aware of and interested in the latest keyboard inventions, and it serves as a renowned general keyboard treatise from the eighteenth century. Throughout the course of this book, C. P. E. Bach will be referred to simply as Bach, since J. S. Bach will not be referenced.

Johann Kirnberger (1721–1783): German theorist and composer known for his theoretical and instructional works. *The New Grove Dictionary of Music and Musicians* explains, "He was among the most significant of a group of [German] theorists, which included Quantz and C. P. E. Bach."[28]

Heinrich Christoph Koch (1749–1816): German theorist and violinist. He is remembered most for his work, *Versuch einer Anleitung zur Composition*, published in three volumes (1782, 1787, 1793), and *Musikalisches Lexikon* (1802), comprehensive studies of music theory and aesthetics.[29]

Leopold Mozart (1719–1787): Composer, violinist, theorist. *The New Grove Dictionary of Music and Musicians* acknowledges that L. Mozart's *Violinschule* (1756, revised in 1769–1770 and again in 1787), was "widely recognized as the most important violin tutor of its time. The work is the source closest to [W. A.] Mozart, and is the most valuable guide to the musical and aesthetic education of the young composer."[30]

Joachim Quantz (1697-1773): German flautist, composer, flute maker, and flute teacher to Frederick the Great (serving in court simultaneously with C. P. E. Bach). His most significant contribution to musical literature is his tutorial *Versuch* (1752).[31]

Daniel Gottlob Türk (1750–1813): Composer, keyboardist, and teacher who was recognized as the leader in musical life in Halle, Germany during his lifetime. He was greatly influenced by C. P. E. Bach's *Versuch*. In 1789, he published *Klavierschule*, based on years of experience and thorough knowledge of the relevant literature. Although *Klavierschule* was intended primarily as a clavichord tutor,[32] Türk was very aware of and interested in the latest keyboard inventions, and it serves as a renowned eighteenth-century general keyboard treatise. Beethoven used *Klavierschule* in 1808 as a teaching resource for the Archduke Rudolph.[33]

Main Players (Present)

Malcolm Bilson (1935–): American pianist, fortepianist, and educator Bilson has been a prominent leader in period instrument performing, scholarship, and teaching for decades. His impressive performing and recording career includes three important complete cycles of works for piano by Mozart and participation in an epoch-making eight-concert series featuring all Beethoven sonatas on historical pianos in Merkin Hall, New York,

New York. Bilson has released two educational videos, *Knowing the Score* (2005) and *Performing the Score* (2011). Professor Emeritus Bilson continues to perform and teach throughout the world.

Robert Levin (1947–): Renowned early music specialist known for his restoration of the Classical Era practice of improvised embellishments and cadenzas. His Mozart and Beethoven performances have been hailed for their active mastery of the Classical musical language. Professor Emeritus Levin continues to perform and teach throughout the world.

In addition to the groundbreaking work and accomplishments of Bilson and Levin, several acclaimed "new generation" fortepianists are worth mentioning and listed below. Visit their websites to see each artist's considerable contributions. Peruse each discography to begin a listening journey for your own discoveries.

- Tom Beghin
- Kristian Bezuidenhout
- Ronald Brautigam
- Alexei Ljubimov
- Viviana Sofronitsky
- Andreas Staier
- Bart van Oort

You will find that each chapter opens with material to provide a historically informed perspective surrounding eighteenth-century style. A section labeled influences applied will follow, with suggestions for concepts to be considered, techniques to be tried, and adjustments to be experimented with on the modern piano. A lesson will close each chapter with pedagogical suggestions for a Mozart dance from The London Notebook, KV15oo.

Throughout the book you will find an icon directing you to the companion website. Here, you will find a variety of resources: in-depth discussions beyond the scope of the written text, diagrams and tables to illustrate a topic, or recordings of examples to bring the written language to auditory life. Each musical example in the book is presented in three instructive versions: (a) an uninfluenced modern piano interpretation, (b) a Viennese five-octave fortepiano rendition, and (c) a reconciled version that demonstrates how *Discoveries from the Fortepiano* influences interpretation for delivery on the modern piano. The objective is to present what has been described in prose in such a way that it may be heard and understood aurally.

Recordings were made by using two pianos in the instruments collection at the University of Nebraska–Lincoln Glenn Korff School of Music between May 27, 2014 and June 6, 2014: a 1978 Belt-Walter fortepiano replica of a circa 1780s Viennese five-octave Anton Walter fortepiano and a Steinway M grand piano. Both instruments were in the same studio space to maintain acoustic consistency.

Although the short recordings on the companion website serve an insightful instructional purpose, you are encouraged to seek out recordings of works in their entirety, as performed by the artists suggested in this section. That is how the essence is captured. Music should be listened to in context—fluid and integrated.

With the ground rules laid, it is now time to dig and uncover *Discoveries from the Fortepiano*.

GOAL #1: THE FORTEPIANO

Today, when most people speak of *the piano*, they envision a very specific sort of instrument: the modern piano, which is (and has been for over 150 years) quite uniform in size, construction, action, and sound qualities. Not so with eighteenth-century pianos.

This first goal—*understand the instrument for which the music was intended*—is most easily achieved by playing and studying eighteenth-century instruments.

Extant and replica period instruments exist today. The machine can be examined, deconstructed, reconstructed, and played in similar venues to very closely approximate a recreated experience, thus providing insight to inform playing today. We look back in order to move forward or risk losing the essence of the Classical Era style. Dart warns of the following:

> The Viennese fortepianos of the Mozart period cannot rival the modern grand in loudness or in speed of repetition, but good surviving specimens suggest that our conception of Mozart's piano music is falsified by our unfamiliarity with the piano of his time.[34]

Because of its importance to Classical Era composition and performance, the Viennese five-octave fortepiano (referred to simply as the fortepiano from this point forward) will be the focus. Specifically, this instrument was integral to Mozart's work, early Beethoven, and many other period composers. It is the appropriate "jumping off" place. If interest in further study is piqued, expand exploration in many directions—earlier to the clavichord and harpsichord, other regions to find other eighteenth-century instruments, or later to explore five-and-a-half- or six-octave instruments.

Fortepiano

Historical background. At the turn of the eighteenth century, two of the most popular keyboard instruments were the harpsichord—known for its comparative strength and bright tone but incapable of gradual dynamic change, and the clavichord—admired for its sensitivity to subtle expressive gradations of tone yet suitable only to very small performing areas. The arrival of Cristofori's *"gravicembalo col piano e forte,"* (harpsichord with soft and loud) circa 1709, gave birth to the dawn of a new era in keyboard instrument development and, by extension, repertoire and style.

Eighteenth-century inventors experimented and developed a wide variety of keyboard instruments. Bach mentions various types of keyboard instruments in passing during the introduction to his *Versuch,* and Türk describes no fewer than twenty types in the introduction to his *Klavierschule.* Suffice it to say there was no standard fortepiano. In *The Pianoforte in the Classical Era,* Michael Cole reports that "it would probably be true to say that never before nor since has there been such a diversity of keyboard instruments available at one time and in one area [Germany]."[35] Nor was there any standard name to describe the instruments. A variety of names were employed, such as *cimbalo di piano e forte, cembalo, clavicembalo, clavecin, instrument, Flügel, Clavier, Hammerclavier, Hammerflügel,* or *hammer harpsichord* to name just a few.[36] Moreover, in *Piano Roles,* James Parakilas points out that publishers were most interested in making sales to *all* keyboard owners, regardless of which specific instrument was in the home. Hence, title pages remained as generic as possible.[37] Today, the *fortepiano* refers to the instrument that was in use from the mid-eighteenth to the early nineteenth century.

As the development of the fortepiano progressed, its popularity grew. In "After Mozart: The Viennese Piano Scene in the 1790's," Katalin Komlós explains that the fortepiano appeared on the music scene just as aristocracy-supported public concerts shifted to smaller venues supported by the growing middle class. Yet "compared to the six performers [keyboardists] who appeared on stage in Vienna in the 1780s, the last decade of the century saw no less than fourteen fortepianists on stage."[38] This upturn clearly supports the claim for rising interest in the fortepiano, particularly since the increase occurred in the midst of a downturn in public concert life during the 1790s. The fortepiano also found its niche through an increase in private patronage. The Viennese soirée in the aristocratic or bourgeois salon was the typical venue that featured forte-pianists. Representative music heard in these settings included various popular forms such as dances, marches, variations, rondos, and the piano sonata. On a good evening, a fine guest artist could be cajoled into bril-liant improvisations on any of the previously mentioned forms.

In his 1753 *Versuch,* Bach describes the "new piano" as an instrument that has "many fine qualities, although its touch must be carefully worked out, a task which is not without difficulties. It sounds well by itself and in small ensembles."[39] Here, Bach was critiquing a Silbermann piano.[40] As with any new invention, there was a flurry of activity amongst inven-tors such as Zumpfe, Silbermann, Schanz, Walter, and Stein. These new pianos were definitely works in progress, for, by his 1762 revised edition of *Versuch,* Bach praises its virtues. "The pianoforte and clavichord pro-vide the best accompaniments in performances that require the most elegant taste.[41] ... [and they] enjoy great advantages over the harpsi-chord and organ because of the many ways in which their volume can be gradually changed."[42] Regardless of whether this is because the instru-ments improved, musicians became more adept at the new invention, or a combination of both, the fortepiano had taken hold. On pages 6–8 in *Performance Practices in Classic Piano Music,* Rosenblum points out that the fortepiano was played publicly as early as 1763 in Vienna's famous Burgtheater, and in Paris and Dublin in 1768. In 1766, J. C. Bach endorsed a new type of piano invented by Johann Zumpe.[43] Mozart became acquainted with and admired Stein's fortepiano while visiting Mannheim in 1777. In *The Fortepiano in the Classical Era,* Cole points to a 1777 Stein coordinated concert (at Mozart's behest), wherein three of Stein's instru-ments were premiered in Augsburg. The concert (with Mozart on the pro-gram as performing his own compositions on Stein's instruments) was a great success.[44] So impressed was Mozart with this instrument that Schonberg observes, "All of his post-1777 keyboard music was conceived for the piano—which means most of the sonatas and all of the concertos beginning with K. 414."[45] By the 1780s, the fortepiano was here to stay.

The Instrument (the Five-Octave Viennese Fortepiano circa 1750–1790)

To explain the mechanics and sound of the fortepiano, I have relied on my years of personal experience with the Viennese five-octave 1978

Belt-Walter replica circa 1780 Walter fortepiano at the University of Nebraska–Lincoln, the variety of historical instruments with which I have become acquainted while participating in international workshops and seminars, and the information provided in Sandra Rosenblum's *Performance Practices in Classic Piano Music*, and Michael Cole's *The Pianoforte in the Classical Era*. Since our point of reference is as modern pianists, the discussion will focus on comparisons between the Viennese fortepiano and the modern piano.

On pages 49–50, Rosenblum notes that Mozart, Haydn, and Beethoven preferred Viennese-built fortepianos. Haydn preferred a five-octave Schanz, which he purchased in 1788. Although Mozart greatly admired Stein's pianos, the cost was prohibitive and he ultimately owned a five-octave Walter acquired sometime between 1782 and 1785.[46] Barth, in *The Pianist as Orator*, and Rosenblum, in *Performance Practices in Classical Piano Music*, point out that Beethoven's lifelong preference was for Viennese instruments from the Stein/Streicher family. These instruments share a number of salient characteristics that, if understood in relation to the modern piano, will lead to genuine and authentic performances today.

Fortepianos were primarily made in two shapes: rectangular (square pianos), which were very popular with the burgeoning middle class, and wing-shaped (grand pianos), which were oftentimes simply the new instrument built into an old harpsichord case. When comparing the overall characteristics of the fortepiano and the modern piano, we find that the differences are considerable. The fortepiano's prevailing quality is its ability to be played with finesse. Everything on the fortepiano is literally and aesthetically lighter and more responsive than the modern piano. A Steinway D eight-foot concert grand weighs almost six times as much as a Walter 1790 fortepiano. The fortepiano soundboard is thinner than the modern piano soundboard. Fortepiano hammers contain sharply tapered shafts that are less than half the size of today's hammers and travel half the distance of a modern piano hammer. The fortepiano action contains a light, simple, single-lever system with the key in direct contact with the jack rather than the twenty-plus parts that propel the hammer on the modern piano. The physical act of playing the fortepiano is lighter and acutely tactual—one can actually feel the key and hammer touch the string. (For further comparison, see Diagrams 1.1 and 1.2 on the companion website. ▶)

A progressive development that Stein brought to the fortepiano was the escapement (specifically touted in Mozart's famous letter of 1777) that improved reliability and responsiveness. Cole describes this improvement:

> By this [the escapement mechanism of Stein] the hammers can be regulated
> to rise very close to the strings without danger of blocking or double-hitting.
> Neither is there any need for more than half a millimetre of lost motion in the
> key—hence the player can have an expressive contact through the key with
> the nice sensation of controlling the speech of the instrument in a very precise
> way. A very minute movement of the key is sufficient to initiate the hammer
> lift, and the reliability of the escapement ensures that a very light touch will
> sound a pianissimo, while the heaviest pressure produces a fortissimo without
> any fear of damaging the instrument.[47]

The lighter key weight and quicker action in the fortepiano facilitates responsiveness. Fortepiano keys are less than half the weight of modern piano keys. The distance traveled and energy required to execute the key on the fortepiano is about one-third of that needed for the modern piano. Couple the light action with the escapement mechanism designed by Stein and the technique required to play the fortepiano is markedly more responsive and lighter than what is needed for the modern piano.

The actual dimensions of keys on the fortepiano are smaller than the modern piano, a difference that dramatically impacts technique further. (Find specifics on the companion website, Table 1.1. ⊙) Everything from judging distances up and down the keyboard to moving in and out from sharps to naturals covers less distance and consequently requires less energy to reach the desired destination. The result is an instrument that has the capability for excellent control, incredible speed in passage work, subtle inflection for voicing changes, crisp articulation, and quick shifts from *forte* to *piano*.

The fortepiano's strings and hammers also markedly influence the sound. Fortepiano strings are made not of steel but of iron, which creates a very silvery tone. Because of the wooden frame, the strings withstand less than a quarter of the strain of modern pianos; this much reduced strain results in a sound rich in overtones. The fortepiano's use of small, pointed hammers on small, light, strings leads to a clear, clean, articulate sound on the fortepiano, compared to a more spongy sound caused by the large, heavy hammers on big, thick strings on the modern piano.

The fortepiano range influenced composers' musical concept. The typical fortepiano range is five octaves, basically that of the human voice. The works of Mozart, Haydn, and Beethoven (up to 1803) fit agreeably within the five-octave range. Compared to the modern piano at seven-and-a-half octaves, the "extremes" are considerably smaller on the fortepiano. (Find comparisons on the companion website, Table 1.2. ▶))

The mechanics of the fortepiano, combined with its sound qualities, result in an instrument with clear tone definition. I find that the voices articulate cleanly, move to the forefront quickly, and just as easily recede. One of the most amazing qualities inherent in the fortepiano is the variety of tone color and character that spans the range of the instrument; a perfect match for a composer or performer wishing to convey varieties of *affekt*. Rosenblum's description paints the tone colors vividly:

> Such differences sharpen the distinctions between parts of the musical texture and enhance polyphonic passages. The bass is sonorous and dark but remains clear, avoiding the wooly quality of the pianoforte. Low trills and closely spaced bass chords sound well on the fortepiano. When pushed, the bass can also growl. The middle register produces a warm singing tone. The treble ... varies more among instruments in its effects than do the other registers. It is sometimes flutelike, but it can also sound metallic and very penetrating.[48]

Understanding fortepiano tone production and decay significantly impacts executing this style on the modern piano (Diagram 1.1). On the modern piano, the tone develops through four phases (attack, sustain, bloom, decay), growing slightly before beginning to gradually decay. Tone production more naturally imitates vowels. The singing line is of utmost importance. The benefit lies in its ability to create a nearly seamless vocal legato with long-line phrasing—all desired elements of modern performing style.[49] The detriment: it is difficult to maintain clarity. Conversely, on the fortepiano, the tone begins to decay from the moment the hammer strikes the key and decays much more quickly than on the modern piano. Tone production more naturally imitates consonants and thus facilitates

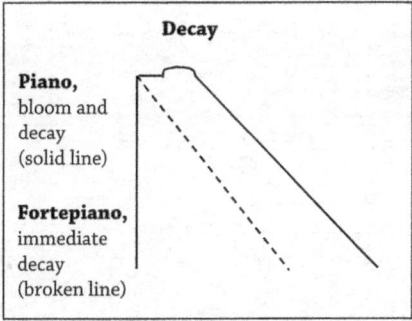

Diagram 1.1. Piano versus fortepiano decay.

clarity—an important goal in eighteenth-century style. It allows the music to emulate rhetoric: to speak, articulate, recite. The disadvantage of the quick decay is that a true legato line is possible only on a *diminuendo*.

During his 2007 presentation, "To Speak or Sing: Mozart and Beethoven on the Fortepiano," Bart van Oort demonstrated one example of Beethoven's creative genius; how Beethoven took advantage of mechanical attributes to create an effective opening to the *Pathetique* sonata (Example 1.1). After van Oort's initial *forte* attack, the opening chord decayed and the appropriate tempo, timing, and *piano* dynamic level presented themselves naturally. Thus, the use of *fp* or *sfz* followed by *p* or *pp* is very effective on the fortepiano.[50] A quick examination of the literature will provide numerous examples.

Music Example 1.1. Beethoven, Piano Sonata, op. 13/i, mm. 1–2. (ABRSM) ⊙

The fortepiano's quickness and clarity of attack, the speed with which its sound is put into motion, and the quick rate of decay all carry sway in tempo choices. For example, notice the original time signature, cut time, in Example 1.2, Beethoven Piano Sonata, op. 27. A slower tempo of common time, as is sometimes heard on the modern piano (and notated in

Music Example 1.2. Beethoven, Piano Sonata op. 27, no. 2/i, mm. 1–5. (ABRSM) ⊙

non-*Urtext* editions), doesn't work on the fortepiano. Because of the rapid decay, a quicker tempo is required. Again, Beethoven made masterly use of the machine at hand to create his desired sound quality.

Generally speaking, on the fortepiano the pedal is executed with the knee, rather than the feet. The dampers are much lighter than today's dampers. They are seated very close to the strings and are very responsive. Pedal is used sparingly and creates very light sustaining. Each pedal choice is intentional, most often for color and special effect, rather than extending a melodic line. More will be said in chapter 12.

By today's standards, the overall sound of the fortepiano is smaller and more transparent, and it decays more quickly than the modern piano. But that makes it no less capable of expressing the breadth of notated musical thought. It is actually the perfect match for expressing the language of the Classical Era style. Although it is not possible to recreate the actual performed sound with absolute certainty, the knowledge of these basic ingredients should profoundly impact understanding the perceived sound of eighteenth-century style. We are then better equipped to make informed decisions from eighteenth-century repertoire to be carried into modern playing.

GOAL #2: THE LANGUAGE (WHAT THEY SAID)

It's not Just What They Said, but What They Meant by What They Said!

In a previous section, it was pointed out that in fact things are not always as they have been; it is an evolving process, this existence on earth. Language is no different. Evolutionary theories of linguistics that date back to the eighteenth and nineteenth century support the premise that as humankind develops and evolves, so does language and vice versa. Nineteenth-century linguists concluded that languages become ever more efficient and progressive in nature. More recent work concludes that as people evolve into more efficient beings, they incorporate a more efficient language. It is generally safe to say that the current accepted belief is that language evolves as does humankind. (For further discussion visit the companion website, Text 1.1. ▶)

When students are first exposed to the cakewalk dance, I begin by asking them to define "cakewalk." Invariably, I receive this answer: "Oh! This is what we do at school on fun-night. We walk around on numbers that have been placed on the floor while music is playing. When the music stops, a number is called out. If your number is called, you win a cupcake!" Hmm . . . a bit different from what was danced in the Deep South in the late nineteenth century or what Debussy envisioned in 1908. The meanings of all languages, spoken or musical, are ever-changing, like a mobile hanging from the ceiling in constant movement. A quick look at comparisons (Table 1.1) between a 1966 and 2010 dictionary cleverly illustrates the point.

Table 1.1. LANGUAGE EVOLUTION OVER TIME

Term	1966 *Funk and Wagnalls College Dictionary*[76]	2010 *New Oxford American Dictionary, 3rd ed.*[77]
Jazz	copulation (US slang derived from Creole jass coition; from brothels in New Orleans→lying or exaggerated talk, idle and foolish→added liveliness and animation→any contemporary popular dance music	a type of music of black American origin characterized by improvisation, syncopation, and usually a regular or forceful rhythm, emerging at the beginning of the 20th century
Gay	happy and carefree→brightly colorful	homosexual, particularly male→stupid

Not only do meanings change over time, but the same word may also have different meanings, depending on the culture. Divergent definitions were surprisingly (and quite hilariously in some cases) revealed in personal travels, as seen in Table 1.2.

Table 1.2. CULTURAL LANGUAGE VARIANTS

Term	Country: Meaning	Country: Meaning
Jello	US: a trademarked treat made with flavored gelatin and boiled water, refrigerated	Australia: fruit preserves
Fanny	US: slang for the buttocks	UK: part of the female genitalia
Beemer	US: nickname for BMW car	Germany: the projector used for PowerPoint presentations

The language of today is not the same language of yesteryear. Acceptance of the naturally occurring variability and malleability of language is imperative in order to approach eighteenth-century music notational language with an inquisitive and investigative mind; be ready to seek out previous definitions and subtle connotations from a nearly 300-year-old vocabulary. It is imperative in order to be successful in expressing the style. Haynes would agree:

> Thus, with musical documents three to four centuries old, there is every prospect that, without special knowledge, we will mistake the meanings of their symbols. It is convenient to ignore this, and Modern style musicians often read Rhetorical [Classic Era] music with results that are not very satisfactory.[51]

PRONOUNCE, COMPREHEND, CONVINCE

To speak any language, from any time period or culture, requires adherence to common rules of pronunciation. Language pronunciation rules must be understood in order to begin to make sense of intent. Van Oort begins the discussion:

> If English were a dead language, we might never have known the differences
> in pronunciation between the following words: Touch Thought Cough Though
> Plough Through.[52]

But mastering pronunciation of a language is only the beginning. It provides no insight into comprehension. In each of the following pairs, the pronunciation is identical. Yet either an animal is being referenced or something quite different. Comprehension is the key, not simply how the words are spoken.

ant-aunt; boar-bore; bear-bare; deer-dear; faun-fawn; flea-flee; gorilla-guerilla; lichen-liken; llama-lama; moose-mousse; tern-turn

Failure to comprehend equates, in essence, to being an English-only reader/speaker attempting to read/speak Voltaire's *Candide* in French, trying to decode the text on the basis of a phonetic key, but knowing nothing of French language rules, vocabulary, or culture in 1759.

The roles of punctuation, articulation, and inflection drastically impact meaning and interpretation. They convince the listener of what is being said. This idea was of utmost importance to Classical Era composers and musicians. Türk explains the elements that go into convincing:

> The single word: "God!" can denote an exclamation of joy, of pain, of despair,
> the greatest anxiety, pity, astonishment, etc., in various degrees. In the same
> way tones, by changes in the execution, can produce a very different effect. It
> is therefore extremely necessary to study the expression of feelings and pas-
> sions in the most careful way, make them one's own, and learn to apply them
> correctly.[53]

Türk further explains how a simple punctuation mark makes an immense difference in how statements are understood:

> "He lost his life not, only his fortune," or "He lost his life, not only his fortune."[54]

Pronounce, comprehend, convince. The key to being understood. Failing to do so may produce something not at all intended, as Malcolm Bilson has warned workshop participants many times. "When you were something in a different way, you were actually something different!" The next section will address how the intended message was expressed notationally in the eighteenth century.

MUSIC NOTATIONAL LANGUAGE

When I interview prospective beginning students, they usually express their desire to learn how to play the instrument and how to "read" music. Indeed, we learn how to decode signs and symbols in order to "read" and "speak" (perform) the language of music, much of which contains common elements, regardless of place and time. But to make a blanket assumption applicable to all music from the full continuum of time leaves the richness of each idiosyncratic musical language sadly forgotten and "the point of it all" entirely missed. Dart supports this belief:

> The musical notation in use today is the logical development of that used in earlier times, but the present-day significance of the symbols may be, and very often is, utterly different from their significance in eighteenth-century France or sixteenth-century England or fourteenth-century Italy. . . .[55]

Just like written speech, music notational language is dynamic and constantly changing. The signs and symbols may be concrete, but the meaning is in constant flux. As Haynes suggests, "The connotations of words change during our lifetimes . . . surely musical meanings are also on the move. But, while this is happening, nothing changes on paper; the old manuscripts abide, speaking a language that was leading-edge in 1750; many lifetimes ago."[56] Yes, the tone A is still an A. But, it is how the A is interpreted at any given particular time in music history that makes it distinct. Through static written signs and symbols, the aural pronunciation, the definition, inflection, and overall meaning change on the basis of written and "understood" rules.

For the pianist, this point raises several questions:

- How are the signs and symbols (notation) typically pronounced on both the original instrument and mine today?
- What did the music notational language mean in its own time?
- How is that meaning expressed (executed) on my instrument today?

Eighteenth-Century Music Notational Language

What then is known about Classic Era music notational language? First and foremost to the eighteenth-century musician, music must *say something*. And once the meaning is ascertained, it is expressed or conveyed through execution. This will be a recurring theme throughout this book. Türk explains thus:

> Whoever reads a poem he does not know and which is not completely comprehensible to him would probably find it difficult to declaim every single passage in such a way that a listener possessing good taste would find nothing left to be desired. This is also certainly the case in music. Not until a musician knows a composition will he be able to play every part of it with complete skill and with the required expression.[57]

Eighteenth-century musical style is projected by reading the score, comprehending its message, and executing that message from accepted practices—and by having something new to say. Kirnberger and others spoke of this point frequently. (See the citation on the companion website, at Text 1.2. ▶) This is not new territory. There are many written and unwritten practices from every period or style, such as Baroque style, rock and roll, blues, and jazz, which require doing just that.

How They Argued and "What Do *We* Know?"

Concerns regarding how expression was best executed was a topic among period musicians that was passionately discussed and debated. Even within the short span of 1750–1789, Türk's views regarding proper execution of the quarter note developed and changed. Deciphering what sound is described through written notation is tricky. Haynes puts it well. "Anyone who has ever tried to convey a musical idea by means of notation knows how approximate it is. No matter how clever one is at accurately writing the idea, no matter how much detail is included, it always seems a small miracle if someone else can seize the meaning by eye without having first heard it."[58]

Composers painstakingly used specific, exacting, concrete, nonemotional media in their attempt to recreate aural intentions and emotions. For instance, in Example 1.3, (page 26) rather than perform concrete and literal mathematical rhythmic breaks as notated, Quantz most likely describes an *accelerando*.

No matter how thorough the notation, it inexactly expresses sounds and emotions in written form. And sadly, we can't reconstruct a sound that no

Music Example 1.3. Quantz, *On Playing the Flute*, Table XII, Fig. 8 right, 146.

longer exists. There are no recordings to substantiate how this notation was expressed. Peres Da Costa agrees. "The evolving meaning of inherited notational signs and terminology adds yet a further layer of complexity. What was once fashionable or accepted may no longer be so."[59]

But all is not lost, as Peres Da Costa encourages. "Although we may never know, we still must strive to be informed as best possible. Clearly, the more we are informed, the more equipped we are to make informed choices and to fill in the gaps in our knowledge."[60] Just as *everybody knows swinging eighth notes in jazz is stylistic*, there were many "understood" rules that eighteenth-century musicians took for granted. And about them, much was said. A great deal can be learned from the documents left behind. The best hope for a rational solution is to learn as much as possible about the language from eighteenth-century letters, pedagogical writings, and treatises.

What is learned from the treatises, coupled with what is known about the mechanics of the fortepiano, informs our understanding in part. Van Oort recommends, "We can try to solve the problem by finding a 'native' speaker; in this case, the eighteenth century fortepiano."[61] However, playing the native speaker alone is not the answer. If I don't know *how* to express and execute the language, the result will be quite unsatisfying. Learning the language and style and discovering how it may be executed on the fortepiano—*that's* how I make new discoveries. I must keep in mind that it is impossible to duplicate the style of fortepiano music on the modern piano. It cannot be translated. But my modern performance of an old style can be informed by my knowledge of the bygone language as performed on its intended instrument.

You are now invited to the debate, fraught with disparities, challenges, and demands, yet also reassured with similarities and much guidance, all found in the primary sources. This remarkable centuries-old language will unfold like a lovely rosebud coming into full bloom.

GOAL #3/4: WHAT THEY MEANT/HOW DO I PERFORM THE LANGUAGE TODAY?

Although the overriding and eventual goal is to get at what the composer *meant*, it is reached only from a reliable source/score that demonstrates what was actually written. There are esteemed annotated scores that provide insight and are of great value, yet those, too, are once-removed from the primary source and can be dangerous if the edits are not clear to the performer. Therefore, the first step in striving to convey the composer's message is to come as close as possible to the original message, the primary source, the composer's "spelling." Dart would concur: "First of all we need to know the exact symbols the composer used."[62]

Urtext editions bring the performer as close as possible to the original notation. Here, scholars examine information from various "first" editions—manuscripts, autographs, first published editions—and come to a learned conclusion regarding what most closely represents an "authentic" score. When there is a discrepancy, *Urtexts* usually provide optional versions of a note, measure, or section from which the performer may make an informed choice.

Score accuracy was extremely important to eighteenth-century musicians. This conviction was stressed adamantly, with fervor, by Beethoven in a letter he wrote to Holz:

> For God's sake please impress on Rampel to copy everything exactly as it stands.... Sometimes the ⟍ are inserted intentionally after the notes. The slurs should be exactly as they are now. It is not all the same whether it is a
>
> 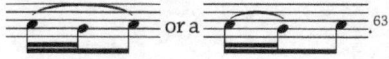 or a [63]

Schulz expresses it slightly differently:

> The few signs with which the composer describes the execution of single notes or phrases [such as slurs, strokes or dots, *forte*, or *piano*, etc.] must be observed as exactly as possible because, *for certain movements, they are as essential as the notes themselves*... [italics added].[64]

For clarification, refer to Example 1.4 (found on page 28). Look at Beethoven's intricate articulation indications of a simple minuet (which, by the way, is considerably more complex than most teaching anthologies). Executing the slurs as Beethoven indicated creates a varied, tasteful, and interesting musical experience.

Modern teaching editions come with problems. With good intentions, they superimpose interpretations that unfortunately change the meaning, sound, and *affekt*: the musical message. For example, compare an edited version of a simple Haydn dance (Example 1.5a, page 29) to an *Urtext* (Example 1.5b, page 30). Listen to the accompanying audio files. The disparities are striking. (Visit the companion website, Diagrams and Audio Files 1.3a–1.4b for more examples of major discrepancies between editions. ▶))

Music Example 1.4. Beethoven, Six Minuets, WoO 10, no. 2. Copyright (1990) by
G. Henle Verlag, Munich.

Music Example 1.5a. Haydn, German Dance in C Major, : Hob. IX:12, no. 10. *German Dance in C Major* by Franz Joseph Haydn, From *Succeeding with the Masters®, Classical Era, Vol.* 1, edited by Helen Marlais. Copyright ©2004 The FJH Music Company Inc. International Copyright Secured. All Rights Reserved. Used with Permission, 18. ▶

Editions from the late nineteenth-, twentieth-, and twenty-first centuries were most interested in promoting the latest development in pianos, the long singing line. These editors consequently changed a great deal of composers' original markings—in essence, changing their "words"—in an attempt to explain them. Again, the differences in notation and resulting musical message are striking. (Visit the companion website, Diagrams and Audio 1.5a–1.6b to compare scores edited by Bartok with Henle editions. ▶)

Obviously, it is impossible to know what the composer meant if it is unclear what in reality was said. It is not feasible to make informed interpretive decisions regarding the composer's intent without an authentic score. It all depends on accurate scores. Dart passionately implores thus:

> Every scrap of information that an early composer conveyed to his performer by means of the written notation he used must be treated as though it were gold; it is very precious, and far more valuable than any editor's opinion, however enlightened this may be.[65]

Music Example 1.5b. Haydn, Twelve German Dances, Hob. IX:12, no. 10. Copyright (1990) by G. Henle Verlag, Munich. ▶.

INFLUENCES APPLIED

Urgency. Playing artfully and successfully does not guarantee the composer's message is being respected or communicated. And that is our responsibility, regardless of the instrument: to learn as much as possible about what the composer intended and allow it to influence us as artists to "say something" in modern performing. Although the attainment of unquestionably complete information is an illusion, musical honesty is possible when the past is accessed and is allowed to excite a sense of correctness and newness for today.

An open-minded approach to discovery brings a wellspring of possibilities. Great thinkers, innovators, explorers, and artists inform their minds by looking back to rich historical experiences. Throughout this book, information will be viewed through the "lens" of the native speaker/writer/composer to draw historically informed conclusions.

Fortepiano. When realized on period instruments, eighteenth-century music takes on fresh meaning and new life, much like a refurbished painting or stained glass window. It will teach us something new about the score and the sound. The task at hand is to develop a "sense" of the fortepiano sound and then develop a sense of how it influences performing on the modern piano. This task is best done by actually playing eighteenth-century repertoire on a period instrument. Do not be discouraged. At first attempt, many modern pianists play too hard, over-attack, and use arm weight, which results in a pressed, forced, and ugly sound. Delicacy, sensitivity to touch, controlled finger action, and finesse are the keywords in capturing fortepiano style on the modern piano. Ideally, play a fortepiano long enough to develop a sense of the instrument, the action, the technique required, and the "sound" or "essence." If an instrument is not available, listening to several quality recordings of accomplished period performers on their instruments will suffice. For it is the "sound concept" that is important.

Active listening is essential. One recent monumental project brings us as close as possible to experiencing a variety of period instruments in their natural environment: *The Virtual Haydn: Complete Works for Solo Keyboard* performed by Tom Beghin. Here, Beghin performs Haydn's solo repertoire on seven recreated historical instruments in nine rooms restored to meet the same acoustical standards Haydn experienced when he lived and performed his music in them.

Take advantage of the opportunity to listen to the esteemed artists previously listed. Each artist, piano, and setting brings distinctive traits and sound qualities to the Classical Era style. They illustrate informed variety within the style and thus provide wisdom.

Cooper embraces an inclusive approach:

> It is not actually essential to use a fortepiano in order to play the early sonatas effectively. For a start, there was a great variety of sound between different pianos, yet Beethoven did not reject any type as positively unsuitable for his music (nor did he find any that were wholly satisfactory).[66]

To expect eighteenth-century music to be reserved for a single instrument from a specific time is to deny an entire world of music lovers the opportunity to experience Classical Era music. Moreover, failure to make application of these tools to the modern piano is to deny the world an entire style. Distinctive common fortepiano traits may well be interpreted and adapted to today's pianos. Simply being careful not to overplay the modern piano is a positive step in the right direction. The fortepiano's lighter, quicker action and responsiveness should influence decisions regarding adjustments for timing and tempo simply by developing a "classically adapted" technical approach to the modern piano. Particularly helpful is Bilson's general advice:

> I believe Mozart will come out best on a modern piano by a player who learns to play it *as if* it were a far lighter instrument than it actually is, *as if* the keys were far easier to depress than they actually are.[67]

Newman suggests an approach to assist development of this lighter "essence" in low registers:

> It follows that on a modern piano one ought to consider a *portato* rather than a *legato* in bass passages and figuration, and at a faster tempo even a quasi staccato . . . .[68]

While developing the lighter approach, keep in mind other inherent qualities of the fortepiano: the ability to shift quickly from *forte* to *piano*, the myriad subtleties available, and the range of "extremes." As the fortepiano's subtle dynamic range is conceptualized on the modern piano, remain aware of differences in sheer volume capabilities and decay. To the fortepianist, *ff* and *sfz* have as much to do with *affekt* as they do with sheer volume (probably even more). Likewise, the fortepiano's five-octave range should influence the concept of where "the limits" are when playing on a modern seven-and-a-half-octave instrument. What is just a bit low or high on the modern piano could well have been the lowest or highest note on the fortepiano, demanding a much more extreme *affekt*.

One of the finest inherent qualities of the fortepiano—clarity of attack—requires an ever-discerning ear. Bear in mind that the modern piano tone develops through four phases (attack, sustain, bloom, decay), growing slightly before beginning to gradually decay. Therefore, attempting to "bite" or "attack" certain passages in the same way on the modern piano as one would on the fortepiano will create a very choked and choppy tone. Likewise, experiencing and remembering the quick decay of the fortepiano should influence the size of any sudden accent on the modern piano. Listen to make sure any accent has the necessary time to decay in the tempo chosen. Each instrument responds differently, and the lengths to which this concept may be taken will vary from instrument to instrument.

The rich overtones and varieties of *timbre* in the fortepiano encourage more exploration of color changes on the modern piano. Newman expounds:

... today [on modern pianos] the tone is more obscure, more thick, and as
regards tone color more uniform in all registers than in the instruments
of Beethoven's epoch. Only in the middle register at a soft [level] does
the tone color of the modern piano not differ from [that of] Beethoven's
instrument. ... [69]

This evaluation suggests a wider range of options prior to considering the
use of pedal for color. And pedal choices should now be intentional for
special effects rather than blanket legato sustaining.

Take these germinal suggestions and try them on the repertoire. Hear
how these simple adjustments make a big difference. Listen to the audio
examples on the companion website as you work your way through the
book. Hear how the traits of the fortepiano may be used to your advantage; allow them to inform your choices. Create new art that is both true
to the composer and truly your own.

The language. Learning how eighteenth-century language was pronounced, what it meant at the time, and how it was interpreted is at
the heart of learning the style. The ultimate goal is not to imitate the
old, or discard it, but determine what is viable for use within reasonable
parameters for artistic playing on today's piano. As van Oort suggests,
we are forced into "making a translation of sorts."[70] Once the challenges
are addressed, discrepancies can be reconciled. The act of speaking an
authentic rendition of eighteenth-century music notational language
is compatible with playing it on the modern piano. Rather than turning your back on the rich history or attempting to imitate the sound
of a fortepiano on a modern piano, you will be able to use the information to better understand the composer's intent and create your own
individual art.

Urtexts. The importance of playing from *Urtext* scores cannot be
emphasized enough. *Urtext* scores are essential in making informed decisions regarding what composers actually wrote (how the language was
"spelled") before attempting to unearth how the notation was executed
("pronounced") or determining how it may be interpreted. Dart supports
this argument:

It is impossible for anyone living today to hear early music with the ears of
those who first heard it, and it is idle to pretend otherwise. But it is more or
less possible for us to look at its notation with the eyes of those who first saw
it, and the least we can do is to try. Too few editors realize their responsi-
bilities not only to the composer but also to the present-day performer [and
listener].[71]

Although *Urtexts* are the essential first step, having an *Urtext* alone does not an informed performance make. It is here where esteemed annotated editions may provide direction through respected interpretations. Willis advises thus:

> Today, while the use of original musical texts is widely taken for granted, many performers and musicologists recognize that this does not in itself guarantee interesting, affecting performances. Thoughtful musicians recognize the need to discover performance implications which go beyond the literal sonic reproduction of the notation—implications grounded in analysis, performance practice research, experimentation with period instruments, and the revival of improvisatory elements of performance.[72]

Annotated editions are valuable for learning a great deal about a different interpretation, plausible variation or improvisation, or the view from a different era. While working from *any edition,* continually ask yourself, "Am I getting the information from the composer or the editor?" Always read the editorial notes. In Cooper's latest edition of Beethoven's piano sonatas, there are nearly 200 pages devoted to explaining, interpreting, and putting the scores in historical context. Appropriate decisions can best be made from knowledgeable sources. Good editions make a clear distinction between accurate scores, learned interpretations, and appropriate instructions for the performer. However, it is still best to play from an *Urtext,* clearly knowing what is from the composer. You, the performer, may then add markings to clarify your personal interpretation taken from all sources.

Urtexts are the recipe. They do not clarify performance practices—the countless unnotated conventions of the day. The crux of this book delves into those intricacies to provide historically accurate, plausible, and applicable answers for today.

One final warning. A predominant post–WW II belief holds that there is an *exactly correct* way to play the score; to literally observe all markings *exactly* as written, using current performance practice standards. Unfortunately, many twenty-first century notational rules don't apply to eighteenth-century notation. Combining this well-intentioned, ill-informed sentiment with the scholarly deficiencies in many teaching editions almost guarantees realizing the score *exactly incorrectly.* Dart compares customs:

> A composer of the eighteenth-century ... also used notation in accordance with the conventions of his own time, but there is therefore every chance in the world that a twentieth-century performer will entirely misinterpret his

music through an inadequate knowledge of these conventions, for the most part long obsolete . . . forgotten.[73]

For the struggling musician, teacher, and performer, purchasing *Urtext* editions requires an additional expense above and beyond conveniently priced anthologies. Marvelous benefits are reaped:

- The opportunity to know the composer's "words"
- The opportunity to make interpretive decisions based on informed research
- To own full musical collections with a wealth of repertoire beyond the "standards"
- To explore new repertoire choices for the "seasoned" teacher or performer

Currently, there are a number of excellent choices available. The following list contains recommended collections for use prior to standard sonatas. They are the foundational scores I maintain in my personal library—an excellent starting point. They are quite user-friendly; one concept at a time can be learned and incorporated, setting a solid foundation for larger works.

➤ Bach, C. P. E. *24 Pieces for Piano* (International Music Co.)
➤ Beethoven, *Klavierstücke* (Henle—12)
➤ Beethoven, *Leichte Meisterwerke für Klavier* (Musica Budapest)
➤ Beethoven, *Sämtliche Bagatellen* (Henle—158)
➤ Beethoven, *Tänze für Klavier* (Henle—449)
➤ Haydn, *Leichte Meisterwerke für Klavier* (Musica Budapest)
➤ Haydn, *Tänze und Märche für Klavier* (Henle—617)
➤ Haydn, *Neun kleine frühe Sonaten* (Henle—645)
➤ (Various), *Leichte Klavierstücke*, Band I (Henle—134)
➤ Mozart, L., *Notenbuch für Nannerl* (Schott)
➤ Mozart, *Klavierstücke* (Henle—22)

For the more substantial works, Malcolm Bilson offers suggestions based on his experience:

- The Bärenreiter NMA (Neue Mozart Ausgabe, or New Mozart Edition) is available free online at http://dme.mozarteum.at/DME/main/index.php?l=, and this is an excellent edition for Mozart.
- The Beethoven and Haydn editions are published by Henle. They exist both with fingerings and without (email communication from December 8, 2013).

Barry Cooper provides some of the most recent scholarship on Beethoven: *The Thirty-five Piano Sonatas by Beethoven* (in three volumes), published by the Associated Board of the Royal Schools of Music (2007).

Once *Urtext* scores are obtained, then and only then can eighteenth-century influences be applied with integrity. As Newman recommends, "The performer must then make decisions between acquiring the most authentic score available and actually performing it."[74] Throughout the course of this book, discussions will continue about the viability (practicality, effectiveness, whether it is convincing) and timeliness (does it work today?) of performing choices to make your interpretive work relevant and applicable.

Some argue, as Newman does, that unedited *Urtext*s are not likely to suffice for intelligent interpretations by most performers. "All too often they still require decisions, choices, and even independent research that demand too much of the performer before the performing itself can begin."[75] It has been my experience as a musician and master teacher that we hunger for knowledge and play much more musically and creatively when we learn the language and make the score our own. We are both willing and capable. . . .

Which is why you are on this journey: to have questions answered in a succinct, pedagogically sound, and practical format while at the same time to ask questions that will make the work your own. It is time to unveil the parameters for eighteenth-century music notational language and open the floodgates to amazing aural and emotional experiences—making what is old new again . . . and yours. So, let's get started!

THE LESSON

Throughout this book, at the end of each chapter, Mozart's London Notebook excerpt KV 15oo, mm. 1–8 (Henle edition) (Example 1.6) will be used to demonstrate how easily, simply, and effectively the topic(s) presented may be applied. A beginning-level piece was purposely chosen to demonstrate how eighteenth-century influences are applicable to all repertoires, from beginning to advanced music. Pedagogical suggestions are based on successful, firsthand experience teaching this piece to early intermediate students who encounter eighteenth-century repertoire on the modern piano for the first time. Advanced musicians may then take these basic concepts and build extended application to complex works.

Play and study Example 1.6 with the following points in mind.

Music Example 1.6. Mozart, London Notebook, KV 15oo, mm. 1–8. Copyright (1983) by G. Henle Verlag, Munich.

1. Play the excerpt with varying style interpretations such as jazz, blues, rock and roll, Classical, and Romantic. Discuss, compare, and contrast the impact of historically informed style contexts.
2. Talk about the instrument for which this piece was most likely composed and the distinct traits of the fortepiano. Listen to recordings of fortepiano performances.

    ✓ Practice strategy: listen to recordings of simple Classical repertoire as performed by accomplished fortepianists, such as van Oort's recording of Mozart's *Klavierstücke (Complete)*
3. Discuss different instruments in the orchestra and the different tone qualities (*timbre*) produced from those instruments. Discuss the *timbre* in the different ranges of the fortepiano, the smaller range of the fortepiano, and how those qualities might be expressed in this piece on the modern piano.
   a. Middle range—perhaps *tutti* (brass, or full strings) in mm. 1–2
   b. Higher range—perhaps a smaller group (winds) in mm. 3–4
   c. Left-hand octave jumps, perhaps imitating bassoon-like qualities
   d. Adding instruments in mm. 5–6, returning to *tutti* on mm. 7–8
4. Discuss tone production and decay. Determine an appropriate adjustment on the modern piano to bring integrity to the eighteenth-century sound.
   a. Determine an appropriate volume to allow for decay and *detaché* between notes.
5. Discuss the fortepiano action and differences in technique between the fortepiano and modern piano.
   a. Play with a compact hand, utilizing fingers more and arms less.
   b. Play lightly, *as if* this were a fortepiano action.

6. Look at the score and notice the sparseness of direction from the composer. Explain that the rules are there; it's just a new game! Introduce the fact that eighteenth-century music notational language has its own rules, such as how the quarter note is to be played (executed), dynamics, and articulation choices, setting the scene for the chapters to come, much like the trailer to an exciting movie!

7. Discuss other styles of music.
   a. Discuss differences in styles of music and how the style dictates, in part, how notes are performed.
   b. Talk about "assumed" rules, such as "swinging" jazz eighth notes.

8. Ask if anyone has ever taken what you (the student) said or wrote and changed it. Even if well-intentioned, would it still be the original words and ideas? Explain that this is the point of *Urtext* editions—to get as close as possible to the "first person."

9. Look at the excerpt pairs from this chapter with different editing. Play the scores to hear how much musical ideas change, depending on the edition.
   a. Discuss what happens when editors fill in the score with their own suggestions—performers have fewer choices.
   b. Notice how changes made by the editor change "the rules of the (interpretation) game."

10. Refer to the previous discussion surrounding jazz.
    a. Understanding the "rules of the game" (stylistic traits) makes it possible to play "true to the style" while at the same time infuse individual ideas.
    b. The same is true with eighteenth-century notation.

Use the quick reference guide on the companion website to summarize. ▶

CHAPTER 2

⌒⌒

Affekt and Good Taste

Haydn speaking to L. Mozart, observing the young Mozart: Your son has
"taste and a profound understanding."
—*etching on a wall at Mozarthaus, Vienna, Austria*

In chapter 1 the door to willingness was opened, some commonly held misconceptions were set straight, a brief overview of the fortepiano was provided, the beginnings for understanding eighteenth-century notational language were broached, and the importance of using *Urtext* editions as a reliable source for the composer's "words" was emphasized. The stage is now set to look at those "words"—to comprehend what they most likely meant, how they were executed, how they sounded on the fortepiano, and, ultimately, how that body of knowledge impacts playing today.

Every musician should comprehend the message behind eighteenth-century music notational language *before* attempting to play it on *any* instrument. Grasping the message provides an account of the character, the mood, the emotion—the *affekt*—behind the pitch, volume, and duration directions on the written page. In turn, interpretive choices within defined parameters are revealed. This is where newfound freedom is experienced.

Affekt. It all begins here. From L. Mozart to Türk, Kirnberger to Quantz, Bach to Koch, every esteemed treatise from the eighteenth century discusses the immense importance of understanding the influence of *affekt* on playing. For instance, in *Klavierschule*, Türk points out that regardless of one's technical prowess, without understanding the *affekt*, it is "not possible to have good execution because the most essential part is missing, namely the expression of the prevailing character without which no listener can be moved to any degree."[1] (See the extended quotation on the companion website, Text 2.1. ⊙)

It is not enough to play with amazing facility and phenomenal dexterity. Nor is it enough to play every pitch and note value accurately. Music must *say something*. It is essential to comprehend the language that is spoken. The primary sources bear this out, as Bach tells us, "What comprises good performance? The ability through singing or playing to make the ear conscious of the true content and affect of a composition."[2] To ignore the meaning sends us back to the word pairs in chapter 1, wondering whether the music is a boar or a bore!

Eighteenth-century musicians believed that, without understanding the content and *affekt*, all effort was in vain. Beethoven was well informed and his work was impacted by the relationships between oratory, poetry, rhetoric, and music. He was also familiar with Bach's *Versuch*, which devotes considerable content to the importance of *affekt*. Badura-Skoda notes that Beethoven held Bach's *Versuch* in high regard, requiring Carl Czerny to obtain and bring a copy along for lessons.[3] It was with intense resolve that period musicians endeavored to express meaning in music. The remembrance from Beethoven's pupil Ferdinand Ries provides a substantive testament:

> . . . He would often have me repeat a single number ten or more times. In the
> Variations in F major, Op. 34, I was obliged to repeat almost the entire final
> Adagio variation seventeen times; and even then he was not satisfied with the
> expression in the small cadenza.[4]

Eighteenth-century musical experience was communal. It was inclusive, as Haynes clarifies: "Rhetorical music had as its aim to evoke and provoke emotions—the Affections, or Passions—that were shared by everyone, audience and performers alike."[5] The interactive intention was so pronounced that the house lights were sometimes left up to encourage audience and performer interaction.[6]

Music must say something to everyone, and it must be done in *good taste*. In eighteenth-century culture, the societal ideal of refinement and finesse was of utmost importance, much more important than we give it credit today—detail down to the slightest nuance. As Koch warns performers, playing that lacks good taste is akin to "clownery . . . telling a dirty joke to a gathering of intellectuals."[7] (See the extended citation on the companion website, Text 2.2. ⊙)

Affekt is the ground upon which eighteenth-century music is built. It provides the foundation for expressing meaning and understanding. It governs the means for good execution. It must be pursued with great resolve. And in good taste.

HISTORICAL BACKGROUND

From the ancients to today, and everything in between, music discussions revolve around *affekt*. We choose to experience music because it touches our heart. The *New Oxford American Dictionary* provides origins. The word "affect" or "affection" comes from the Latin *afficere*, "to have an effect on, influence," or *affectare*, "aim at." The original sense of the meaning was to stir emotions of "like or love."[8] Notice the connecting thread—music as it projects *affekt*—in each of the following styles.

Doctrine of Affections

Musicians of the late Baroque Era, particularly in Germany, fully embraced this belief system. *The Harvard Dictionary of Music* explains, "This belief, widely held in the 17th and early 18th centuries, that the principal aim of music is to arouse the passions or affections (love, hate, joy, anger, fear, etc.). By the later seventeenth century, the view also included the notion that a composition (or at least a single movement or major section of a larger work) should have a unity of affection."[9]

Beyond the *doctrine of affections*, several schools of thought were cultivated. They all contain a common focus or goal, to express *affekt*, yet individual characteristic specialties emerged.

Galant Style

This early eighteenth-century style was in contrast to the dramatic, learned contrapuntal Baroque style. It comes from the root "to amuse oneself" and was a fancy of the upper classes and nobility. The purpose was to keep up with the latest "style." The cultural belief was that the latest fashion or composition was never expected to last more than five years, as the next new fad would then be in vogue. This is a free or homophonic style. *The Harvard Dictionary of Music* lists specifics. "Traits attributed to the *galant* style by various 18th-century theorists include light texture, periodic phrasing with frequent cadences, liberally ornamented melodies, simple harmony, and free treatment of dissonance."[10] The appearance of this style accompanied the shift from sacred to secular, church to salon, fugal (polyphonic) to accompanied melody (homophonic).

Empfindsamer Stil

The Harvard Dictionary of Music provides a succinct description: "The north German 'sensitive' or 'sentimental' style of the mid-18th century . . . The goal [in this style] was the direct, natural, sensitive, and often subjective expression of emotion. [It] may be considered a dialect of the international *galant* style. Particular traits of *empfindsam* style are the liberal use of appoggiatura or sigh figures, exploitation of dynamic nuance, and frequent melodic and harmonic chromaticism. . . . The keyboard idiom . . . is often exceptionally intricate and refined, incorporating extensive ornamentation and complex rhythmic differentiation below the beat level."[11]

This style is well-represented by W. F. Bach, C. P. E. Bach, and Quantz circa 1750–1780, and is characterized by frequent changes or alternations between affections within a given section or movement.[12]

Sturm und Drang (Storm and Stress)

The Harvard Dictionary of Music concisely describes a movement related to "German literature in the second half of the 18th century that had as its goal the powerful, shocking, even violent expression of emotion."[13] Here, *affekt* is realized through angular, abrupt shifts in expression, unpredictable themes, large leaps, rapid changes in dynamics, pulsing rhythms (perfectly suited for Alberti bass; see chapter 3), and syncopation.

"Defining" Affekt

Affekt is a foundational pillar for eighteenth-century style. When the ability of music to stir emotions was discussed in the period literature, it was described in many ways, including character, affections, expression, affect, and emotion. For consistency, unless in a direct quotation, the Germanic term *affekt* will be used.

How *does* one define or describe and then develop the ability to express *affekt*? Instructions from treatises such as those written by Bach and

Quantz charge us to, first and foremost, be surrounded by good compositions and great artists, whose mastery will influence and promote development of *affekt*. Most interesting and insightful is the advice from these
two instrumentalists: listen to good singers. Quantz impels us thus:

> The beginner must seek also to listen to as many good and generally approved
> compositions as possible. By this means he will greatly facilitate his path
> toward good taste in music. He must seek to profit not only from good instru-
> mentalists of every kind, but also from good singers.[14] (See Bach's advice on
> the companion website, Text 2.3. ▶)

It is largely through experiencing great music that sensitivity may be
discovered and cultivated. A recent personal experience highlights the
profound impact of actively doing, rather than talking about, art. While
traveling throughout Italy in the summer of 2010, absorbing museum
after museum of great sculptures, I had the opportunity to visit St. Peter's
Basilica in Vatican City. Although I am not an art specialist by any means,
I am familiar with many of the pieces I was about to experience. As
I turned the corner, my eyes befell *Pietá* by Michelangelo. I was awestruck
by a greatness I had never before experienced. Ineffable. I wept as I reacted
to the *affekt* Michelangelo captured in Carrara marble. I had read about
and seen pictures of *Pietá*, but couldn't be so moved until I *experienced*
the sculpture. It spoke profoundly and deeply to my heart. By being surrounded by analogous excellence in music, one may develop sensitivity to
affekt. Türk echoes the essential role that experience plays in discovering
beauty:

> There are some means which can more or less contribute to the strengthening
> of expression and which to some extent can be put down in the form of written
> instruction, although it is even in this regard incomparably better to listen to
> singers and players of great sensitivity. For as has been said, certain subtleties
> of expression cannot really be described; they must be *heard*.[15]

It must be experienced. *Heard.* I can describe gorgeous colors of blue,
pink, violet, and orange. I can scientifically explain the effects of humidity
on visibility and hue. I can share the exact sunrise timetables at 15°N and
86°W. Yet none of that expresses what I *felt*, the *affekt* that wafted over
me, when I actually sat on the dock by a small Honduran island at those
coordinates and beheld a most breathtaking sunrise over the Caribbean
Sea. Then I *knew* beauty.

We must move from the desk, where we read about music to the concert hall, where we experience it. We are thus instructed: listen to renowned specialists performing on period instruments. Begin with those artists listed in chapter 1. Invite the beauty to wash over you. Nurture sensitivity.

Still, Türk admits the benefit of some form of written direction. "There are some means which can more or less contribute to the strengthening of expression and which to some extent can be put down in the form of written instruction."[16] The information that is available is informative and suggestive. Delve into the literature to uncover many clues in the quest to foster personal sensitivity to eighteenth-century music notational language.

BLUEPRINT OF AN INSPIRED SOUND

An architect first conceptualizes an idea, next creates a blueprint, and finally executes the written plans to build a tangible, physical structure. The concept and blueprint shape the specifics of the final creation. For example, the concept and blueprint behind grand amusement parks such as Denmark's Tivoli Gardens or Florida's Disneyworld are markedly different from the plans behind lovely sacred places of worship such as London's St. Paul's Cathedral or Washington National Cathedral in Washington, DC. Likewise, eighteenth-century musicians began with an inspired blueprint for a particular sound.

Türk devotes Part Three of *Klavierschule* and Bach devotes the entire section "Performance" in his *Versuch* to get at and then execute the underlying concept. During a master class at The Art of the Fortepiano, van Oort provided direction along these lines, explaining that a sensitive composer or performer with good taste determines the *concept* before addressing the details, decides *what* is wanted before playing to avoid reworking material later, and then makes decisions regarding how the concept will be achieved to prevent relying on "intuitive" playing, which usually results in sentimentality.[17] "Mind before fingers on the keys" is a good adage. There is an etching attributed to Haydn on a wall at Mozarthaus in Vienna, Austria. Observing the young Mozart, Haydn says to L. Mozart that his son has "taste and a profound understanding." Indeed, the concept is important!

To develop "taste and a profound understanding" begin with the blueprint, build the foundation, and then beautify the structure: *affekt*, formal structure, and harmonic function, followed by individual elements such as dynamics, note values, articulation, and ornamentation.

Music is organic, not the sum of separate inanimate parts, but the culmination of many parts working together to create a living, ever-changing art. Although the elements will be discussed separately, be mindful that they are part of a fluid, dynamic, complete musical whole. Aristotle reasons that the whole *is* greater than, and something altogether different from, the sum of its parts:

> In the case of all things which have several parts and in which the whole is not, as it were, a mere heap, but the totality is something besides the parts, there is a cause of unity.[18] (See the extended citation on the companion website, Text 2.4. ⏵)

AFFEKT AND STRUCTURE, METER, INHERENT TEMPO

Conceptualizing a formal structure intentionally advances a particular *affekt*. To this end, Sulzer expresses just how important the sonata was: "There is no form of instrumental music that is more capable of depicting wordless sentiments than the sonata."[19] Indeed, many believed the sonata was the most pure or perfect form for delivery of *affekt* because it does not rely on words. The Classical Era sonata is, in many ways, a culmination of growth out of the Baroque dance suite, both socially and musically. Socially, dance suites were sets of incidental music that moved from the countryside to the dance hall to royal court ballrooms. They were part of the culture. Composers and performers were consciously (perhaps even subconsciously) aware of the dances. Musically, decisions surrounding form and meter were indispensably entrenched in, and inextricably interwoven with, these socially significant dances. As the dances moved from the countryside (as expanded incidental dance music) to salon settings of middle- and upper- class society, and later to the concert hall, they grew into the Classical piano sonata. And were very popular. Therefore, it is imperative to look at dance forms to better comprehend underpinnings of Classical Era *affekt* and sonata structure.

A bird's-eye view has been created to serve as a useful tool when you encounter repertoire from the Classical Era. Essential musical traits of popular Baroque dances have been sorted from Türk's *Klavierschule*.[20] They are synthesized and presented in Table 2.1. Notice how each dance is inextricably linked to meter, inherent tempo, special traits, *affekt*, and execution.

All of the elements work interdependently, much like a circulatory system—each element being dependent upon one another and working

Table 2.1. BAROQUE DANCES AND *AFFEKT*

DANCE	METER	INHERENT TEMPO	SPECIAL TRAITS	*Affekt*	EXECUTION
Allemande in suites/partitas	$\frac{4}{4}$	Not too fast	Begins with upbeat	Serious	
Allemande in dances	$\frac{4}{4}$	Rapid tempo	Begins with upbeat	Lively	Light
Bourée	$\frac{2}{2}$ or $\frac{4}{4}$	Moderate	Begins with quarter note upbeat	Spirited	Light
Canarie	$\frac{3}{8}$ or $\frac{6}{8}$	Faster than gigue	Strongly accented dotted notes that are very detached		
Ciaconne (chaconne, ciaccona)	$\frac{3}{2}$, $\frac{3}{4}$	Moderately fast	Every first note of a measure is rather strongly marked		
Courante (corrente)	$\frac{3}{2}$ or $\frac{3}{4}$	Not very fast	Commonly begins with a short note as upbeat	Serious	Almost more detached than legato
Gavotte	alla breve ₵	Moderately fast	Begins with an upbeat of two quarter notes	Pleasant and rather lively	
Gigue (giga, gique)	$\frac{6}{8}$, $\frac{12}{8}$, or $\frac{3}{8}$	Fast		Cheerful	Short and light fashion
March	$\frac{4}{4}$	Moderate enough to allow for two steps in each measure	Dotted notes especially call for full and emphatic playing	Brave, bold, rousing	Forceful
Minuet (menuett, minuetto)	$\frac{3}{4}$ (more seldom $\frac{3}{8}$)	Moderately fast and agreeable	Executed without embellishments	Well-known dance of noble and charming character	
Musette		Slower tempo than the gigue		Naive, gentle, and pleasant	Very beguiling and legato manner
Rigaudon	alla breve ₵	Fast	Begins with a quarter-note upbeat	Lively, cheerful	Light execution
Romanze			Simple, agreeable, and naive melody		Made more poignant by increasing expression rather than ornaments and additions
Sarabande	$\frac{3}{2}$ or $\frac{3}{4}$	Rather slow	Particularly used in Spain	Serious nature joined with expression and dignity	Heavy execution
Waltz	$\frac{3}{4}$	Rather quick			Light execution

together in order for the desired *affekt* to be expressed. Notice the relationship between each particular dance and *affekt*. Kirnberger explains that meter indications and note-value choices influence *affekt*. "This difference of meters is very well suited to express particular nuances of the passions . . . a more ponderous or lighter meter depending upon whether the affect in its particular nuance requires one or the other."[21] (See the extended citation on the companion website, Text 2.5. ▶)) This "ponderous or lighter meter"[22] refers to the weight of the meter, as Türk now clarifies: "A composition in $\frac{3}{2}$ is played more heavily than it would be if it were in $\frac{3}{4}$ [which is lighter] or even in $\frac{3}{8}$ [which is lighter yet, regardless of any tempo marking]."[23] Return to Table 2.1. Those meters with a 2 in the denominator are associated with heavy and serious *affekt*, while those with an 8 are associated with light and cheerful *affekt*.

Note values chosen within a given meter provide direction as well. Simply put, long note values are heavy, short values light. Kirnberger provides a specific example. "The character of $\frac{3}{4}$ meter is entirely different when quarter notes are used almost exclusively throughout than when many eighths and even smaller notes occur."[24] And Kirnberger addresses how they interact with tempo: "Tempo in melody can also be violent or tender, skipping or monotonous, fiery or bland even when the degree of fast or slow motion is the same, depending upon the type of note values chosen for the melody."[25] See chapter 5 for further discussion.

Inherent tempo rounds out the discussion of rhythmic organization as it relates to the *affekt* of dances. Table 2.1 illustrates the relationship between *affekt* and tempo. And Türk speaks to the effect of tempo on *affekt*. "Whether a heavy or light execution [of any given rhythm] is to be chosen may also be determined from the tempo."[26] Sulzer flips the coin and clarifies how *affekt* influences tempo:

> However, tempo in music is not limited just to the different degrees of slow and fast motion. There are passions in which the images flow monotonously like a gentle brook; others where they flow faster with a moderate stir, but without delay; some in which the succession of images is similar to wild brooks swollen by heavy rains, which rush violently along and sweep with them everything that stand in their way; and again others in which the images are similar to the wild sea, which violently beats against the shore and then recedes to crash again with new force."[27]

Even so, when explaining parameters of *affekt* and emotion, there are probably more exceptions than rules. Thankfully, it is not rules we are looking for, but understanding of a sound. Kirnberger admits, "However, it is not possible to give definite rules that would specify the most suitable tempo and meter for every type of sentiment. For the most part, it depends on a refined and accurate sensitivity."[28] It falls back on understanding the *affekt* of the piece at hand.

So, from the name of the dance, the meter indication, and the chosen note values alone, the performer is given much information about the *affekt*. Their interaction creates a smooth and interdependent system of *affekt*. And yet period musicians knew that this was still sometimes not sufficient in "telling the story." Türk adds the following to the discussion:

> Every composition has a certain (predominant) character. In order that the player know beforehand what character is predominant in a composition, and how he should generally prepare its execution, more careful composers are accustomed to indicate the character of a composition as well as its tempo. For this reason there are a number of terms which are employed as an attempt to define the required execution.[29] (See the extended citation on the companion website, Text 2.6. ▶)

Another overview, synthesized from Türk's *Klavierschule*,[30] proves useful. On page 49, Table 2.2 defines common period terminology that was utilized when determining *affekt* and appropriate execution.

For further investigation, visit *Klavierschule*, page 348, where Türk discusses the use of these qualitative terms in relation to heavy or light execution to arrive at the appropriate *affekt*. More will be said about tempo in chapter 13.

All of these components—dance forms, meter, note values, inherent tempo, and qualitative terms—interact with and feed off one another to notationally describe the desired *affekt*. How to execute that description will be discussed in detail in subsequent chapters.

AFFEKT AND MODE, MOOD

Now that fundamental principles of the interaction between meter and affect are established, the next step is to move to mode and mood to reveal how the sound shapes *affekt*. According to Kirnberger, "for the invention of a good and expressive melody, the first consideration of the composer must be directed at the choice of mode."[31]

Table 2.2. COMMON TERMINOLOGY USED TO CLARIFY EXECUTION
OF *AFFEKT* IN TEMPO

afffettuoso; con affetto	Touching, with much expression of the effect, with sensitivity
con afflizzione	With grief or sadness
agitato	Agitated, impetuously, anxiously restlessly
amoroso	Tenderly, affectionately
animoso	Bravely, lively, valiantly
appassionato	Passionately
ardito	Boldly, briskly, plucky
arioso	Melodically, in a singing fashion
brillante	Glittering, brilliant, spirited, lively
con brio	Fiery, heatedly, glowing, noisily
burlesco	Jocularly, drolly
cantabile	In a singing style
dolce	Pleasant, sweet, gentle
doloroso	Painful
con fuoco	With fire (very lively)
furioso	Furiously
giocoso	Jocular
grave	Serious, grave with dignity
grazioso, con grazia	Pleasant, agreeable, charming, with grace
gustoso, con gusto	Tasteful, with taste
lamentoso, lamentabile	Lamenting, sad, tearful, in a lamenting fashion
languido, languente	Languishing, sighing
legato	Bound together (slurred)
leggiere, leggiermente	Lightly executed
maestoso	Majestic, sublime
mesto	Sad, distressed
pastorale	Pastoral; that is, gracefully and with noble simplicity
patetico	Pathetically; that is, touching to a very high degree, also with a certain greatness
pesante	Emphatically, ponderously
risoluto	Resolute, courageous
scherzando, scherzo	Jocular, dallying
serioso	Seriously, emphatically
sostenuto	Grave; that is, with sustained (and not too short) duration of tones
spiritoso, con spirito	Fiery, heated
staccato	Struck very quickly
tempestoso	Stormy, impetuous, violent
tenor, con tenerezza	Tender, touching, soft
tenuto	Held, held out
vivo, con vivezza, vivace	Lively

In the Classical Era style, key choice is an intentional decision that expresses a particular *affekt*. Kirnberger describes the major mode as "joyous and gay ... has nothing but euphonious and cheerful progressions from its final."[32] Major keys may relate happiness, joy, innocence, purity, simplicity, pastoral scenes, or majesty and triumph, whereas minor keys may relate sadness, melancholy, the dramatic or horrid, darkness, disaster, passion, stress, storms, or devilishness.

Much of the differences in *affekt* are derived from the relationship of the third and the sixth. Kirnberger reasons thus:

> Since thirds and sixths are the intervals heard most frequently in melody, it can be seen from this that the difference in character between the major and minor keys must be considerable, and that the major modes are generally more pleasant, joyous, harmonious, and fuller sounding than the minor modes, since major thirds and sixths are more consonant than minor ones.[33]

Mode choice, in large part, determines mood. Beyond whether a piece is simply in the major or minor mode, there are differences in *affekt* that are dependent upon the purity of the key. The concept of key purity is grounded in Classical Era tuning norms, which make the differences even more striking. Classical Era practice employs mean-tone tuning. The mean-tone system allows for the pure intervals (and keys) to be more at rest and non-pure intervals (and keys) to be more tense. This tuning has a tremendous effect on the *affekt*. Haynes describes mean tone in relation to the modern tuning practice of equal temperament. "Tuning of chords in equal temperament ... is very active, in contrast to the stability and calm of the pure thirds of mean tone."[34] In essence, if *everything* is active (equal temperament), then there is no opportunity to feel at rest and then later excited.

When one uses the mean-tone system, the further from purity a key choice moves, the more intense the *affekt*. Kirnberger descriptively teaches the following:

> A basic rule for judging scales [is] that the major keys whose thirds are completely pure possess most strongly the quality of the major mode, and the greatest roughness and finally even something like ferocity enter into those major keys farthest removed from this purity. The same must also be assumed of minor keys: Those whose thirds are purest have the most gentle and pleasing tenderness and sadness, but those that are farthest removed from this purity blend the most painful and adverse qualities into this character.[35]

Table 2.3. TUNING PURITY AND KEY RELATIONSHIPS

Classes of Major keys (from most to least pure):

First class	C major, D major, F major, G major
Second class	E major, F♯ major, A major, B major
Third class	D♭ major, E♭ major, A♭ major, B♭ major

Classes of Minor keys (from most to least pure)

First class	D minor, E minor, A minor, and B minor
Second class	C♯ minor, D♯ minor, F♯ minor, G♯ minor
Third class	C minor, F minor, G minor, B♭ minor

Table 2.3 provides simply presented parameters regarding tuning purity, as discussed by Kirnberger.[36]

Discussions that address aesthetics in conjunction with choices in modality date back to medieval times. Later, in 1713, German theorist Johann Mattheson expressed grave concerns about simplistic and naive views regarding key choice.[37] (Find more from Mattheson on the companion website, Text 2.7. ⏵) There is much more to it than "major is happy, minor is sad; flats are soft or melancholy and sharps are harsh or bright." To the Classical Era composer with sensitivity and good taste, much effort was expended to choose the right mode.

Every major and minor mode brought with it an associated *affekt,* so much so that Rosen remarks, "Beethoven did say that he could distinguish between music in D flat and C sharp. . . . What Beethoven was talking about was the 'character' of the different tonalities."[38] In *A History of Key Characteristics in the 18th and Early 19th Centuries*, Rita Steblin provides a thorough discussion and compendium of descriptions from over thirty treatises dating from 1690 to 1840. The richness of detail can only be hinted at here; interested readers are urged to visit Steblin's catalogue, found in Appendix A.

In consideration of the scope of this book, the following chart provides a useful summary, including vivid, detailed descriptions from Germanic treatises, circa 1750–1800 (the height of the fortepiano era). At the conclusion of each key characteristic, I have provided suggested works for listening to corroborate the suppositions from the text, translating the abstract into verifiable sound. You are invited to listen to each work and focus on how each key choice relates to its associated *affekt,* for as Türk advises, "certain subtleties of expression cannot really be described; they must be *heard.*"[39] As you listen, compare and contrast sets of instructions and charts. Take in the remarkable agreement between mode purity, key relationships, and composers' repertoire choices. Undeniably, *affekt* and modality are intimately connected.

C Major	Simplicity, joy, purity, innocence, pastoral
	Majestic, grand, noble, militant, firm resolution
	"Most fit for a painting, for pure water arias"[40]
	(Haydn: *The Creation,* Hob. XXI:2, "The Marv'llous Work Behold Amaz'd", Piano Sonata, Hob. XVI:50;
	Mozart: Piano Sonata, K. 545, K. 309)
C Minor	Plaintive, tender, extreme lamenting, pathetic
	"The color of a pale rose and also the aroma of the same"[41]
	"The sighing of the lovesick soul lies in this key"[42]
	Melancholy (Quantz, 164)
	(Beethoven: Piano Sonata op. 13, *Pathetique;*
	Haydn: Piano Sonata, Hob. XVI:20)
D♭/C♯ Major	Leering, degenerating into grief and rapture
	"It cannot laugh, but it can smile; it cannot howl, but it can at least grimace its crying"[43]
	Unusual characters and feelings
	Remains on the outer limits of the musical world
	(Reported in Schindler's *Biographie:* Beethoven: D♭ Major soft/ C♯ Major hard)
	"In this remote key, Haydn and Beethoven have written their sublimest thoughts. They never enter it but for tragic purposes."[44]
	(D♭ Major: Beethoven: Piano Sonata, op. 26/ ii;
	Haydn: Piano Sonata, Hob. XVI:46/ii)
	(C♯ Major: Beethoven: String Quartet, op. 131, final section)
C♯ Minor	Despair
	(Beethoven: Piano Sonata, op. 27, no. 2;
	Haydn: Piano Sonata, Hob. XVI:36)
D Major	Bright, gaiety, brilliance, joyful dancing, funny, boisterous praise
	Martial, pomp, festive, jubilation, exultation
	"Even the god of thunder has a claim to this key" [45]
	(Handel: *Messiah,* "Hallelujah";
	Haydn: Piano Sonata, Hob. XVI:37)

D Minor	Serious subjects, melancholy, sorrowing
	Horrible, gloomy lament, deep suffering
	"A ghost must speak in d minor"[46]
	(Beethoven: Piano Sonata, op. 31, no. 2, *The Tempest*;
	Mozart: Fantasia, K. 397)
E♭ Major	Religious, solemn, priestly
	"The key of love, of devotion, of intimate conversation with God; through its three flats it expresses the holy trinity"[47]
	Night, dark, plaintive
	"Cinnamon with orange blossom"[48]
	(Haydn: Piano Sonata, Hob. XVI:52;
	Mozart: Piano Sonata, K. 282)
E♭ Minor	Anxiety, the soul's deepest distress, brooding despair
	"If ghosts could speak, they would have to speak in this key, with its frigid, gripping, and convulsive clanging"[49]
	(Mozart: Prelude in E♭ Minor, no. 1, K. 404a)
E Major	Noisy shouts of joy, fiery
	"Hilarity, uplifting, sharp, piercing, laughing pleasure and not yet full delight"[50]
	"Yellow is its colour and mace its aroma"[51]
	(Beethoven: Piano Sonata, op. 14, no. 1, op. 109)
E Minor	Sweet and tender, lamenting, naive, womanly
	"Its color is pale orange; neither good nor bad"[52]
	(Beethoven: Piano Sonata, op. 90;
	Haydn: Piano Sonata, Hob. XVI: 34, iii)
F Major	Horns used in hunting calls were in F major, majestic, gentle dignity, joyful, confidence, polite, clever
	(Beethoven: Piano Sonata, Op. 10, No. 2;
	Mozart: Piano Sonata, K. 280, K. 332)
F Minor	Sad, gloomy, despair, pathetic, mournful, sorrow, grief, anguish, weeping, agitation, lament
	"Black, helpless melancholy ... causes the listener to shudder with horror"[53]
	Melancholy[54]
	(Beethoven: Piano Sonata, Op. 2, No. 1, Op. 23, *Appassionata*)

F♯ Major   Very brilliant and piercing, dark feeling, lofty
            pride, awe
            Outer limits of the musical world
            (Beethoven: Piano Sonata, op. 78)

G♭ Major   Splendor, magnificence, triumphant
            (Schubert: Impromptu no. 3, D. 899)

F♯ Minor   Melancholy, gloomy, mournfully grand,
            discontented
            "It tugs at passion as a dog biting a dress"[55]
            (C. P. E. Bach: Prussian Piano Sonata, Wq. 48,
                no. 6/ii, Fantasia in F♯ Minor)

G Major   Pleasing, lyrical, tender, simple, gay, charm
            "innocent rustic pleasures"[56]
            "The color white"[57]
            (Beethoven: Piano Sonata, op. 49, no. 2;
            Mozart: Piano Sonata, K. 283)

G Minor   Sadness, discontent, uneasiness
            "worry about a failed scheme; bad-tempered
                gnashing of teeth"[58]
            Color and aroma: purple and violets[59]
            (Haydn: Piano Sonata, Hob. XVI:44,
            Mozart: Piano Sonata K. 312)

A♭ Major   Solemn, splendid majesty, gentle night key, dark,
            stillness
            "Key of the grave, judgment, eternity lie in its
                radius"[60]
            "Plutonian realm"[61]
            "Black like the night"[62]
            (Beethoven: Piano Sonata, op. 26, no. 12,
            op. 110)

G♯ Minor   Wailing lament, misery
            The color: "everything struggling with difficulty"[63]
            (Beethoven: String Quartet in C♯ minor, op. 131/
                vi, Adagio)

A Major   Playful and jesting, gaiety, brilliance, uplifting,
            merry, full of spirit
            "Beautiful Saxon-green, refreshing aroma of
                lemons"[64]
            (Beethoven: Piano Sonata, op. 2, no. 2)

A Minor	Sorrowful, laments, expresses grief, womanly, most naive of all
	"Melancholy"[65]
	(Beethoven: Für Elise, WoO 59;
	Mozart: Piano Sonata, K. 310 (his first minor sonata)
B♭ Major	Masculine energy, majesty, quiet in its greatness, noble
	"Hope, aspiration for a better world"[66]
	"Shiny deep crimson and smells of cloves"[67]
	(Beethoven: Piano Sonata, op. 22, Piano Sonata, op. 106, Hammerklavier)
B♭ Minor	"Surly, often dressed in the garment of night, mocking God and the world; discontented with itself and with everything; preparation for suicide sounds in this key"[68]
	(Beethoven: Piano Sonata, op. 106/ii, semplice section)
B Major	Brilliant and playful, loftiness
	Anger, rage, jealousy, fury
	"Composed from the most glaring colors … announcing wild passions"[69]
	(Beethoven: Fantasia in G Minor, Op. 77, concluding section)
B Minor	Sweet and tender, gloomy, melancholy, simple
	"Deep, fine dark-blue"[70]
	(Haydn: Piano Sonata, Hob. XVI:47; Mozart: Adagio in B Minor, KV 540)

As Türk, Bach, and Kirnberger assert, Mattheson, too, compels the performer to act within suggested parameters when determining *affekt* (here, relating to key relationships), but that ultimately the choice is left to individual "good taste." And so Mattheson concludes his general remarks on *affekt* and key relationships with a disclaimer:

> The opinions on this subject are almost countless and I do not know of any other reason for this than the difference in human temperaments. Doubtless, it may be that one key, which appears merry and rousing to someone with a sanguine temperament, seems lamentable and distressed to the phlegmatic person, etc. We … want to make it clear once again that everyone is free to attribute such properties to the keys which best suit his natural inclination.[71]

AFFEKT AND CONSONANCE, DISSONANCE

Thus far, *affekt* as prescribed from decisions regarding form, meter, rhythm, inherent tempo, mode, and mood has been illustrated in a rather broad, theoretical sense. As the focus narrows to the inspection of consonance and dissonance, duality is intensified.

Human nature finds comfort in the familiar. Remembering that peaceful feeling experienced upon returning home from an extended trip is evidence enough. But too much relaxation becomes dreary, tedious, and lackluster. There is something about people, places, and things out of the ordinary that is intriguing and piques interest. And, if there is a bit of devilment in the mix, so much the better! "To prevent this [a dull melody]," Kirnberger describes, "there is nothing more effective than to use a note that does not belong to the scale, particularly when it falls on the main accent of the phrase."[72] To the Classical ear, this "something that doesn't belong" is a dissonance.

Bach explains how this is done. "But in general it can be said that dissonances are played loudly and consonances softly, since the former rouse our emotions and the latter quiet them."[73] Is it truly that simple? Yes and no. Alas, there is much to sort through in regard to this consonance versus dissonance idea in eighteenth-century music notational language.

In Classical Era melody, there is a general understanding of naturally occurring consonant and dissonant intervals, presented in Table 2.4.

Table 2.4. INTERVAL RELATIONSHIPS WITH CONSONANCE AND DISSONANCE

Perfect Consonances	Imperfect Consonances	More Imperfect Consonances	Dissonances	Most Dissonant
Perfect unison	Major third	Minor third	Major second	Major seventh
Perfect octave	Major sixth	Minor sixth	Minor second	
Perfect fourth			Minor seventh	
Perfect fifth				

Kirnberger explains how the overall combination of intervals influences *affekt* and compositional technique. "Leaps are most effective for the expression of anger and also joy; but for the expression of tender sentiments, gently flowing progressions are more appropriate than leaps."[74]

More specifically, Tables 2.5 and 2.6 (page 57 and 58) present an easy-to-follow format to illustrate how intervals created within any melody may function to depict *affekt*. The information is based on instruction from Kirnberger's *The Art of Strict Musical Composition*.[75]

Table 2.5. ASCENDING MELODIES

Augmented Prime	Anxious
Minor 2nd	Sad
Major 2nd	Pleasant, but also pathetic
Augmented 2nd	Yearning
Minor 3rd	Sad, melancholy
Major 3rd	Joyful
Diminished 4th	Melancholy, plaintive
Small Dim. 4th	Happy
Large Dim. 4th	Sad
Augmented 4th	Intense
Small 5th	Tender
False (dim) 5th	Graceful, imploring
Perfect 5th	Happy, courageous
Augmented 5th	Anxious
Minor 6th	Melancholy, imploring, caressing
Major 6th	Merry, vehement, intense
Diminished 7th	Painful
Minor 7th	Tender, sad, also indecisive
Major 7th	Intense, raving, expressing desperation
Octave	Happy, courageous, encouraging

An expeditious rule of thumb provided in Bach's *Versuch* is that ". . . all tones of a melody which lie outside the key may well be emphasized regardless of whether they form consonances or dissonances and those which lie within the key may be effectively performed piano, again regardless of their consonance or dissonance."[76] (The second half of Bach's statement is referring to the inherent consonance and dissonance within a scale—thirds and sixths being consonant, sevenths being dissonant.) In other words, go to the dissonance; this is where the passions are aroused. (For more, see the extended text on the companion website, Text 2.8. ▶)

Kirnberger again points to the interactive and flexible nature of our work. Here, he bridges melodic and harmonic considerations:

I do not mean to imply that these melodic progressions have only the effects indicated [in Table 2.5 and 2.6] and cannot be changed in any way. Rather, I mean only that these effects seem to me to be most appropriate to them. Much depends here on what precedes and follows and, in general, on the totality of the melodic phrase . . . ; it also depends on the position of the intermingled [intervals] of the scale or mode, and above all on the beat of the measure on which they are used and on the harmony that is placed under them.[77]

Table 2.6. DESCENDING MELODIES

Augmented Prime	Extremely sad
Minor 2nd	Pleasant
Major 2nd	Serious, soothing
Augmented 2nd	Plaintive, tender, caressing
Diminished 3rd	Very melancholy, tender
Minor 3rd	Calm, moderately cheerful
Major 3rd	Pathetic, also melancholy
Diminished 4th	Melancholy, anxious
Small Dim. 4th	Calm, content
Large 4th	Very depressed
Augmented 4th	Desperately sad
Small 5th	Tenderly sad
False (dim) 5th	Imploring
Perfect 5th	Content, soothing
Augmented 5th	Timid
(only in bass)	
Minor 6th	Depressed
Major 6th	Rather timid
Diminished 7th	Lamenting
Minor 7th	Rather frightful
Major 7th	Tremendously frightful
Octave	Very soothing

Just how much and in what way these dissonances or high points should be emphasized is a matter of execution—the final topic of this chapter.

AFFEKT AND EXECUTION

Documents from the Classical Era support the commonly held view that eighteenth-century expressive performance of *affekt* in good taste is the result of execution and attention to detail. Türk explains as follows:

> Whoever performs a composition so that its inherent affect (character) is expressed (made perceptible) to the utmost even in every single passage, and that the tones become, so to speak, a language of feelings, of him one says that he has a good execution. Good execution, therefore, is the most important, yet at the same time the most difficult aspect of music making.[78]

So creating the desired *affekt* is achieved through attention to detail, which comes about through good execution—effective physical interaction with the instrument. This topic was addressed repeatedly amongst period musicians. Türk alone strongly addressed this issue no fewer than five times (see the citations on the companion website, Text 2.9. ▶)), covering everything from the need for extraordinary facility to execute ornaments, detaching, slurring, or sustaining notes; appropriate judgment and execution of heaviness/lightness, loudness/softness; and clarity of ideas; all to achieve an end—expressing *affekt*.

To the eighteenth-century musician, conveyance of *affekt* in good taste is everything and it is achieved through good execution.

INFLUENCES APPLIED

When period musicians considered the blueprint for a piece, they began with *affekt*. So this is where we begin. How might the composer have notated the *affekt*? While participating in The Art of the Fortepiano, I heard Malcolm Bilson ask a student, "Was the composer questioning, exclaiming, concluding, pausing, or reflecting? Does your performance convey that sentiment?"[79] Ask yourself, "Where is the ?!.,?" And what notational tools were used to convey this message? Consider mode, tempo, meter, dynamics, touch, and articulation.

The concept. Seize any opportunity to play on a period instrument that is tuned with mean-tone tuning. It will dramatically impact your concept of *affekt* and key/interval relationships.

Attention to *affekt* should impact and influence performing decisions on *any* instrument. As Tilman Skowroneck advocates in *Beethoven the Pianist,* we must learn what the score tells us about the music and what the score tells us to strive for or expect from the instrument. And we must listen to feedback from the instrument, as it will tell us something new about the music.[80]

Digging into and searching out the composer's intended *affekt* will promote historically informed music making and original playing. The time invested prior to taking a piece to the piano will pay handsomely, both in terms of efficiency in practice and in developing sensitivity and good taste.

For the sake of discussion and to validate these concepts in practice, take Beethoven's well-known Für Elise. Answer the following questions (in italics), one by one, relying on the historical information section of this chapter. Plausible answers are provided in brackets.

- *What is the* affekt? [forlorn, sweet, melancholy]
- *Where does the* affekt *change?* [ms. 8, 24, 30, 59, 77]

- *What elements in the music support this* affekt? [dance form/meter/ rhythm and note-value choices; mode/mood/melodic interval choices; harmonic choices]
- *Are there elements of* Sturm und Drang? [foremost shift of *affekt* is at mm. 59–76]
- *Listen to recordings in which the works are performed on period instruments by esteemed artists who are knowledgeable regarding period performance practice.*
- *Listen to recordings of works in similar mode(s) and mood(s).* [A Minor: Mozart, Piano Sonata, K. 310, or Beethoven, Piano Sonata, op. 2, no. 2/ iii, m. 57 ff; F Major: Beethoven Piano Sonata, op. 10, no. 2; C Major: Mozart Piano Sonata, K. 545]
- *Attend concerts in which works are performed on period instruments by esteemed artists who are accomplished period performance practitioners.*
- *What influence does Baroque dance have on this work?* [This is a minuet, agreeable, charming character]
- *What influence does the meter have on the* affekt? [$\frac{3}{8}$ is a light meter]
- *What influence do note values have on the* affekt? [As the work becomes more expressive, the note values become longer (ms. 23, ms. 59), which translates to heavier and more expressive.]
- *Are there qualitative tempo indications to direct the movement of the affekt?* [*con moto*]
- *How does the mode impact* affekt? [Table 2.7 lists the pure key choices and complementary mood relationships.]
- *What consonances and dissonances impact the* affekt? [As the melodic *affekt* becomes more expressive, the intervals become wider (mm. 9–12). The melodic intervals throughout the work are in agreement with the melodic interval suggestions from Kirnberger (refer to Table 2.5 and 2.6.) As the harmonic *affekt* becomes more intense, the harmony becomes more dissonant (mm. 60, 62, 65).]

Table 2.7. AFFEKT AND KEY RELATIONSHIPS IN FÜR ELISE

Measures	Key	Purity	Related *Affekt*
1–8	A minor	Pure	Most naive of all, womanly, lamenting
9–14	C major	Pure	Simple, joy, pure, innocence
23–30	F major	Pure	Joyful, polite, clever, gentle dignity
59–81	A minor	Pure	Sorrowful, lament, grief

Expressing *affekt* is arrived at through execution. If we change execution, we change *affekt*. Composers only give us execution. It is our job to use that as a tool to get at the *affekt*. Consider more questions to arrive at execution possibilities:

- What is the musical concept? What does the notation describe? What is the composer's story? What is going on here? What is my story? How will I execute this?
- Decide *what* you want before you play.
- When you have decided exactly what you want, you will be able to play it.
- Use the mind and inner ear to first feel what you are after.
- Be sure you have hold of the reins. Do you just have beautiful horses (technique) with no control (concept)?
    - Sentimental (superficial) playing disguises details and depth.
    - Taking away superficial/sentimental playing often exposes some not-so-good playing, which now provides something to work on during practice.
- Orchestrate your piece.
- How does your idea belong to the whole concept? What is its function? Isolate each part and decide if this part or section is
    - complacent
    - in opposition
    - in contrast
    - in unison
    - accompanying
    - a dancing partner
- Remember that two parts are never completely equal: one is always more "equal" than the other.
- Written speech uses punctuation to articulate ideas. Look for hints in the score to do likewise.
- Playing slowly and listening to interaction will help form execution decisions.
- The importance of singing cannot be emphasized enough, particularly for an instrument where breathing is not essential to creating the sound. Quantz reiterates the importance:

> Taking breath at the proper time is essential in playing wind instruments as well as in singing. Because of frequently encountered abuses in this regard, melodies that should be coherent are often broken up, the composition is spoiled, and the listener is robbed of part of his pleasure. To separate several

notes that belong together is just as bad as to take a breath in reading [words] before the sense is clear, or in the middle of a word of two or three syllables.[81]

- Not only is it necessary to emulate singers in the approach to breathing, but the approach to the type of sound created is important. Continually ask, "Is what I am creating tasteful and beautiful?" Quantz emphasizes setting high standards.

  Each instrumentalist must strive to execute that which is *cantabile* as a good singer executes it.[82]

- Don't play out of habit and blind repetition, but from a conscious, musical choice. Quantz cautions thus:

  Excessive playing weakens the body, blunts the senses, and destroys the desire and appetite to perform a piece with true fervor.[83]

Concept building was discussed during a master class at Early Music Days. Bilson suggested the following plan to pursue when contemplating appropriate choices.

- Sing the section *away from the piano* convincingly until it becomes clear and a part of you.
- Sing and play the section.
- Perform, incorporating what you have learned from these previous steps.

Good taste is a combination of knowing when to use exact ingredients (when to strictly follow performance rules) versus knowing when to use a little of this and a little of that (bending the rules). My son-in-law is a mathematician. When he first became acquainted with my cooking style he was amazed (and quite alarmed) at how little I followed some recipes—mathematically is not a good descriptor! A common joke at the dinner table comes when compliments on the dish arise and I respond, "You know, I should probably write down what I did so I can make it like this again sometime!" My adventuresome nature has developed over many, many years of exactly following recipes. It helps to know the rules before bending them! As I heard Malcolm Bilson say at Early Music Days, "Great composers follow the rules . . . *most of the time.*" The trick is finding the exceptions. Finding them makes practice and good performance interesting.

The next challenge is to take a work that you have studied and played without benefit of this orderly, informed investigative process. Compare the conclusions you made on your own after time-consuming and intensive work to the insight quickly and readily available from this chapter.

You may be surprised at how quickly you came to some of the same conclusions, how shocked you are by some of the dramatic differences, and
perhaps, how delighted you are with some new insights.

The final challenge is to take a work you have never before studied.
Apply the extensive parameters of the previously outlined principles.
Enjoy the efficiency, clarity, and creative direction the data communicates
for interpretive choices.

When encountering a new piece of music, view it through the period
lens. Remember that musicians of the day would have been much more
aware of the *affekt* as it related to the composer's key choice or intervallic
choices. They were "in the midst of it" rather than being nearly 300 years
removed, as we are today. Today, we must become reacquainted with these
relations and let them impact how we develop concept. We, too, can benefit from the internal tensions created by key and intervallic choice.

Applied affekt *and execution.* The million-dollar question now presents
itself: How does one tastefully *execute affekt* either on the fortepiano or as
an informed musician on the modern piano? Perhaps your head is swim-
ming, or maybe even drowning, by this point. Your mind is paralyzed with
so many "helpful suggestions" from the past. Fear not! The remaining
chapters of this book address the sole concept: execution. (Not of yourself,
but execution of *affekt* on the instrument!) *Affekt* is conveyed through execution. The concepts presented in this chapter inform "comprehension" of
the language. Knowing how to execute, or "speak," this language stylistically and allow the historical influences to instruct and suggest creative
solutions within informed parameters on any instrument is the goal of
the remainder this book.

Unlike other instrumentalists, fortepianists of yesteryear and modern
pianists of today can control only the intensity and duration of tones.
Thus, they are unable to swell a tone or control its rate of diminution.
To be sure, at broader levels, pianists can extend the resources available.
Newman assures us that it may be done by "creating the illusion of con-
trolling tone quality, even *timbre*—that is, by connecting or disconnecting
tones, grouping them rhythmically and dynamically, pedaling in different
ways, balancing textural strands appropriately, and suitably employing
agogics [accents produced by lengthening the time value of a note]."[84] At
this practice, the eighteenth-century composer/performer was master. We
have much to learn from the eighteenth-century mindset and skill set. We
do have the opportunity to yield prodigious musical dividends from the
variety of options offered for execution in the Classical Era style. Many
new interpretive options are at our disposal when eighteenth-century
music notational language is understood and "spoken." Paradoxically, the

strictures of this language wildly, widely, and wisely open doors beyond the confines of twenty-first-century music notational rules.

THE LESSON

Play and study Example 2.1 with the following points in mind.

Music Example 2.1. Mozart, London Notebook, KV 15oo, mm. 1–8. Copyright (1983) G. Henle Verlag, Munich.

1. Demonstrate the work. Ask questions to develop a concept.
   a. What is the overall *affekt*? Where does it change? How could this be achieved at the piano? (Try many possibilities.)
   b. Address specific issues.
      i. What dance influenced this work? What is the appropriate inherent tempo?
      ii. How does the meter influence the tempo?
      iii. What note values are employed? How does that influence the mood?
      iv. Where are the dissonances ("crunches" to the young musician) and how may they best be highlighted?
      v. Dynamics (discuss ideas, knowing more will be revealed in chapter 6)
      vi. Touch—*legato, detaché, staccato* (discuss ideas, knowing more will be revealed in chapter 8)
2. With guiding questions based on the information above, the concept may be determined before playing a single note.
   a. This is a *courante*.
   b. $\frac{3}{4}$ *courante* is not very fast.

   c. Quarter notes are somewhat heavy and detached, adding to the serious *affekt*.

   d. With a serious *affekt*, there are appropriate options:

      i.   mm. 1–2 *forte*, *detaché*, and heavy (perhaps imitating brass instruments)

      ii. mm. 3–4 *piano*, more *legato*, and light (perhaps winds)

      iii. mm. 5–6, following slurs (leaning into dissonances), terraces dynamics *crescendo*

      iv. mm. 7–8 *forte*, *detaché*, heavy (perhaps *tutti*)

3. Determine a personal concept.

This working out of ideas is all done on the modern piano. With basic information about the fortepiano, *Urtext* editions, and a bit of basic performance knowledge for expressing one's musical concept, students have many more musical tools and options at their disposal within informed parameters to make decisions.

As do you.

Use the quick reference guide on the companion website to summarize. ⏵

CHAPTER 3

⌀⌀⌀

Formal Structure
and Harmonic Function

Great composers follow the rules . . . most of the time!
—Malcolm Bilson at Early Music Days

For the purposes of this book, it is assumed the reader has a working knowledge of binary, ternary, and rondo form, as well as sonata allegro form. A basic understanding of Western functional harmonic concepts, including the ability to analyze the form and harmonic function of repertoire, is also assumed. This chapter highlights distinctive Classical Era features and exceptions. Utilization of these tools will significantly enhance performing style and the ability to project *affekt*.

FORMAL STRUCTURE

Experiencing formal structure is a journey. Whether the journey is begun by modulating away from the tonic key as is found in binary or sonata allegro form, creating a contrasting mood as in ternary form, or ever intensifying variations with each reprise as in rondo form, the interesting part of the journey is the tension created in the departure from tonic, the interplay between ideas, and the ultimate anticipation of the return home. The journey is crafted carefully. Excitement is created by manipulating the structure "in good taste."

In *Music in the Galant Style*, Robert Gjerdingen methodically examines distinctive eighteenth-century formal structures. He provides excellent insight to specific organizational concepts. Gjerdingen reminds the reader to look for "schemata"[1] to discern the formal structure of eighteenth-century repertoire. These schemata fall into formal patterns that Gjerdingen presents as prototypes. It is a fascinating working out of the skillful interplay between the descending bass line patterns, an ascending "do-re-mi" treble, and various harmonic cadential formulae.

We must know about skeletal foundations to truly understand this style. And, don't discount the small ones; eighteenth-century musicians didn't. Gjerdingen echoes the strong connection between smaller and larger formal structure:

> The same general sequence of schemata used in a minuet could be used in the large movement, though with other schemata added or interpolated. And if one could not write a good minuet, there was little point in attempting a larger format.[2]

This concept, equally true in performing, is served well with a good understanding of each foundational structure—big and small. *Music in the Galant Style* is a valuable resource to better grasp these concepts at a much deeper level.

There are interesting "out-of-the-ordinary" prototypes to be on the look-out for when determining eighteenth-century formal structure, clever clues from the composer. Many of these elements are interconnected with other components. For instance, consider the Beethoven Allegretto movement in Example 3.1. Although the "A" section is of typical eight-measure length and modulates from the minor tonic to the major mediant, Beethoven sets it a bit on edge with a six plus two measure grouping rather than four plus four *vierhebigkeit* (the divisibility of music into units of four).

Music Example 3.1. Beethoven, Piano Sonata, op. 10, no. 2/ii, mm. 1–8. (ABRSM) ▶

Another interesting twist worth noting is the interruption of *vierhe-bigkeit* with two-measure groups. The development section of Beethoven Piano Sonata, op. 10, no. 2 is an excellent case in point. Beethoven cleverly begins with a two-bar introduction, proceeds with four bar groupings, and then surprisingly inserts two bar groups at measures 81, 87, and 89. Knowledge of and highlighting this type of formal structure will greatly enhance *affekt*. These creative compositional tools will be further examined in chapter 5.

It is also advisable to be on the look-out for interruptions or surprises in harmonic progressions. Bach instructs that the unexpected and dissonant should be highlighted. "So-called deceptive progressions are also brought out markedly to complement their function."[3]

It is *upon* the foundation of formal structure and harmonic function that melody is laid. Again, patterns may be found. Gjerdingen devotes an entire chapter alone to "The Do-Re-Mi."[4] Knowledge and application of melodic skeletal structures greatly shape performance in eighteenth-century style. Again, they provide direction to the unexpected, influencing *affekt*.

HARMONIC FUNCTION

Return to the analogy from chapter 2—beautiful structures, like St. Paul's Cathedral or the Washington National Cathedral. The footings, pilings, and frame hidden underneath the façade support and give form or shape to the building. Likewise in eighteenth-century music, the thoroughbass (commonly called figured bass today) is the solid footing. Bach devotes a full twenty-five percent of his *Versuch* to this fundamental component, and Türk advises his readers to study distinguished works on this subject, starting with Bach's *Versuch*. Türk makes the connection between figured bass and good execution:

> A knowledge of thoroughbass is indispensable to good execution because without this knowledge, the various rules concerning appoggiaturas and ornaments, the required strength or weakness of consonant and dissonant harmonies, and the like, cannot be followed.[5]

It's not just the harmony. It's the relationship between harmony, melody, and formal structure. Willis reports, "Much more than other musicians, the eighteenth-century keyboard player had to learn to link melody to its underlying harmonic support. He could not function as an accompanist or chamber player without mastering figured bass realization; it was fundamental to his musical training."[6] Although most modern pianists do not study figured bass, this knowledge is a compelling reminder to be vitally aware and make use of harmonic implications in determining how Classical Era music is performed.

Pay attention to harmony. In *The End of Early Music,* Haynes provides two different recordings of J. S. Bach's Air on the G String (Air, Suite 3, BWV 1068). Although both recordings may serve as examples of beautiful music, the artists in the first recording perform a modern view rendition, building from the melody down. Consequently, Haynes observes how "real harmonic events that could act as cues for nuance, like suspensions and dissonances, are ignored."[7] The artists in the second recording take their cues from the bass line and harmonic function, which serves as the catalyst for projecting Bach's formal structure and intended *affekt.* In comparison to the first recording, the second, Haynes believes, "'puts out' less but gets good mileage from what Bach actually wrote."[8] This distinction is really worth a listen!

Harmonic function drives expression. The dominant preparation, I_4^6, becomes expressive as a result of its structural importance. The I_4^6 equals arrival. Return to Example 3.1. Beethoven left several clues that directs the performer to this point of arrival: six plus two measure grouping, setting off by articulation, texture shift from linear to vertical, and the I_4^6. In *Beethoven on Beethoven,* Newman agrees. "The peak on the penultimate strong beat in this example [Beethoven Piano Sonata op.10, no. 2/ii/mm. 1–8] is supported further by the six-four chord on the feminine cadence at that point."[9]

At the Westfield International Fortepiano Academy, van Oort laid out a formulaic structure that corresponds with Newman's observation about the penultimate strong beat: two plus two plus four, with the climax occurring on bar six or seven. The high point is often bar six; it is the expressive bar. It provides direction and focus to the line. As the cadence is approached, it is helpful to keep in mind two important harmonic considerations. First, I_4^6 is *always* a heightened dissonance and an anticipation of tonic. It is a point of arrival. Eighteenth-century style dictates it be made special—louder, softer, more intense, rhythmically heightened. Second, from the dominant preparation to the dominant and concluding on the tonic ($I_4^6 \rightarrow \rightarrow V_7 \rightarrow \rightarrow I$), a clear path is made. The resolution is usually not louder, but builds to V_7, then resolves.[10]

Türk explains the importance of harmonic implications all the way down to isolated events:

> A composition with many [harmonic] dissonances must be executed more heavily than another in which for the most part light, consonant harmonies are employed.[11]

The dominant seventh chord, V_7, particularly when placed under a fermata, requires special attention. When a V_7 appears, the scene is changing and anticipation should be heightened. Consider the diminished seventh chord, which is even more intense. Made up entirely of minor thirds, it depicts *complete* uncertainty and tension. Performers with good taste bring this harmonic tension to the listener's attention.

Knowledge of formal structure and harmonic function lays interpretive and expressive answers at our feet. Once these are worked through, embellishing components that may bring richness and clarity are more easily determined. An extremely useful embellishing harmonic accompaniment pattern from the eighteenth century is the Alberti bass.

THE ALBERTI BASS AND OTHER ACCOMPANYING FIGURES

In its simplest sense, music of the Baroque Era (circa 1600–1750) may be defined as a polyphonic style based on linear melodies grounded harmonically in figured bass, seen in Diagram 3.1.

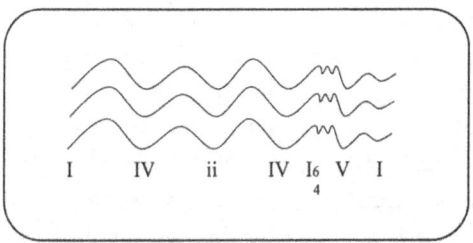

Diagram 3.1. Counterpoint.

Both linear and vertical structural elements underwent dramatic change in the eighteenth century because of the influence of broken-chord patterns (that date back to the seventeenth century),[12] the best known of which is the Alberti bass. The Alberti bass breaks down the independence of contrapuntal voices by absorbing them into the accompaniment pattern, seen in Diagram 3.2.

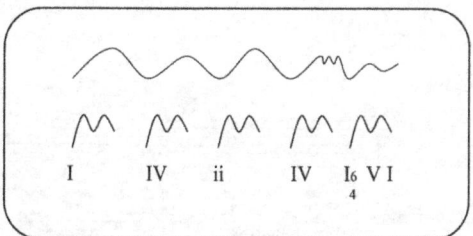

Diagram 3.2. Alberti Bass.

According to *The Harvard Dictionary of Music*, the Alberti bass is "an accompaniment figure, found frequently in the left hand of 18th-century keyboard music, in which the pitches of three-pitch chords are playing successively in the order lowest, highest, middle, highest, as in ... Mozart (Sonata in C major K. 545)."[13] The figure is named after Italian singer, harpsichordist, and composer Domenico Alberti (1710–1740?), who used this figuration extensively.[14] Today, the various configurations of arpeggiated broken harmony are simply named the Alberti bass for ease in identification. Once it appeared on the scene, the Alberti bass took hold. It was very popular around 1800. It went out of fashion quickly as new pianos appeared that contained a more resonant soundboard with more overtones that resulted in a naturally louder, longer-lasting tone. The effect of the pattern is much more difficult to achieve on pianos from the Romantic Era forward.

The perfect genre for the Alberti bass configurations was the sonata; the perfect instrument to execute it on was the fortepiano. The Alberti bass establishes harmonic function through a simple periodic structure with symmetrical four-bar phrases, complementary to the Classical Era sonata. The pattern is extremely conducive to the mechanics of the fortepiano, lending energy to the declamatory nature of the instrument and rhetorical style of the time.

The bright, clear attack on the fortepiano lends itself to this figuration perfectly. What is often described as simply an accompaniment pattern today is much more important and instrumental in creating *affekt* in eighteenth-century style. The Alberti bass motives create rhythmic and harmonic energy, drive, and momentum—pulse and forward propulsion—whether dramatic or lyrical. Although the Alberti bass configurations do break down polyphony to a certain extent, polyphonic contours remain or are implied, and may be highlighted to create more interest in secondary melodies.

The Alberti bass shapes vary according to need. The most intense figuration that provides optimal rhythmic energy, drive, and opportunity for polyphonic implications outlines a 5-1-3-1-5-1-3-1 pattern, seen in Example 3.2.

Music Example 3.2. Mozart, Piano Sonata, K. 309/I, mm. 73–74. Copyright (2005) G. Henle Verlag, Munich. ▶

As the intensity of the *affekt* relaxes, so does the activity of the figuration. In mm. 15–16 of Example 3.3, the *affekt* is less intense than that of Example 3.2. The texture is thinner and the implied polyphony has been reduced to two voices. Yet the intervals and 1-5-1-5-1-5 figuration keeps things quite "live." Drive is lessened further at mm. 22–24, when the figure shifts to a rolling and relaxed 1-3-5-3-1-3-5-3 in the right hand. (Here, the suspense comes from the melodic motive in the left hand.) The *affekt* is the least dramatic and almost lyrical in mm. 18–21, where the left-hand pattern outlines a simple harmonic progression with arpeggiated four-note chords 5-3-2-1-5-3-2-1.

Music Example 3.3. Mozart, London Notebook, Anh. 109b no. 3 (15p), mm. 15–25. Copyright (2005) G. Henle Verlag, Munich. ▶

Example 3.4 illustrates another common practice in the eighteenth century. Here, the Alberti bass is used to embellish and make the harmony more sonorous through configurations conducive to finger legato (over-holding notes).

Music Example 3.4. Mozart, Piano Sonata, K. 280/ii, mm. 45–47. Copyright (2005) G. Henle Verlag, Munich. ▶

An accompaniment figure can make a melody better if it joins the character of the melody. If the bass notes follow the melody, it is common to use the same articulation as the melody. In Example 3.5, the left hand follows the right hand's articulation lead.

Music Example 3.5. Beethoven, Bagatelle, op. 119, no. 1, mm. 47–52. Copyright (1978) G. Henle Verlag, Munich. ▶

Accompaniment figures give the listener clues about the *affekt* of the section. Play them strongly in the beginning and then decide if, on the basis of the *affekt,* they should fade into the background or remain strong.

ARPEGGIATED CHORDS

Arpeggiation as a means to embellish and enhance expression is a wonderful tool from the Baroque Era that is found in the Classical Era as well. In *Off the Record*, Peres Da Costa explains how playing vertically notated music in a dislocated manner, one note after the other, has "been a long-standing [practice] in the early keyboard scene—particularly by harpsichordists and clavichordists. And, it is gradually infiltrating fortepiano playing."[15] The companion website to *Off the Record* provides audio files to hear this practice.

Peres Da Costa unearthed evidence that suggests notated arpeggiation was only "part of the story." For instance, the first movement of Piano Concerto op. 58 by Beethoven begins with a full four-note chord in each hand. Arpeggiation is not indicated in either the first edition or the copy corrected by Beethoven himself. Yet Carl Czerny, who studied with Beethoven, later added the marking.[16] Perhaps this was Czerny's way of keeping the "unwritten" tradition alive through notation that would have been unnecessary for Beethoven to mark, much as adding the staccato marking at the ends of phrases was done to explain the "understood" tradition after the fact.

Whether notated or unnotated, arpeggiation is dependent upon *affekt*. It can fill out and sustain expressive sounds on instruments with a quick decay (such as the fortepiano). It "softens the blow" to enhance expression on a *forte* or an accented note, yet it can enhance brilliance if snapped rapidly. It is used frequently in slow movements. Timing is an important consideration. When contemplating use of arpeggiation, performers should keep in mind that the structure, harmonic function, and melodic line must be kept intact. Appropriate use of arpeggiation will, in fact, enhance those elements.

In his *Versuch*, Bach explains how arpeggiation is notated and executed in this style. "The usual signs of arpeggiation and their execution appear in Figure 176 [Example 3.6].[17] The asterisked example represents an arpeggio with an *acciaccatura* (the diagonal line between the E and F). Türk explains that when this symbol appears the notes are to be "played broken (struck one after the other)." [18] Bach concludes the definitions. "The word 'arpeggio' written over a long note calls for a chord broken upward and downward several times."[19]

Music Example 3.6. Bach, *Versuch*, Figure 176.

Türk lists more performing options. "When there is a succession of broken chords, composers are accustomed to write the word *arpeggio* above (a) and leave the manner of execution up to the discretion of the player, or they show the degree of speed, etc., for the first chord of a series with a *segue* following, indicating to the player that the following chords are to be played in the same manner (b)."[20] (See Example 3.7.)

Music Example 3.7. Türk, *Klavierschule*, 282–283.

INFLUENCES APPLIED

Heed the significant implications from Gjerdingen's work: begin with the formal structure—that's where period composers and musicians began. And, begin here from the very beginning, with simple folk songs and dances. Musicians at all levels are quite capable of learning about tonic and dominant harmonies and how to distinguish their functions. Furthermore, a great opportunity is afforded to introduce secondary dominants, a device that paves the way for understanding modulations in small binary forms and, later on, in sonatas.

The first essential step in understanding the *affekt* behind any composition is to analyze and "know" the function of the notes. Determine the form, harmonic function, and phrase structure. Examine the score to expose any "extra" measures, hybrid structures, or any unexpected changes that should be emphasized for good execution. The time spent in uncovering these items will pay handsomely in developing a concept for the work, thus saving countless hours of blind practice. Next, look for each of the distinctive Classical Era harmonic traits previously delineated that may bring extra energy, beauty, or shape to the piece.

Examine your score to see how it stacks up to period norms. Where did the composer follow the rules? Where did he creatively bend or break the rules? As I heard Malcolm Bilson observe while teaching at Early Music Days in Hungary, "Great composers follow the rules . . . *most* of the time!"[21]

For an expanded knowledge base, listen to recordings from *The End of Early Music* and *Off the Record*. They provide startling insight to period practice and marvelous options to explore as personal authentic performance style is developed.

Often, it is when the Alberti bass appears that the momentum picks up and the real action takes place. I'm reminded of another clever quip I heard Malcolm Bilson share during one of his master classes in Early Music Days: "When it shows, the music goes!"[22] One of the biggest challenges for the modern player is what to do with it "when it shows" because *it* (the Alberti bass) is *not* conducive to execution on the modern piano. Attempting to minimize the Alberti bass figuration on the modern piano is a common mistake. Not only is this minimizing extremely difficult to accomplish but, as van Oort advised in a workshop during The Art of Fortepiano, "Trying to play the Alberti bass too quietly actually draws attention to itself and creates exactly the opposite intended effect, and usually just becomes annoying."[23] Rather, highlight rhythmic drive, dramatic or beautiful qualities, or any secondary melody. This effort will bring energy and focus to the motive, as was historically intended. Envision "orchestrating" Alberti bass figurations and harmonic contours to add depth and substance to the voices. This practice also brings the figure into focus and provides clarity.

During a master class at Fortepiano at Villa Bossi, Bart van Oort provided helpful instruction to develop Alberti bass technique. He suggested that when constructing Alberti bass figurations, begin by creating a pulse. Practice in pulses of one pulse per measure, two pulses per measure, one pulse with each beat. The *affekt* of the section will determine the appropriate number of pulses.[24] As intensity increases, tempo stretches (more to be revealed in chapter 5). Pulsing the Alberti bass provides many benefits. The pulse will be defined. Rhythm will be defined and enlivened. The intermediary notes will naturally be softer. Rushing, that ever-present nemesis, will be kept at bay!

When shaping the Alberti bass, I have found it helpful to begin with the bass notes (in pulses) alone in conjunction with the melody. This clarifies voice leading. Next, "divide" the hand in half. The bass note is a downward rotation, and the remaining notes are the upward rotation, creating a stroke for each unit. Devoting time to these exercises will develop cleaner technical execution that will be easier to control.

Search out opportunities to incorporate arpeggiation to enhance the *affekt*. Look first wherever any full chords in long notes appear in the score. A word of caution: each choice should maintain and enhance structure, harmonic function, and melodic line.

Formal structure and harmonic function provide the solid groundwork on which eighteenth-century style and *affekt* are built. The Alberti bass and arpeggiation are two of the tools available to enhance the foundation. Taking great care with the "unseen elements" (formal structure and harmonic function) will bring meaningful and long-lasting beauty to that which is seen or heard on the surface.

THE LESSON

Play and study Example 3.8 with the following points in mind.

Music Example 3.8. Mozart, London Notebook, KV 15oo, mm. 1–8. Copyright (1983) G. Henle Verlag, Munich.

1. Discuss the formal structure (binary form). This is the "A" section.
2. Look for skeletal aspects (formal structure) that may inform and influence *affekt*.
   a. Look at the downbeats of mm. 1–4 and find "do, do, re/fa, mi" in the melody against the bass line of 1–1–6(7)–1. Therefore, ms. 3 is more dissonant and contains more tension.
   b. The most dissonant chord in mm. 1–4 occurs on beat 3 of ms. 3. Taking time to emphasize this dissonance will actually be of assistance in dealing with the double thirds in the right hand.

3. Discuss the modulation from tonic to dominant in mm. 5–8.
4. Determine ways in which the tension from tonic to dominant may be emphasized.
   a. Terraced dynamic *cresc.* at mm. 5 and 6
5. Discuss the cadential treatment at ms. 4 versus ms. 8.
   a. The imperfect authentic cadence at ms. 4 has less tension and drive.
   b. $I_4^6 \rightarrow V \rightarrow I$ in the dominant key creates tension and should be highlighted.

Use the quick reference guide on the companion website to summarize. ▶

CHAPTER 4

✧

Technique—Execution

Three questions must be answered to get at the heart of any systematic approach to technique:

How does one *make* sound—approaching the instrument?
How does one *release* the sound—exiting the instrument?
How does one *communicate* with the audience—engaging the listener?

Salient mechanical features of the fortepiano were examined and inherently distinctive traits were highlighted in chapter 1. It was discovered that the fortepiano contains many differences when compared to the modern piano:

- Lighter, quicker, and more responsive action
- More tactile feel
- Volume capabilities derived from a different spectrum
- More immediate attack and decay
- More clarity in speaking; more overtones that provide a rich sound
- Wider-ranging timbre varieties

General answers to technical questions were supplied that concerned how to adjust physically when one plays fortepiano music on the modern piano.

Getting into the nitty-gritty of execution requires examining period beliefs, traditions, and practices. Theories will be explained and developed.

Simple and straightforward information regarding eighteenth-century technique will be provided to achieve the ultimate end goal: reconciled, relevant, and practical application for playing today.

BELIEFS AND TRADITIONS

Common sense dictates that developing skill and good technique is attained through a good instrument, excellent instruction, and appropriate instructional materials. Eighteenth-century musicians firmly held this belief as well. Bach's *Versuch* and Türk's *Klavierschule* are the two single most important keyboard treatises from the second half of the eighteenth century. In the beginning pages of each, period instruments are discussed and, not surprisingly, recommendations are made to ensure the use of good and appropriate instruments when one is learning to play a keyboard instrument. Next, Türk firmly stresses the need for a good teacher:

> The teacher, even if he is not a player of the first order himself—for to teach well and to play superbly are two very different things—must have at least a well-developed sense of musical taste and the ability to perform well, aside from the necessary knowledge.[1]

Pedagogically, both books offer extensive insight and advice that was instructive then and is still relatable today. Türk's commitment to good teaching materials is demonstrated in the twelve teaching pieces he supplied at the end of *Klavierschule*. I find them extremely helpful as a "post-test" of sorts, checking to make sure information has been sufficiently processed to be able to depend on reasonable application. Beethoven personally relied on Bach's *Versuch* when teaching young Carl Czerny, a point that further demonstrates the importance of these tutors at the time.

With a good piano at hand, a good teacher employed, and good teaching materials on deck, the student is ready to learn how to read music and physically play it on the piano. The term *execution* is most frequently used in period literature to describe technical action at the keyboard. In eighteenth-century style, execution is much more than pressing a key and getting a sound. An enlightening passage by Türk emphasizes the connection between *affekt* and execution:

> He who performs a composition so that its inherent affect (character) is expressed (made perceptible) to the utmost even in every single passage, and

that the tones become, so to speak, a language of feelings, of him one says that he has a good execution. Good execution, therefore, is the most important, yet at the same time the most difficult aspect of music making.[2]

Quantz stresses the responsibility of the performer to develop good execution:

The best composition may be marred by poor execution, just as a mediocre composition may be improved and enhanced by good execution.[3]

In his *Versuch*, Bach clearly lays out the three factors essential to the "true art of playing keyboard instruments: correct fingering, good embellishments, and good performance."[4] Bach warns that failure to meet these requisites results in a dire state of affairs:

Owing to the ignorance of these factors [correct fingering, good embellishments, and good performance], keyboardists can be heard who after torturous trouble have finally learned how to make their instrument sound loathsome to an enlightened listener. Their playing lacks roundness, clarity, forthrightness, and in their stead one hears only hacking, thumping, and stumbling.[5]

Following such foreboding, warning, and strong advice, all three authors proceed with specific guidance for a good technical approach. Bach and Türk's beliefs regarding body and hand position at rest are so similar to today's approach that a quick review suffices: sit directly in front of middle C at an appropriate distance from the keys, at a comfortable height on the bench, with a curved finger position that allows for ease of movement both up and down and in and out of the keys. Descriptions of Mozart's deportment at the piano and his personal letters substantiate the commonly held view that a naturalness in playing and posture was appropriate. Czerny's description of Beethoven at the piano further supports this philosophy. "His [Beethoven's] bearing while performing was ideally restful, noble, and beautiful, without the slightest grimace."[6] Türk addresses the issue head on:

In the very beginning, distorted facial expressions, writhing, grimaces, or whatever you might want to call them ... shaking or nodding of the head, snorting during a trill or during a difficult passage, and the like, must never be permitted of the pupil, regardless of social position or sex ... for although music is perceived only through the sense of hearing, the sense of sight should not be offended in the process.[7]

The Classical Era ideal regarding deportment is copacetic to today's view. What is it then that defines "typical" Classical Era technique? The musculature involved and function performed? The guiding components that provide reliable outcomes in this style? To find the answers requires turning to specific practices.

PRACTICES

Physical roles in execution. Eighteenth-century style begins with the gesture. Musical concepts are germinated through small gestures that combine and develop into phrases, sections, and the complete whole. The small gesture is as imperative to the composer as is each brush stroke to the painter or each ingredient to the baker.

Execution of the gesture is initiated with the wrist leading. While the wrist leads, the fingers carry the majority of the work in all touches—*legato, detaché, staccato*—and everything in between. The forearm carries the hand sideways to each new location and the next gesture. The full arm works from the shoulder and is used to shift the hand into or back from the raised keys as well as navigate large shifts in keyboard location.

The forearm lies naturally, just as it is attached to the arm, and the hand extends naturally from the forearm. The arm supports the hand, the hand the fingers. The best position is with a compact hand. It is the default position. The calmer the arm and hand, the more sure the motion of the fingers, as Czerny instructs. "Generally, the arm and forearm use as little motion as needed; just enough to facilitate or support the fingers."[8]

Czerny remembers instruction from Beethoven about the importance of a good hand position to carry the fingers so they may do their work efficiently:

> In the first lessons, Beethoven had me concentrate exclusively on scales in all the keys, showed me the only correct position of the hands and fingers (unknown as yet to most players at that time), and especially the use of the thumb—rules whose value I came to appreciate only much later.[9]

Czerny believed so strongly in the virtue of good technique that he wrote a delightful tutor, entitled *Letter to a Young Lady on the Art of Playing the Pianoforte,* for beginning students to instruct them along these lines. It lightheartedly encourages pianists to develop reliable technique as soon as possible and is still relatable today. I use it with beginning students to provide context and to bring credibility to the message. They find it "quite cool" that how I instruct them to play is the same as how Beethoven and his student, Carl Czerny, taught and played.

Function. Bach devotes twenty-five percent of his *Versuch* to thorough-bass. Clearly, the bass line is important to Classical Era repertoire. For the pianist, this means the left hand. During the Westfield International Fortepiano Academy, fortepianist Bart van Oort built upon Bach's advice while presenting a succinct outline of the use of the hands:

> Each hand serves a specific function. The left hand carries great responsibility. It sets the tempo by providing direction and timing, clarifies harmony and harmonic rhythm, spells out formal structure, provides balance, determines dynamics, and sets the underpinnings of rhythm. Built upon the strong foundation provided by the left hand, the right hand provides expressivity and ornaments the harmony—that is to say, carries the melodic material.[10]

Keeping a consistent hand shape provides greater reliability in outcomes. For instance, if a gesture is repeated in a different place on the keyboard and the hand shape remains consistent, it is more likely that the same type of sound will be duplicated in the new location. Or, as dynamics change, the focus of the tone will be sustained with a consistent hand shape. To play at a *piano* dynamic level takes more effort and focused energy than playing *forte*. A firm hand is required for both.

The wrist functions for pianists much as the bow does for string players. Up bows (upward gestures) must begin with the wrist up, and down bows (downward gestures) must begin with the wrist down. This action sets the stage for the appropriate gesture.

The fingers. The fingers play a significant role and do the lion's share of the work. Like the hand, fingers should be natural in shape, relaxed, compact, yet not stiff or tense, while holding their position. Bach provides specifics:

> In playing, the fingers should be arched and the muscles relaxed. . . . Stiffness hampers all movement, above all the constantly required rapid extension and contraction of the hands. All stretches, the omission of certain fingers, even the indispensable crossing of the fingers and turning of them demand this elastic ability.[11]

Beethoven relied on and taught this method.[12] In 1860, Mähler recalled to Thayer that "Beethoven played with his hands so very still; wonderful as his execution was, there was no tossing of them to and fro, up and down; they seemed to glide right and left over the keys, the fingers alone doing the work."[13]

The best finger placement on the keys is when they lie as a D major pentachord is formed, with fingers on the outer edges of the raised sharps. Fingers are curved and work with quick strokes. The physical makeup of shorter keys on the fortepiano (see chapter 1) facilitates a constantly curved, at-the-ready attitude, resting lightly on the keys unless extending for a large interval.

Independence of fingers is vital to successfully execute this style. Equal facility promotes the freedom to execute subtleties and nuances in expression, such as phrasing, ornamentation, and dynamics.

Although a non-legato, strike-from-above-the-key approach was clearly established in the Baroque Era, a legato touch with the attack being initiated with fingers on the keys came to be the preferred approach in the Classical Era and remains so today. An anonymous review of an article published in London in 1829 paints a clear pedagogical picture:

> The legato style . . . [a new phenomenon] is produced by . . . pressing [the fingers] down more firmly on the instrument . . . the fingers seem all strung upon one wire, and one is not taken up till the other is fairly set down . . . they seem to flow into one another.[14]

Period musicians believed the gesture must match the music, that what we do with our bodies *completely* affects the sound. It *is* easier if the body and fingers are doing what the music says!

Fingering choices. Bach understood the dangerous pitfall awaiting keyboard players that does not exist for other instrumentalists. "In the case of other instruments the slightest incorrectness of fingering is usually betrayed by the downright impossibility of performing the notes."[15] For non-keyboardists, in other words, wrong fingering equals wrong note! But for the pianist, we can stumble along, playing the right pitches, while all the while making a complete mess of the musical message because of inept fingering. It behooves us to heed Bach's advice and take it seriously, as it is still true: "Today, much more than in the past, no one can hope to play well who does not use his fingers correctly."[16] (See the extended citations on the companion website, Text 4.1. ▶) Sadly, though, Bach observes that application and consistent use of fingerings is "a secret art, known and practiced by very few."[17] Bach and Türk both demonstrate their belief in the importance of beginning with good fingering by choosing to place the topic at the start of their treatises. Bach devotes thirty-seven pages to fingering in the first chapter of *Versuch*, and Türk devotes sixty pages to fingering in the second chapter of *Klavierschule*.

In addition to its importance for good execution, fingering is completely interconnected to musicality. It is unequivocal. Fingering is inseparable from interpretation. In eighteenth-century style, fingering serves a musical function that is equally important to (and to Bach, surpasses) the technical role. Bach accentuates the need for good fingering:

> After mastering the requisite knowledge of keys, notes, rests, rhythm, and so forth, students should be made to spend a good deal of time practicing only the examples of fingering [all scales as outlined in *Versuch*], slowly at first and then more rapidly until in due time good fingering, as difficult and varied as it is at the keyboard, will become so much a matter of habit that it may be put out of mind.[18]

After scale fingerings in combinations of all colors and stripes are mastered, true Classical Era style may be engaged. In the choice of fingering, the *affekt* should be at the forefront of the performer's mind. It is here that the final question of execution may be answered: *How does one communicate with the audience—engaging the listener?* If that is truly the goal, then the best *effect* in choosing fingering should be the first consideration; the easiest fingering will not always be the *best* choice. Clementi believed that "to produce the *best effect*, by the *easiest means*, is the great basis of the art of fingering."[19] Notice the *best effect* trumps the *easiest means*. But what is amazing is that determining the best effect will oftentimes produce the easiest means. The following examples clarify.

In Example 4.1, the *best* fingering is achieved by the *easiest* means: the suggested consistent fingerings. Beethoven (who provided more fingerings in his scores than his contemporaries)[20] likewise favored consistent fingerings for repeated or similar figures. Inconsistent fingering was reserved for special technical or interpretive situations. To demonstrate the point, take Example 4.1 to the keyboard. First, try the excerpt with consecutive fingering (*1-2, 2-3, 3-4, 4-5, 5-4, 4-3, 3-2 . . .*) while at the same time following the slur indications. Now, play it with Türk's suggestions. Türk's choices require one gesture, one muscle movement, gliding up and down the keyboard—the *best* effect by the *easiest* means.

Music Example 4.1. Türk, *Klavierschule*, 158.

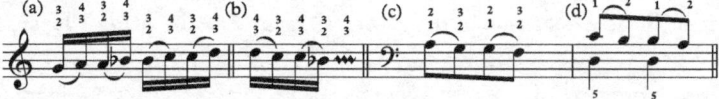

Example 4.2 shows how Clementi's advice applies to repertoire. In beats 1 and 2 of measure 33, the editor suggests fingering: *2-1-2-4-5*. This choice encourages slurring beat 1 to 2, which directly contradicts Mozart's articulation indication. Articulating the second beat requires the performer to consciously break the finger *legato* after the fourth finger. Playing *1-2-4-5-3* produces Mozart's articulation by using the natural inclination of the fingers: starting with a heavier gesture (and naturally heavier fingers) at the beginning of the slur, breaking the *legato* after finger 5, and landing with a rich, thick finger 3 on the second beat. Again, the *best* effect by the *easiest* means: one natural gesture followed by one newly articulated stroke.

Music Example 4.2. Mozart, Piano Sonata, K. 309/ II, mm. 33–36. Copyright (2005) G. Henle Verlag, Munich.

An often-employed modern practice is the use of changing fingers on repeated notes. Nothing in the literature, including Bach's *Versuch* or Türk's *Klavierschule*, promotes this modern school of thought. On the contrary, emphasis is placed on developing facility with *all* fingers to promote ease of execution in repeated-note passages. Only two specific situations in Bach's *Versuch* (page 33 and pages 73–74) promote changing fingers on repeated notes: during a long extended passage of repeated notes in a fast tempo, and in order to musically set up a new gesture in a moderate tempo.

Warning! Most *Urtext* editions offer fingering suggestions provided by an editorial staff, not the composer. Newman points out that "Beethoven provided more fingerings in his scores than any of the other Classic masters,"[21] and he placed special emphasis on fingerings in his teaching. For instance, Sonatina in F Major, WoO 50/I, which was written pedagogically for a student in 1788–1790, is replete with copious fingerings. In most editions, Beethoven's fingerings are indicated with italics. All other fingerings in any edition, unless specifically clarified as those of the composer, should be considered with great caution. And even at that, as Türk points out, fingering is ultimately determined by each performer's specific hand shape and finger length, for, "it would not be easy to find two clavichord players who in a somewhat longer composition would make use of the same fingering throughout."[22]

This technical approach provides rational solutions to the perceived "problems" of executing eighteenth-century repertoire. The added bonus? An eighteenth-century style that is easier to execute, that contains new palettes of color, and that provides unimagined sound energy through intentionally executed technical paths.

INFLUENCES APPLIED

Much as science is forced to look back to the leech and the maggot to inform modern medicine, modern music is forced to return to the fortepiano to inform technique. Those fortunate enough to play a fortepiano will more readily gain insight into a period approach.

During the initial experience at the fortepiano, most modern pianists feel as if everything happens too quickly and too easily, in a rude way, much like shifting from manual steering to power steering. Octaves are over-jumped, notes sound before intended or when not intended at all, scale passages fall apart, trills no longer respond, dynamic range is nonexistent ... general chaos abounds! The initial experience is usually fraught with frustration, and any return to the instrument is certain to come with a level of trepidation. However, if the best answers come from looking back to and learning from the primary source (the fortepiano), and if a remedied approach to resolve the execution conflict between the fortepiano and the piano is the goal, there must be willingness to develop and incorporate some of these concepts into modern technique.

Nobody wants to have weaknesses glaringly exposed. And yet that is *exactly* what happens when modern pianists first have a go at the fortepiano. We feel naked and exposed. Any technical deficiencies are magnified and become quite transparent, which is a humbling experience, to say the least. There is no hiding behind the long legato line, the thick pedal, or weighty chords. Do not be discouraged. Working through issues, whether on the fortepiano or on the modern piano in the ways suggested, provides great opportunities for improvement. The hand and body will adjust and improved responsiveness and control will emerge.

Application of Classical Era technique will make executing repertoire from any era better. It is worth the effort. Incorporate the following concepts into your playing and enjoy the freedom to express old ideas with new facility. Entirely new capabilities will materialize in the process as well.

From Bach and Türk to Beethoven's student Czerny, a compact, consistent hand shape is found to be fundamental. In Czerny's *Letters to a Young Lady on the Art of Playing the Pianoforte*, he discusses and diagrams a proper hand shape.

Drawing from several sources, a synthesized approach provides an excellent pedagogical progression for a sound technical regimen:

- As van Oort suggests, begin with the wrist. Start *on* the key—the wrist initiates the action. If the wrist is stiff, musicality and technical facility become harsh at best, [23] and at worst, paralyzed.
- Using Beethoven's advice from a comment in a Cramer Etude, develop the feeling of musical impulse while playing several two-note slurs. "The purpose is to withdraw the hand lightly. This will be achieved if it [the hand] is always placed firmly on the first of the two slurred notes and is lifted almost vertically as the second note is touched."[24]
- Develop uniformity in the fingers. Keep a small, closed hand position with very curved fingers. From this position, as recommended in a London 1829 article, fingers glide on the keys as if "all strung upon a wire."[25]
- Van Oort offers an exercise to develop facility while in the uniform, compact position. Practice scale segments in beats with a very compact hand, being aware of the center of balance in the hand, finger 3.[26] This exercise should be played in all keys.

- Accents and beats take time. As van Oort clarified in a master class during the Westfield International Fortepiano Academy, beats should be ruled by musical needs. The fewer the accents, the more easily one may play with speed and agility. Bringing down the activity of the fingers (which happens when accents or beats are reduced) enables faster execution. Practice trills or long groups of sixteenth notes with four beats, two beats, and finally one beat per bar.[27]
- Rosenblum suggests that "agility and finesse are more valuable than power."[28] This is true to a certain extent. Be careful to avoid confusing a light touch with feathery, uncommitted execution, as it provides very few

options for conveying varieties of *affekt*. Van Oort warns that "dusting" the top of the keys creates unfocused, uncontrolled, and unreliable playing.[29] It also lacks depth, like skimming the surface of a Caribbean ocean and missing all the beautiful colors and the interesting life down below. Baseball players strive for "soft hands," which in no way implies weakness but is powerful and calculated control, much like what is desired at the fortepiano.

Begin with a piece never before studied to avoid habitual technical responses. Something simple is recommended to allow focus on one issue at a time. Start with isolated gestures. Systematically work through the Practices section (physical roles, function, fingers, fingering choices). Initially, this will be a painstakingly slow process. Be patient. You are adding entirely new tools to the "technique toolbox," and they will be available for access time and time again in the future. Once a technique is consistent and reliable, determine where else it may be applied throughout the piece and in future repertoire.

When making fingering choices, keep it simple. There are two kinds of keys (high and low) and two kinds of fingers (high and low); begin here. Now ask yourself, does my fingering choice reflect the musical gesture? Is fingering for *musical* gain? Just because a particular fingering is *possible* doesn't mean it is the most plausible or that it is the most musical choice. Remember Clementi's observation: "To produce the *best effect*, by the *easiest means*, is the great basis of the art of fingering."[30]

When fingering is thoughtfully applied, many musical problems and concerns dissolve, like the case in Example 4.3. Using 3 on both the A♭ *and* G (mm. 103–104) will better ensure musical execution of Mozart's written gesture:

Music Example 4.3. Mozart, Piano Sonata, K. 309/I, mm. 103–106. Copyright (2005) G. Henle Verlag, Munich. ▶

Take into account the instrument on which you are playing. Many of today's pianos contain a stiffer action that may require incorporation of some forearm to support gestures. Regardless, be careful never to overplay, force, or overpower the style. When determining whether to use more forearm or full arm, make an intentional, conscious decision for a specific reason as needs arise for adjustments rather than deferring to the bigger (and less easily controlled) muscle groups out of habit.

Think twice. If you employ the full arm and the top capabilities of today's instrumental volume, the tone will be harsh and uncharacteristic. Furthermore, the sound will not decay quickly enough to articulate the succeeding sounds appropriately. The sound will either be too muddy or too choppy; certainly not the intended *affekt*.

With increased awareness of the demands of both instruments, you may find reasonable solutions to performing music on the modern piano that was originally intended for the fortepiano. It is a process of continually listening, experimenting, and adjusting to feedback from the music, the instrument, and the hall. The means and energy expended to this end will provide results beyond recreating old music on a new instrument, but rather, creating new music all your own with authenticity while respecting the originally intended message.

THE LESSON

Play and study Example 4.4 with the following points in mind.

Music Example 4.4. Mozart, London Notebook, KV 15oo, mm. 1–8. Copyright (1983) G. Henle Verlag, Munich.

1. Prior to introducing this work, students should be developing basic technical proficiency in several areas:
   a. Five-finger patterns
   b. Good hand position
   c. Finger independence
   d. Two-note slurs, executed as described previously by Beethoven

   e. Moving to different locations on the keyboard
   f. Playing in musical gestures, the wrist leading the gestures
2. Discuss the importance and benefit of using fingering choices for musical gain.
3. Make decisions regarding fingering and technical approach.
   a. Use finger energy to maintain crispness and separation (even on mm. 1–2, where the *affekt* is heavy).
   b. Lighter touch on mm. 3–4 will facilitate the desired piano dynamic and light *affekt*.
   c. Use *2-3* fingering in ms. 5 to create the desired "down-up" musical gain.
4. Introduce the *appoggiatura*, which relates to the fingering choices in ms. 5.

Use the quick reference guide on the companion website to summarize. ▶

CHAPTER 5

✺

Rhythm

Time makes melody, therefore, time is the soul of music.

—L. Mozart, *Violinschule*

T his is the crux of the matter. It all rests on rhythm. And there is no better instrument than the fortepiano for achieving this goal. From his presentation, "To Speak or Sing," van Oort clarifies, "The bright attack of the fortepiano tone makes rhythm one of its strongest inherent qualities."[1]

A discussion of eighteenth-century rhythmic practices is a multifaceted and deeply interwoven affair—much more than simple, clear-cut, one-size-fits-all note values and rests. Influencing attributes include *affekt*, tempo, meter, individual rhythms, rhetoric, and phrase structure. It is time to peel away the layers involved to understand the practices and to reveal a kaleidoscope of possibilities for expression.

HISTORICAL BACKGROUND

Music notational language is full of signs and symbols whose meanings continue to change over time. Eighteenth-century music notational language is a complete language. Now, nearly 300 years later, many twenty-first-century musicians apply modern era judgments to Classical Era scores. Ferguson connects with the past. "It is generally assumed nowadays that a composer writes the precise note values and rhythms that he requires in performance; but this was not always so."[2] Although Ferguson reminds us that notation practices are different today, I think a more important overriding point is missed by implying that eighteenth-century notation was more imprecise than modern notational practices. We come to this "new" old language with preconceived notions from our current twenty-first-century understanding, which does not serve us well. Although a quarter note is still a quarter note on paper, what it means today and what it meant yesterday may be completely different. Yes, judging by today's standards, this centuries-old language is not precise. But a deeper understanding is that both languages are whole. Classical Era musicians wrote completely what was required for performance in their time. Our task is to unearth the hidden treasure chest and open it to see that it is full of precious gems for decoding the meaning of Classical Era rhythmic notation.

With the flip of the lid, common symbols are exposed that exist both in eighteenth- and twenty-first-century notation. But the execution of those symbols is distinct to the style, instruments, and notational practices of each era. Attempting to apply twenty-first-century music notational rules to eighteenth-century music notational language most certainly assures imprecise delivery of an informed, adjusted, and authentic eighteenth-century style. Expressing (performing) the language can be achieved only through developing a working knowledge of bygone principles, as Ferguson later acknowledges. "Various notational and rhythmic conventions were recognized by both composer and performer, and to ignore them today is to falsify the music."[3] Much of modern pedagogy manifests this limited understanding of eighteenth-century rhythmic notation practices by either relying on ill-informed editions or minimizing the point and ignoring the elements that define the Classical Era style—the "ostrich head in the sand" syndrome. Failure to recognize and apply these principles leaves musicians four undesirable options:

- Depend on the expertise (or lack thereof) of another musician.
- Depend on an edition that might or might not be historically informed.
- Adhere strictly to the written page while using twenty-first-century practices.
- Ignore historical stylistic considerations altogether and impulsively interpret the score.

Learning to decipher eighteenth-century music notational language provides a wide range of parameters to guide choices. Uncovering crucial clues to the language offers fresh insight and freedom that allows musical interpretations that are both historically informed and truly our own.

Consider Example 5.1. The score may be played according to assumed modern rhythmic notational conventions:

- Quickly (from the Allegro tempo marking)
- *Legato* (as no separations are indicated)
- Quarter notes receiving full value, lasting until the beginning of the next beat
- No prescribed direction regarding heavy or light execution

Music Example 5.1. Clementi, Piano Sonatina, op. 36, no. 1/I, mm. 1–4. Copyright (2011) G. Henle Verlag, Munich. ▶

Sadly, these assumptions are ill informed. Yet, the pertinent directions are right there in the notation. We simply need to know the "rules of the game." As the chapter unfolds, the eighteenth-century rules necessary to comprehend and perform the notation will be explained. The excerpt will then be revisited to uncover a historically informed and very different interpretation from the one initially proposed.

The treatment of rhythm in this book is selective, covering customary practices typically understood by eighteenth-century musicians. Though it would be impractical to attempt rigid application of these practices to all notation encountered in eighteenth-century repertoire, it provides the basic and clear beginning necessary for comprehending this language. For extensive delineation of exceptions and extensions to these practices, go to primary sources such as C. P. E. Bach's *Versuch*, Türk's *Klavierschule*, or other superb volumes that codify eighteenth-century performance practice in depth, such as Clive Brown's *Classical and Romantic Performing Practice 1750–1900* (Oxford University Press) or Sandra Rosenblum's *Performance Practices in Classic Piano Music* (Indiana University Press).

BASIC TENETS

As articulated by Aristotle in chapter 2, the whole is greater than the sum of its parts. This precept is true when one looks at rhythm, too.

Diagram 5.1 illustrates how eighteenth-century rhythm principles are organic, not the sum of many separate inanimate parts, but the culmination of many parts working together to create an ever-changing, living art. For purposes of examination, however, the elements will be treated separately, then rejoined as a fluid, complete rhythmic whole.

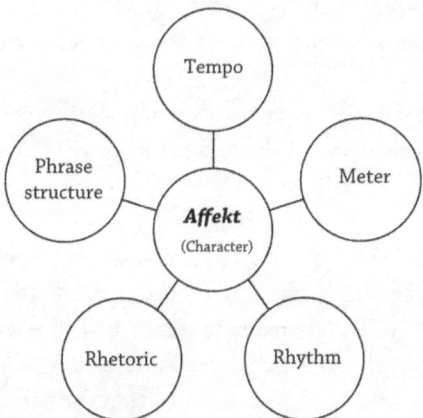

Diagram 5.1. Rhythm Schemata.

Affekt (character). The centerpiece that is rarely acknowledged or discussed by modern players when explaining rhythmic notation *must* be included in order to understand eighteenth-century rhythmic notational language: *affekt.* In eighteenth-century style, music notational language is complete. Everything required for performance is present in the score, including *affekt.* The composer chooses the rhythm required to project the intended *affekt.* In turn, *affekt* induces variables that offer choices in how that rhythm may be performed. Just as structure, harmonic function, and consonance/dissonance interact with *affekt* to steer the performer in execution, rhythmic elements interact as well. Learning some rudimentary rhythm-reading rules will facilitate projecting *affekt* through rhythm.

Again, the elements are interdependent. According to Kirnberger, tempo, meter, and rhythmic choices interact to create *affekt*:

> Tempo, meter, and rhythm give melody its life and power. Tempo defines the rate of speed, which by itself is already important since it designates a lively or quiet character. *Meter* determines the accents in addition to the length and brevity of the notes and the lighter or more emphatic delivery; and it shapes the notes into words, so to speak. But *rhythm* establishes for the ear the individual phrases formed by the words and the periods composed of several phrases. Melody is transformed into a comprehensible and stimulating speech

by the proper combination of these three things. It must be kept in mind that none of these elements is sufficient by itself to give the melody a precise *affekt*; the true expression of the melody is determined *only by their synthesis and their interaction* [italics mine].[4]

Tempo. To the eighteenth-century musician, tempo is much more complex than a speed direction (which, in many cases, did not exist) written at the beginning of a movement. Kirnberger captures the essence:

> *Tempo* . . . can also be violent or tender, skipping or monotonous, fiery or bland even when the degree of fast or slow motion is the same, *depending on the type of note values chosen* . . . [italics mine].[5]

In the eighteenth-century style, appropriate tempo is imperative to convey the desired *affekt*. Determining factors include *tempo ordinari* (basic understood tempi), well-known dance tempi, passions, meter, note values, and rhetoric. Qualitative designations, such as *allegro assai, maestoso,* or *scherzando,* may be added to provide additional expressive direction, as discussed in chapter 2. A tempo marking may be specifically indicated by the composer (see chapter 13), although many eighteenth-century works do not carry an indicated tempo. For, as Kirnberger concludes "[an appropriate tempo]. . . *tempo giusto* [is] determined by the meter and the note values that are employed in it."[6] Aha! So tempo (along with *affekt*) is influenced by, and interconnected with, rhythm choices.

Returning to the opening Clementi example, we find that the generating *tempo ordinari* is a moderate march (see chapter 2). Clementi most likely intended the notes to move along quickly, but not fast. Yet the *Allegro* tempo marking gained speed from 1750 through 1810. The first printing of op. 36, no. 1 in 1797 indicates *Allegro* tempo and common time signature. By the sixth printing, around 1820, Clementi changed the meter to cut time, indicating an increase in momentum.[7] So an eighteenth-century *Allegro giusto* was probably not as speedy as is interpreted today. More will be discovered about indicated tempi in chapter 13.

Meter. In addition to direction regarding the organization of strong and weak beats and the relation to period dances (see chapter 2), meter choices tell us about *affekt* and the weight of the music. The time signature $\frac{3}{2}$ is heavier, $\frac{3}{4}$ is lighter, and $\frac{3}{8}$ is lighter yet, regardless of any tempo marking.[8] Mozart's Piano Sonata in F Major, KV 280 is an ideal example of the progression of *affekt* from heavier to lighter. The sonata moves from a stately triple meter in the first movement (Example 5.2) to a lighter duple meter in the second movement (Example 5.3) and closes with a very light triple meter (perhaps even one pulse to the measure) in the final movement (Example 5.4).

Music Example 5.2. Mozart, Piano Sonata, KV 280/I, mm. 1–4. Copyright (2005) G. Henle Verlag, Munich.

Music Example 5.3. Mozart, Piano Sonata, KV 280/ii, mm. 1–5. Copyright (2005) G. Henle Verlag, Munich.

Music Example 5.4. Mozart, Piano Sonata, KV 280/III, mm. 1–8. Copyright (2005) G. Henle Verlag, Munich.

A comparison to the opening Clementi example is strikingly similar: the first movement is in common time (C), moving to $\frac{3}{4}$ in the second movement, and $\frac{3}{8}$ in the third movement. And, as is now understood, the first movement is relatively heavy (but not as heavy as if it were written in cut time).

This notion regarding heavy and light time signatures warrants further discussion. It brings with it answers to the paradox of slow second movements that have what many of today's performers would label as "fast" notes (six-teenth/thirty-second/sixty-fourth notes)—now understood as "lighter" notes. The second movement of Mozart's Piano Sonata in C Major, KV 309 is just one of many examples that utilizes this compositional tool (Example 5.5).

Music Example 5.5. Mozart, Piano Sonata, KV 309/II, mm. 1–4. Copyright (2005) G. Henle Verlag, Munich. ▶

The downbeat. In eighteenth-century music, *the downbeat rules.* L. Mozart writes, "Generally, the accent of the expression or the stress of the tone falls on the ruling or strong beat, which the Italians call *Nota Buona*."[9] Furthermore, period practice dictates beats 1 and 3 as *gut,* good or stronger beats; 2 and 4 as *schlicht,* light or weaker beats. *Excitement* often happens on the *schlicht* beats, eventually leading to *agitato*.[10] Unless otherwise notated, the direction is *to* the downbeat—and it (the down-beat) should be clearly articulated. The downbeat is essential in maintaining one's bearings throughout the course of a piece. Period tutors instruct that when several notes are tied together, the held tone may (and perhaps should) be re-struck to accentuate the metric energy and maintain the sustained tone (refer to the discussion of rapid decay in chapter 1).

Quantz explains how this concept of good and bad beats extends to good and bad notes:

> Where it is possible, the principal notes always must be emphasized more than the passing. In consequence of this rule, the quickest notes in every piece of *moderate tempo* or even in the *Adagio,* though they seem to have the same value, must be played a little unequally, so that the stressed notes of each fig-ure, namely the first, third, fifth, and seventh, are held slightly longer than the passing, namely the second, fourth, sixth, and eighth, although this lengthen-ing must not be as much as if the notes were dotted.[11]

This has dramatic implications for any modern player who feels it sac-rilege to play any long runs of sixteenth notes with anything but unwav-ering evenness! In *The End of Early Music,* Haynes delves deeply into this much-accepted period performance practice. This practice permits and encourages leaning into and taking time on carefully chosen beats and notes.

Within a given meter, there are beats that will naturally be stronger/louder and those that will naturally be weaker/softer. According to Türk, a strong dynamic marking on a naturally weak beat indicates that the marking will "expressly specify the opposite."[12] But there is no mention of shifting the downbeat. An accent or surprise on an off-beat may *counterweigh*—but not replace—the downbeat. In Example 5.6, notice the wonderful surprise effect when *forte* interrupts the third beat and mitigates the downbeat. The downbeat must be securely established or the surprise is lost.

Music Example 5.6. Beethoven, Six Minuets, WoO 10, no. 1, mm. 1–4. Copyright (1990) G. Henle Verlag, Munich.

In Example 5.7, if the downbeat and meter are securely established, the tie over the bar line creates the surprise—an exciting syncopated effect to *counterweigh* (not replace) metrical accents.

Music Example 5.7. Beethoven, Piano Sonata, op. 10, no. 1/i, mm. 37–44. (ABRSM)

The importance of the downbeat has far-reaching implications. Not only does the downbeat rule, but the first note of a section or period receives more emphasis than the first note of a phrase, as Türk's explanation validates: "The beginning tone of every period and the like must be given an even more marked emphasis than an *ordinary* strong beat."[13] In Example 5.8, therefore, the most emphasized note is not the dynamic surprise at the upbeat to ms. 33, but the downbeat A♭ on beat 1 of ms. 33. Its importance is noteworthy; not only is it the downbeat, but it is also the dramatic *subito forte* downbeat to the beginning of a phrase *and* a section.

Music Example 5.8. Beethoven, Piano Sonata, op. 10, no. 2/III, mm. 30–34. (ABRSM) ⊙

The central role of metrical accentuation is of such significance that the first note of each group is at times clearly marked in many ways. Türk outlines the hierarchy. "As necessary as it is to place an emphasis on the first tone of a section or phrase member, it is also important to keep the following limitation in mind: only the first tone that falls on a strong beat must be so stressed."[14] In Example 5.9, the downbeat, which also is the first note/chord of the group, is accentuated by dynamics, texture, register, articulation, and a separation of silence that is then released with the responding slur.

Music Example 5.9. Beethoven, Piano Sonata, op. 10, no. 1/i, mm. 1–4. (ABRSM) ⊙

Conversely to downbeats being crucial and consequently longer and heavier, upbeats are of slightest importance and are always shorter and lighter. The illogicality of scores wherein the entire line is marked *staccato* save the upbeats(s), as seen in Example 5.10, now makes sense: play the upbeat lightly even when the staccato indication is absent. (See chapter 9 for further discussion of the function of staccato.)

The meter may be further supported by accompaniment figures with repeated patterns (often in the left hand). When executed well, they supply

Music Example 5.10. Beethoven, Piano Sonata, op. 10, no. 2/III, mm. 1–6. (ABRSM)

great rhythmic energy and provide tasteful timing. In Example 5.11, the structure and accompaniment pattern are driven through L. Mozart's meticulous and ingenious treatment of the eighth-note groups. Hence, the *affekt* of the carefully crafted quartet-like figure supports the underlying structure, meter, and rhythmic energy.

Music Example 5.11. Mozart, *A Treatise on the Fundamental Principles of Violin Playing*, 220.

Example 5.12 illustrates how this concept applies directly to solo piano literature.

Music Example 5.12. Mozart, Piano Fantasy, K. 397, mm. 12–15. Copyright (1983) G. Henle Verlag, Munich.

Metrical structure does not exist in a vacuum. Brown sorts it out a bit. "The metrical structure of the music, seen from the point of view of the composer, is intimately connected with such things as phrase structure, the rate of harmonic change, and the fullness or lightness of texture at any given point."[15] Phrase structure will be addressed in the next section. A brief look at the other salient points Brown raises is worth consideration. When the harmonic rhythm generally speeds up, or when the line shifts from horizontal to vertical, particularly at cadences, it is the responsibility of the performer to bring notice to these changes. In Example 5.13, texture, harmonic rhythm, and slurring all change concurrently while the bass speaks 2-5-5-1, articulating the authentic cadence. These actions will be of interest to the listener if the performer executes them well.

Music Example 5.13. Beethoven, Piano Sonata, op. 10, no. 2/ii, mm. 1–8. (ABRSM) ▶

In eighteenth-century style, rhythmic gestalt is established through tempo, meter, phrase structure, harmonic structure, accompaniment patterns, and texture, all working in concert. Yet Brown interjects the role of artistic taste:

> While the performer was ideally expected to be aware of the metrical scheme that provided the framework for the composer's musical ideas, it was nevertheless acknowledged by many writers throughout the period that it was unnecessary, indeed inartistic, to make purely metrical accentuation obtrude upon the listener's perceptions, except in special cases (for example dances and marches) where distinct accentual patterns were an essential feature of the genre.[16]

The next section addresses Brown's concern: how is eighteenth-century practice concurrently metrical and expressive?

Rhetoric and musical expression of rhythm. According to the *New Oxford American Dictionary*, rhetoric refers to "the art of effective or persuasive speaking or writing; language designed to have a persuasive or impressive effect on its audience."[17] Haynes provides context. "Rhetorical music had as its aim to evoke and provoke emotions—the Affections, or Passions—that were shared by everyone, audience and performers alike."[18] It was a communal experience rather than an outsider-looking-in event. Everyone participated, performer and artist alike. It must *say something*—to everyone. Every period treatise impels the performer to understand and project *affekt*. Use of rhetoric as it applies to rhythm is one of the tools to achieve that goal. And, the fortepiano was perfectly suited to a music aesthetic that was predicated on passionate, rhetorical speech.

Classical repertoire abounds with correlations to grammatical accentuation—commas, colons, semicolons, exclamation points, question marks, etc.—through musical segments containing varying levels of importance that are stressed rhythmically. This is the essence of rhetoric: it provides the means for delivery of meter and rhythm. Haynes observes that many of today's performances contain a strictly "seamless legato, long-line phrasing, lack of beat hierarchy, unyielding tempos, unstressed dissonances, and rigidly equal 16th notes."[19] When imposed on eighteenth-century style, the result is a shallow sound that may be beautiful on the surface, but contains little depth, leaving the performer and listener wanting.

Eighteenth-century rhythmic declamation is conveyed through two basic types of accentuation: rhetorical (metrics) and pathetic (pathos). Rhetorical declamation implies expected metrical stress (strong beats, first notes of groups). With it comes predictability and comfort. Examples 5.14 and 5.15 illustrate Türk's observation of how composers express rhetorical intent by taking care in shaping groups through slurs, dynamics, and beaming:

> More painstaking composers make phrase members . . . recognizable by separating the note(s) on which the phrase division falls from the following notes.[20]

Music Example 5.14. Mozart, Marche funèbre del Signor Maestro Contrapunto KV 453a, mm. 1–4. Copyright (1983) G. Henle Verlag, Munich. ▶

Music Example 5.15. Beethoven, Bagatelle, op. 119, no. 1, mm. 59–65. Copyright (1978) G. Henle Verlag, Munich. ▶

Example 5.16 demonstrates another common metrical grouping. Here, the alternation between strong and weak groups is supported rhythmically, harmonically, dynamically, and texturally. The first two measures are strong, heavy, *forte*, and thick, followed by a light, airy, *piano* rhetorical response in mm. 3–4.

Music Example 5.16. Mozart, Piano Sonata, K. 309/I, mm. 1–5. Copyright (2005) G. Henle Verlag, Munich. ▶

Pathetic (pathos) rhythmic declamation implies passion in the delivery of an emotion, more complex than sentimental feelings. Projecting pathos requires informed choices that appeal to the audience's sympathies and imagination. Opportunities to project pathos may occur anywhere in the meter. This type of direction is often *not* indicated by the composer per se, but alluded to through other hints. Van Oort sheds light on rhythmic pathos: "The most important liberty which was taken for granted in the eighteenth century was rhythmic flexibility and, within the basic tempo, minimal fluctuations of tempo. I would call this true rhythmical playing as opposed to metrical playing."[21] All period treatises point out that pathos depends on a personal sense of good taste.

Within informed boundaries, pathos both permits and requires the most input from the performer. Here is where the paradox presented in the definition of eighteenth-century music notational language in chapter 1 comes to life. Indeed, notation does represent a specific pitch and duration (complete). The performer is then afforded the freedom and called to the responsibility to read "between the lines" to interpret and project *affekt* (imprecise and malleable). Koch describes this the aspect "by which the spirit of the piece must be made palpable in performance [and] can never fully be represented by signs."[22]

Here, modern performers are called to great responsibility and to respect informed parameters by learning as much as possible about the style. We are not immersed in eighteenth-century culture and context. We do not have the benefit of eighteenth-century recordings to understand the true spirit of the style. Haynes would agree that notation and written commentary tell only part of the story.

> An antique manuscript or print is hardly all of the composer's deed; at best it is only a record of certain aspects of it. Not only is music invariably under-notated, but those signs—the ones that are there—can mean different things.[23]

Peres Da Costa makes a very convincing case with recordings from the late nineteenth and early twentieth century. Listening to the recordings makes it become quite clear that what music theorists wrote as common practice was often not actually how musicians performed. This phenomenon continues today. So we must make do with what we have: the sizable sampling of musical scores from period composers, the wide swath of surviving literature, and the discussions surrounding the performances to offer guidance. This is the deepest insight we are afforded as we determine *pathos* today.

To help clarify the great freedom that *pathos* provides, consider the following limerick. Several appropriate interpretations are possible by applying rhythmic rhetoric and pathos. The rhetorical meter is a typical lyrical limerick. However, pathos is created by the chosen delivery of emphasis within the established form and meter. Each decision impacts the meaning of the limerick.

> There once was a lady named Donna.
> The new style she exclaimed, "I gotta!"
> She'd study and study (it made her quite nutty),
> She now teaches others who wanna.

Read the limerick aloud. Experiment with a variety of rhythmic deliveries: anticipate or delay a word, hurry or slow a phrase, single out a word more heavily or lightly, change nuance, vary attack of certain rhythms (words), use rests, change rhythmic demarcation, or try an unexpected syncopation. With each new delivery, a new *pathos* is created within the metrical rhetoric. The limerick can become silly, serious, mysterious, dangerous, ominous, angry, or boring, depending on the pathos chosen.

Now move this concept to the repertoire. Rhythmic pathos creates the "spice" in the repertoire, allowing the conflict between predictable metrical direction and contrary emphasis to unfold. In Example 5.17, notice the use of *pathos* to exact the rhythmic struggle: the *syncopated* sf *on the weakest beat 3* in ms. 23 that completes a dominant seventh chord, the *tie that mitigates the downbeat* in ms. 24, the non-harmonic chromaticism to blur the expected cadence on the subdominant on beat 1 of ms. 24, and the final deceptive cadence in ms. 24 *on beat 2 rather than an expected downbeat*. The performer then has the freedom to make tasteful decisions regarding *timing*. An abundance of "flavorful" choices in one measure!

Music Example 5.17. Beethoven, Piano Sonata op. 26/II, mm. 17–24. (ABRSM) ▶

Phrase structure. When introducing phrase structure in his tutor, Kirnberger begins with an explanation of the norm: "The best melodies are always those whose phrases have four measures."[24] *The Harvard Dictionary of Music* describes this phrasing, *vierhebigkeit*, as "the divisibility of music into units of four, whether of beats, accents, measures, phrases, etc. [Musicologist and music theorist] Hugo Reimann (1849–1919) was largely responsible for elevating this to a universal principle of Western music."[25] It eventually became a foundational underlying structure of eighteenth-century compositional style as well as the Western music model. Yet a survey of period literature clearly demonstrates that *vierhebigkeit* is simply the point of departure for great composers. In Rosen's discussion of eighteenth-century phrase structure, he supports this observation. "It [four-measure phrase structure] is not the model, but only, at the end, the most common."[26] Such is the foundation for eighteenth-century phrase structure. Every musician, even the earliest beginner, has experienced playing and writing in this short, periodic, symmetrical phrase structure. For the scope of this book, a solid working knowledge of this organizing structure is assumed. Those seeking further instruction are invited to visit Charles Rosen's *The Classical Style.*

Kirnberger encourages structural variety. "There are, of course, situations where individual phrases of more or fewer measures than the others are very appropriate for the sake of a particular expression."[27] Surveying the opening movements of piano sonatas by Haydn, Mozart, and Beethoven revealed a particular feature that positively facilitates *affekt* and was found to occur with enough frequency to demand special attention here. It is a tool of particular interest beyond the common *vierhebigkeit* structure. It involves a forward-moving configuration that lends itself to the passionate nature of rhetoric. It is sometimes called compound sentence structure, or as Caplin coins it, "a hybrid form of eight bar sentence structure."[28] It goes beyond the hybrid of the four measure question and answer. It makes exciting *pathos* possible.

All good things happen in threes in the Classical Era style, and this structure is the pinnacle of that notion. It was important from Bach to Brahms and permeates eighteenth-century compositional style in particular. Caplin describes it as "presentation + continuation."[29] This is another way of looking at Newman's observation in chapter 3. Or, as van Oort suggested at the Westfield International Fortepiano Academy, a simple way to locate this structure in the repertoire is to look for the signs shown in Diagram 5.2.[30]

Small...	Small...	Big→ →→→→
ms. 1, 2...	ms. 3, 4....	ms. 5, 6, 7, 8
(Static)	(Static with variant)	(Begins static but becomes dynamic)
⌣	⌣	⌣ ~
		Climax at ms. 7 (oftentimes ms. 6 in slow movements)

Diagram 5.2. The 2 + 2 + 4 formal structure.

This structure lends itself beautifully to the forward propulsion in Classical *pathos*. Examples 5.18 and 5.19 exhibit this concept.

Music Example 5.18. Beethoven, Piano Sonata op. 2, no. 2/I, mm. 1–8. (ABRSM) ▶

Music Example 5.19. Beethoven, Piano Sonata op. 10, no. 2/I, mm. 1–8. (ABRSM) ▶

Other examples for exploration include the Beethoven Piano Sonata, op. 53; Haydn Piano Sonatas, Hob. XVI:22, and Hob. XVI:33; Mozart Marche funèbre del Signor Maestro Contrapunto, KV 453a; and Mozart Piano Sonata, KV 545.

The rhythm pyramid on page 109 (Diagram 5.3) brings the individual parts of this section together to form a cohesive whole through a visual representation. Beautiful music begins with the foundation—the structure. Although the skeleton under the glowing melody does not come to mind, it really does begin here with rhetoric, structure, and foundational meter. Upon this foundation, phrases, measure groups, and rhythmic accents are chosen to communicate (or mitigate) the meter and *affekt*. Decisions regarding pathos are then made, again to either clarify or mitigate: phrases, measure groups, rhythmic accents, or the meter as a whole. The performer works from the foundation upward, always building, striving to reach the zenith of eighteenth-century musicianship—conveyance of the composer's *affekt* through performing. The top of the pyramid (*affekt*) determines the bottom, and from the bottom up, everything is decided to get to the top again.

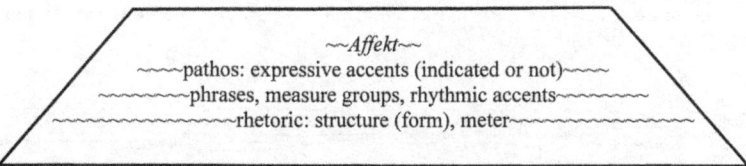

Diagram 5.3. Rhythm pyramid.

How this pyramid is in actuality executed requires examination of more specific facets: note values, rests, cross rhythms, dotted notes, and more on rhetoric.

Note values. Three directions are typically specified when a composer notates rhythm: the assumed "ordinary" way of playing (such as *legato* or *staccato*), indications for deviations from "ordinary," and *affekt* indications. The manner in which any given note value is interpreted has changed quite dramatically over the last 300 years.

Generally speaking, for the twenty-first-century musician, legato is the norm; all notes are connected (see chapter 8), and therefore each note receives full value. In common time, the quarter note is exactly that: a note held for one full beat, releasing with the beginning of the succeeding beat. Not so for the eighteenth-century musician. In music before 1800, the quarter note receives full value *only* when under a slur or *tenuto*. Türk explains the usual way and the exceptions.

> For notes that are to be played in the usual way, that is, neither detached nor slurred, the finger is raised from the key a little earlier than the duration of the note requires. . . . If there are some notes intermingled that should be held for their full value, then *ten.* or *tenuto* is written over them.[31]

In Examples 5.20, 5.21, and 5.22, the quarter notes should all be separated, save those under the slurs in mm. 29 and 32 of Example 5.21 and ms. 3 of Example 5.22 (See page 110).

In modern style, if a composer wishes to clarify or modify the duration of a note, a variety of symbols such as *staccato, detaché,* or *portato* are introduced to so indicate. In eighteenth-century music, *affekt* determines deviations from "ordinary" playing. This was a point of intense discussion for period musicians and theorists (see chapter 8). It boils down to this simple guideline: starting from the foundational base of "ordinary" detached playing, a note's actual duration is lengthened or shortened further, depending on the *affekt.* This technique allows the performer informed freedom of expression. In the same preceding examples, the quarter notes in Example 5.20 should be shorter than those in Example 5.22, and those

Music Example 5.20. Clementi, Piano Sonatina, op. 36, no. 1/I, mm. 1–4. Copyright (2011) G. Henle Verlag, Munich. ▶

Music Example 5.21. Bach, Prussian Sonatas for Piano, Wq 48, no. 6/ii, mm. 29–33. (Barenreiter) Copyright (1988) Bärenreiter-Verlag, Kassel. ▶

Music Example 5.22. Mozart, Piano Sonata, KV 280/I, mm. 1–4. Copyright (2005) G. Henle Verlag, Munich. ▶

in Example 5.21 will be the longest of all, based solely on the *affekt* of the music. Just how much shorter or longer is left for the performer to decide "in good taste."

In present-day practices, the *affekt* or meaning of the notes is prescribed through added expressive instructions such as *pesante* or *leggiero*. Again, not entirely true for the eighteenth-century musician. Although expressive instructions can be found, the mere choice of note values prescribes the *affekt* to be executed. From whole note to sixteenth note is not faster, but gradually lighter. As Quantz describes, "*Gaiety* is represented with short notes . . . *Majesty* is represented with long notes."[32] Return once again to our examples;

on the basis of this information, Example 5.20 should be performed more lightly than the others because of the prevalence of thematic eighth notes.

When eighteenth-century scores are read, the performer can discern from rhythmic notation alone—without any extraneous direction in the score—where to play "ordinary," where to deviate from the usual method, and how to convey the *affekt*. Incidentally, this approach further supports the claim made in chapter 1: play from reliable scores. To the uninformed, *Urtexts* may appear vague or barren, but when the language is understood, *Urtexts* provide the clearest description available today regarding specific rhythmic execution, exceptions to the norm, and *affekt,* straight from the horse's mouth—or composer's pen!

Rests. Music is made up of sound *and silence.* Clever composers employ the use of silence, which greatly enhances *affekt*. Rests provide power, suspense, and energy. Vigilant scrutiny of how rests are used uncovers clues and opens avenues for heightening *affekt* to a greater extent. Silence is sometimes more effective in punctuating the musical point than sound is. In Example 5.23, Beethoven sneaks in a clue to an exciting climax. As the sound diminishes from mm. 74–76, the suspense increases. Beethoven accomplishes this effect by skillfully employing three tools: textural adjustment from mm. 74–75, note value change (heavy to light) from mm. 75–76, and increased silence (eighth rest to two eighth-note rests) from mm. 75–76. Such are the characteristics to search out and highlight in performing.

Music Example 5.23. Beethoven, Für Elise, WoO 59, mm. 72–76. Copyright (1978) G. Henle Verlag, Munich. ▶

This brings us to the final examination of the opening Clementi, Example 5.1. With historical information, score reading and execution are now more clearly directed without the need for any superfluous editorial markings. The interpretation from the beginning of the chapter now takes a completely new turn:

- Quickly and swiftly; not fast
- "Ordinary" non-legato touch
- Quarter notes *detaché*, as they are not under a slur or *tenuto* marking. Although the repeated quarter notes in the right hand cannot receive full

time by virtue of being repeated, they may receive a wide range of length, depending on *affekt*. Here, the *affekt* calls for a crisp *detaché* in both voices.
- Downbeats clearly accentuated
- Light and energetic, as directed from the eighth notes and rests
- Yet not overly light, due to the choice of common time

Cross-rhythms. Today's mathematically exacting music notational system freely intermingles rhythms from differing meters. It is not uncommon to find modern scores wherein the performer is asked to play duplets in one voice with triplets juxtaposed in the other. In eighteenth-century style, what appears on the surface to be a combination of rhythms from two different meters may not be the case. Conventions change over time. Prior to 1775, there was no established form of compound metrical notation. If there was a triplet figure against a duplet figure, oftentimes the figure from duple time was realized in line with the triplet figure:
♩ ♪

The *affekt* of the piece and surrounding notation are also influencing factors. The following contrasting examples clarify this point. In Example 5.24, the first beat of ms. 8 contains what may appear to be a cross rhythm. However, the A sixteenth note in the right hand, should be performed simultaneously with the last A in the left-hand triplet to align itself with the surrounding *affekt*. Both voices sound together to project an F Major pastoral scene.

Music Example 5.24. Clementi, Piano Sonatina, op. 36, no. 1/II, mm. 6–8. Copyright (2011) G. Henle Verlag, Munich. ▶

Example 5.25 (see page 113) presents a situation in which the sixteenth notes should be placed as late as possible after the right-hand triplet figures. The use of a very crisp dotted eighth/sixteenth combination is appropriate here. Intensity is increased and the desired *affekt* is achieved.

The music notational practice of marking the use of triplets in a duple meter was not yet standard in the eighteenth century. However, as Bach states, "Triplets can be recognized simply by their beam."[33] And Türk adds, "When the number 3 is missing, it is necessary to recognize the triplet by context or by counting the numbers of quarters or eighth

Music Example 5.25. Beethoven, Piano Sonata, op. 2, no. 2/III, mm. 56–58. (ABRSM)

notes in a measure."[34] Referring again to the two preceding examples, notice that the triplet figures are notated differently. In Example 5.24, they are made clear through beaming and simply by "doing the math." In Example 5.25, Beethoven marks the figures with the now-familiar *3*. Work out the math and work through the *affekt* to determine tasteful rhythmic groupings.

Double dotting or over dotting. Today, when a performer finds this notation in the score: ♩. ♪, the common assumption is to perform it mathematically accurately, with the dotted eighth note receiving three parts of the quarter note and the sixteenth note receiving the fourth part. In eighteenth-century style, dotted notes were *never* performed in such a manner. The dotted note is always "the big guy." Just how big? In *Klavierschule*, Türk provides several examples to clarify how length is determined by *affekt*. Execution may range anywhere from a very crisp double dotted eighth note followed by a thirty-second note, unwinding all the way down to a much more relaxed quarter note followed by an eighth note as a triplet figure. Dart warns modern performers thus:

> This conventional lengthening of the dotted note and shortening of the complementary note was in very widespread use over a very great length of time, and ignorance of this fact is one of the gravest defects of present-day performances of old music. It is a fashion that lasted from the early years of the seventeenth century down to the last years of the nineteenth.[35]

The dotted note was generally held a bit longer to energize the line. L. Mozart instructs and encourages, "The dot should in fact be held at all times somewhat longer than its value. Not only is the performance thereby enlivened, but hurrying—that almost universal fault—is thereby checked. . . ."[36] Quantz would agree: "[in majestic music] dotted notes must be attacked sharply and must be executed in a lively fashion. The dots are held long, and the following notes are made very short."[37] Period musicians considered many factors when determining the length of the dotted note. As always, the first consideration is *affekt*, followed by the role of the rhythmic motive, consistency of the motive (whether the figure had been established and was thematically important earlier in the work), tempo, and the mere physical ability of the performer to execute the desired rhythm.

Examples 5.26, 5.27, and 5.28 illustrate three excerpts with contrasting *affekt* that require different execution. Under no circumstances would an exact mathematical ratio be appropriate. In Example 5.26, the *affekt* calls for a more relaxed dot, perhaps close to a rocking quarter/eighth triplet combination. However, L. Mozart cautions, "if the dot were held its usual length it would sound very languid and sleepy. In such cases dotted notes must be held somewhat longer. . . ."[38] Here, there are two issues with which to contend: Mozart's reminder to use the dot to enliven the line and Türk's reminder to consider the *affekt*. The performer is left with the freedom to make an informed choice. Example 5.27 calls for a much longer dotted note to enliven the *affekt* and move the action forward. The dotted quarter note in Example 5.28 is the longest of all, emphasizing a dramatic conclusion to the separated

Music Example 5.26. Clementi, Piano Sonatina, op. 36, no. 2/II, mm. 1–4. Copyright (2011) G. Henle Verlag, Munich. ▶

Music Example 5.27. Beethoven, Piano Sonata, op. 10, no. 1/i, mm. 1–4. (ABRSM) ▶

Music Example 5.28. Mozart, Piano Sonata, K. 309/I, mm. 1–5. Copyright (2005) G. Henle Verlag, Munich. ▶

Allegro con spirito

half notes in the grand, opening statement in mm. 1–2. As is now evident, eighteenth-century music notational language departs significantly from the twenty-first-century premise of one "right way" to play dotted rhythms under all circumstances.

One final, extremely important practical consideration must be noted. In eighteenth-century style, the sixteenth note almost always belongs to the eighth note to which it is beamed, not the next note. The next note is a new articulation that must be separated and clear. It is a new stroke. Articulating the new idea makes it clearer and better.

Eighteenth-century music notational language is complete. It provides rhythmic direction and guidance for the performer to effectively choose how to provide the listener an auditory experience of the composer's description. There are very few hard and fast "do's and do not's" but a wide range of "possibly's" for tasteful consideration. Now that these principles are established, it is time to discuss how to judiciously make appropriate adjustments for playing this style on the modern piano.

INFLUENCES APPLIED

Rhythm-reading tools for a logical and systematic approach to reading eighteenth-century rhythmic notation are now available. This availability does not provide a single final answer, but provides direction along informed appropriate paths. The significance of reading the score by using these historically informed tools is that it brings fresh ideas and the potential for new passion in performing. Willingness to undertake these concepts with an open mind and ear is vital for success. Ever striving for more vibrant and rhythmically energized playing will be greatly rewarded.

As has been previously stated, applying this language on a modern instrument is in many ways no different from what period musicians were called to do in their own time. We must learn what the score tells us about the music and what the score tells us to strive for or expect from the instrument. And we must listen to feedback from the instrument, as it will tell us something new about the music.[39]

Bear in mind that the strength of the modern piano is its capability to create a long, singing, connected melodic line (see chapter 1). Rhythmic clarity, that extremely important trait of eighteenth-century music, is produced less naturally on the modern piano, but nonetheless can and should be achieved agreeably. Rhythmic clarity is vital to eighteenth-century style and is oftentimes missed, as Brown, Sadie, and Beethoven all believe. "Virtually all performances on modern pianos are sorely lacking in the strong metric pulse considered of prime importance in all eighteenth-century treatises. Beethoven himself, in his annotations of the Cramer etudes for his nephew Karl, stresses metrical accent almost above any other performance consideration."[40] Knowledge of the rhythmic crispness inherent in the fortepiano, along with knowledge of period rhythmic practices, should foster creative experimentation to search for ways to bring pointed, rhythmic energy to any figure on the modern piano. An eighteenth-century "sense" is truly a viable option on the modern piano.

It is ideal to begin with a piece never before played. Choose a piece that is perhaps a bit simple to limit the number of concepts with which to contend. Any piece from Mozart's London Notebook or any of Beethoven's German Dances will do nicely. An interesting option is the first movement of Mozart's Piano Sonata, KV 545. This movement is written in a two-voice texture. There are no dynamic markings, and only five types of slurs appear that are used fewer than twenty times in the entirety of the movement. This is a great opportunity to test understanding of rhythmic implications by creating a musical rendition based on stylistic norms.

Uncover the structure and underlying concept: the *affekt*. Closely follow each and every guideline presented in the historical section of this chapter. Decide the desired sound to be created and which elements must be brought to the forefront to support that decision. Make sure it supports the *affekt* on which you settled. Do your choices bring a holistic sense to the music?

Next, as a "purist," begin strict application of the guidelines regarding heaviness/lightness and note duration. This task must be done in combination with execution of any slurs, dynamics, and gestures, using other chapters for guidance to avoid a chopped and unattractive sound. Listen to the sound created. Evaluate. Experiment with adjustments. The ear and body must constantly orient and adapt itself to the instrument at hand, rooting out the *affekt*. At master classes, Malcolm Bilson suggests, "When in doubt, exaggerate in one direction or the other—the answer will become readily and abundantly clear when listening (in good taste) with your inner ear."[41] Singing any questionable line is also helpful in deciding how to treat lines rhythmically. Keyboardists often forget the power of this simple yet highly effective tool. Oftentimes students come to me with questions regarding *affekt*, note length, attack or release, and heavy or light execution. By singing the line, students can immediately solve the problem nearly every time. Keep in mind that each instrument, performing space, and performer is strikingly diverse. The process will require practice, persistence, patience, and willingness to shape and mold the sound with the mechanics at hand.

Don't be afraid of the articulated silences. When my children were very little and had "mastered" the art of continual verbalization and chatter, I would set the kitchen timer and tell them they couldn't talk until the timer went off. Yes, silence is golden! The listener will lean into and excitedly anticipate the next sound. It allows the ear to cleanse and refresh. Live through the notes; play the silences. Just because the modern piano is capable of creating a long connected line doesn't necessarily mean continual sound is the ultimate goal. Retire the security blanket (the damper pedal). Playing is not better without rests!

With willingness, creating an eighteenth-century "sense" is feasible. *Affekt* will jump off the page. Vibrancy will emerge. Many "ah ha" moments, as described in the preface, will be created. Exciting revelations will erupt. New paths will continually appear. Expressing musical thoughts with eighteenth-century rhythmic clarity enlivens *Sturm und Drang*.

THE LESSON

Play and study Example 5.29 with the following points in mind.

Music Example 5.29. Mozart, London Notebook, KV 15oo, mm. 1–8. Copyright (1983) G. Henle Verlag, Munich.

1. Determine the *affekt*.
   a. Waltz or minuet in a heavy time
2. Discuss how the hybrid sentence structure (two mm. static, two mm. static, four mm. dynamic) facilitates *pathos* within the organized metrical rhetoric.
3. Discuss possible orchestral instrumentation being employed, as this impacts heaviness or lightness of tone.
4. Separate the quarter notes that are not under a *slur* or *tenuto*.
5. Make decisions regarding quarter notes.
   a. Heavier in mm. 1–2 (march-like), perhaps *tutti*
   b. Quarter notes lighter in mm. 3–4 (range gets higher), perhaps small ensemble
   c. *Legato* quarter notes under the slurs in mm. 5–6 (allowing for more contrast)
6. Feel the section in groups: two strong measures plus two weak measures plus four responsive measures that grow to the dominant.
   ✓ Practice strategy: practice these groups as independent gestures to develop the concept more quickly and easily
7. Pathos emphasis on the F♯ (a bit more the second time) to build to the cadence on the dominant in ms. 8. Introduce the term *agogic*.
   ✓ Practice strategy: play the first note of each measure alone to hear the *agogic* concept, with each downbeat stretched a bit longer

Use the quick reference guide on the companion website to summarize. ▶

CHAPTER 6

⌀⌐⌐

Dynamics

Louder doesn't make it better; it just makes it louder.

HISTORICAL BACKGROUND

The Harvard Dictionary of Music states that no expression marks of any kind have been found in music prior to 1500. The earliest dynamic indication is found in a score for lute circa 1517, directing the performer to *play very softly*. By the end of the sixteenth century the novel style of contrasting sonorities arose with the popularity of madrigals. The use of abbreviations to indicate dynamics appeared as late as 1638—F. [*forte*], P. [*piano*], E. [echo], t [trill].[1] With the rise of the famous Mannheim school, all dynamic effects were used for the first time in the modern way. Mannheim is where Mozart first traveled in his search for employment after having been released from the "oppression" of Salzburg. He was so elated by the music culture and opportunities in Mannheim that he dilly-dallied until he was "forced" to winter there, surrounded by great musicians, the popular Mannheim school of music, and the "new" fortepiano.

"ABSOLUTE" DYNAMICS (*FORTE/PIANO*)

Rosenblum's detailed work as laid out on pages 60–61 in *Performance Practices in Classic Piano Music* concludes that as the fortepiano took hold, notational practices followed. Concrete evidence found in the scores of Haydn, Mozart, and Beethoven's piano sonatas bear witness to the gradual increase in the use of dynamic direction in the score. Haydn (1732–1809) lived the longest (seventy-seven years) and, therefore, offers longitudinal perspective. Overall, Haydn used the fewest absolute dynamic markings. His early sonatas contain none, and sporadic use from 1770 through 1774. From Hob. 40 (1763) to the last sonatas, the number of dynamic indications gradually increased. Statistical analysis from Audun Ravnan provides more insight. Haydn employed a total of 991 absolute dynamic markings (26 percent *forte*, 26 percent *piano*).[2] Mozart (17561791) used this "new" tool more than twice as much as Haydn, with a total of 2,244 absolute dynamics (41 percent *forte*, 44 percent *piano*).[3] His first six sonatas are replete with markings (exploiting the capabilities of the fortepiano he encountered in Munich in 1775). The sonatas K. 280 through 283 contain indications specifically for right hand and left hand. And Beethoven (1770–1827), who came on the scene a bit later, incorporated dynamics as a full-fledged, integral part of his compositions. More numerous markings appear: 9,297 dynamic markings of all type. Twenty-four percent are absolute soft versus 15 percent absolute loud[4]—four times the number used by Haydn. Furthermore, they are more varied, are more subtle, and contain more contrast: *ppp, piu cresc., cresc. poco a poco, leggiermente, teneramente, ben marcato, sanft.*[5] With time, dynamic indications grew in frequency and variety.

One additional contributing factor is worth mentioning—the mere presence of the composer. In the eighteenth century, the composer was often the performer. Or at the least, the composer was frequently present when his work was performed. With the rise of amateur performers and an increase in publishing, composers may have been concerned with how their music was performed in their absence. Most likely, the situation was a result of a combination of both influences. Whatever the situation, basic ground rules were understood.

Definitions. Interestingly, both Bach and Türk speak very little about dynamics. Bach writes three sentences:

> P. means *piano* or soft; two or more of the letters standing together denote greater softness. M.F. means *mezzo forte* or half loud. F. means *forte*; to denote greater loudness two or more of the letters are placed together.[6]

Türk defines five terms:

> *ff* means *fortissimo,* very (extremely) loud, loudest
>
> *f—forte*, loud
>
> *mf—mezzo forte*, medium (moderately) loud

    p—piano, softly, lightly

    pp—pianissimo, very (extremely) soft, softest[7]

Notice there is no mention of *mp*. Rosenblum reports that "*mezzo piano* was used not at all by Haydn or Mozart and apparently only once by Beethoven in Piano Sonata op. 111/i/22–23."[8]

    What they *do* speak to at great length is—you guessed it!—the performer's ability to project *affekt* through execution. Bach's comment here seems most pertinent to the argument:

> It is not possible to describe the contexts appropriate to the forte or piano because for every case covered by even the best rule there will be an exception. The particular effect of these shading depends on the passage, its context, and the composer, who may introduce either a forte or a piano at a given place for equally convincing reasons.[9] (See Türk's comments on the companion website, Text 6.1. ⊙)

    Implications. How do we weave our way through the eighteenth-century understanding of dynamics? Today, *forte* and *piano* are generally associated with an absolute volume that has a very wide range from loud to soft. The novelty with the fortepiano wasn't an extreme range of volume as we know today, but its ability to quickly alternate and facilitate finesse. *Forte* and *piano* are the backbone, indicating more and less rather than an absolute extreme loud or soft. Quantz illuminates thus: "It [*forte* and *piano*] forms the musical light and shadow to be expressed by the performer, and is of the greatest necessity. It must be used with great discernment, however, lest you go from one to the other with too much vehemence rather than swell and diminish the tone imperceptibly."[10]

    Forte→piano is not necessarily an absolute direction specifically for the notes under the marking all the way to the next indication, but serves as a guide for dynamic direction from one marking to the next on the basis of melodic, harmonic, and contextual clues. The marking *f→→→→p* is actually giving direction to begin *forte* and work toward *piano*, not an absolute *f→f→f→f→f→f→f→p*. In Example 6.1 (see page 122), ms. 4 is the appropriate place to begin a *diminuendo*, thus bridging the opening statement to the response at ms. 5. At ms. 6, *poco crescendo* is appropriate in preparation for the dominant key, second-theme group, and upcoming *forte*.

    Likewise, in Example 6.2 (see page 122), ms. 19, Mozart provides direction from *forte→piano* rather than an absolute *forte* on beat 1 that continues until *piano* in the middle of beat 2. The performer should be moving from *forte* on beat 1 to *piano* on beat 2.

Music Example 6.1. Clementi, Piano Sonatina, op. 36/I, mm. 1–4. Copyright (2011) G. Henle Verlag, Munich. ▶

Music Example 6.2. Mozart, Piano Sonata, K. 309/II, mm. 17–19. Copyright (2005) G. Henle Verlag, Munich. ▶

If you have ever put together a jigsaw puzzle, you already understand this concept of shading. There is never just one color of green in a forest or blue in the sea. *Forte* and *piano* were used similarly in the eighteenth century to indicate shadings rather than dramatic volume shift. Not only is the instrument incapable of the powerful *forte* found in the modern piano, but such severe accents may force the particular pitches out of tune and shocking changes might also very well be considered in bad taste. In Example 6.3, Mozart is clearly shading the line or creating a swell, as Quantz previously described.

Music Example 6.3. Mozart, Piano Sonata, K. 280/III, mm. 42–47. Copyright (2005) G. Henle Verlag, Munich. ▶

Forte followed by piano. Forte followed by *piano* or *piano* followed by *forte* (*fp, pf*) are often declarative in nature. Or they may give direction regarding a terraced *crescendo* or *diminuendo*. Again, the breadth is determined by the *affekt* of the piece, instrument, and size of the hall. In Example 6.4, Mozart is providing expressive direction more so than volume. Notice the *fp* over a long note in the bass. The nature of the instrument facilitates the proper decay without any work needed from the pianist if the *forte* is executed at an appropriate level.

Music Example 6.4. Mozart, Piano Sonata, K. 280/III, mm. 55–59. Copyright (2005) G. Henle Verlag, Munich. ▶

Quick alternation of *f* and *p* were also used by the composer and performer to clarify themes, enhance the underlying structure, delineate harmonic relationships, augment texture, and illuminate rhythmic energy. To execute these nuances requires discernment and "good taste." In Example 6.5, the dynamic markings provide expressive direction within the musical line, which leads the performer to execute in a manner other than *ordinari* (the weaker beats receiving stress). As the intensity increases, terraced dynamics may be employed and the breadth of the *forte* may be widened.

Music Example 6.5. Mozart, Piano Sonata, K. 309/I, mm. 48–51. Copyright (2005) G. Henle Verlag, Munich. ▶

The dynamic *fp* can serve a declarative expressive function. In Example 6.6, mm. 1 and 2 build bit by bit, leading up to the *forte* in ms. 3, all within context of the character of a delicate second movement. From the *forte* forward, the phrase is completed with a subtle *diminuendo*, arriving at *piano* by the end of the phrase in ms. 4. Understanding and executing this type of specific direction creates an exquisitely beautiful line.

Music Example 6.6. Mozart, Piano Sonata, K. 309/II, mm. 1–4. Copyright (2005) G. Henle Verlag, Munich. ▶

Further, use of *fp* as *subito* is appropriate to heighten a particular harmony or rhythm, or to provide melodic interruption, as demonstrated in Example 6.7. The natural decay of the fortepiano allows the *fp* to "time out" appropriately, heighten the harmony, and prepare the subsequent rhythm. In Example 6.8, the *fp* slightly interrupts and emphasizes the appoggiatura in the lyrical first theme.

Music Example 6.7. Beethoven, Piano Sonata, op. 13/i, mm. 1–2. (ABRSM) ▶

Music Example 6.8. Mozart, Piano Sonata, K. 283/I, mm. 1–6. Copyright (2005) G. Henle Verlag, Munich. ▶

Understood practices. Today, *dolce* is commonly understood as "sweetly" with a side serving of soft. According to Türk, it indicates "pleasant, sweet, and gentle."[11] On pages 60 and 63 of *Performance Practices in Classic Piano Music,* Rosenblum unearths instances in Mozart and Clementi that point to the belief that *espressivo, dolce,* and *piano* were synonymous. One mark-ing rarely seen today is *pf*, which indicates play *poco forte* or *piu forte*. Fortunately, it is usually spelled out.

In the Classical Era style it is understood that low notes are naturally heavier, high notes lighter. This practice follows the natural inclination of the human voice and is well suited to the mechanics of the fortepiano. Common period practice dictates that the top note of a musical line may be louder *only* if it is on the downbeat. By relying on the inherent qualities of the fortepiano, the top note will sing out and be accentuated naturally when this tool is used. In Example 6.9, the high G will *not* be the loudest note because it occurs under a slur (see chapter 8) and on the weak beat of ms. 3. Rather, the F appoggiatura in ms. 4 will receive the special empha-sis dynamically and rhythmically.

Music Example 6.9. Mozart, Piano Sonata, K. 332/I, mm. 1–7. Copyright (2005) G. Henle Verlag, Munich. ▶

Melodic tones that create dissonance are brought out in this style. In his *Versuch*, Quantz works out an elaborate plan for executing various levels of dissonance. Bach explains simply:

> But in general it can be said that dissonances are played loudly and consonances softly, since the former arouse our emotions and the latter quiet them ... all tones of a melody which lay outside the key may well be emphasized.[12]

GRADUAL AND TERRACED DYNAMICS

The desire for a keyboard instrument that could sustain a gradual and wider volume range was realized in the fortepiano. Augsburg, Munich, Mannheim, and Vienna, all fortepiano-building hubs, were within a small distance from Salzburg. Mozart was smack dab in the middle of these new developments. While striking out on his own for employment, he arrived in Mannheim on October 30, 1777. As mentioned earlier, so entranced was he that although it was evident no employment opportunities were going to materialize in the near future, and in spite of letters from his father urging him to move on, he managed to stay until March 14, 1778. Mozart must have felt like a kid in a candy store, experiencing the amazing musical and cultural life in Mannheim. Schubart describes an exquisite music culture:

> No orchestra in the world has ever surpassed that of Mannheim in performance. Its *forte* is like thunder, its *crescendo* a cataract, its *dim.* a crystal stream burbling into the distance, its *piano* a breath of spring.[13]

Gradual dynamics enhance phrases, sections, and structure. Context is supplied by *The Harvard Dictionary of Music*: although gradual changes were in use in performance from 1600, notation of gradual dynamic changes came over time. The earliest known use of modern signs for *crescendo* and *diminuendo* appeared in 1739.[14] Rosenblum notes that the *crescendo/diminuendo* hairpin signs (< >) began appearing in the 1780s and 1790s.[15] Haydn first used them in 1784 (Hob. 40), Clementi in works after 1800, and Beethoven right from the start with op. 1 for shading one note or two-, three-, or four-note groups.[16] Although origins of the extended *crescendo* can be traced to the Italian opera overture, again, Charles Burney describes where the significant developments took place: "It was [at Mannheim] that the *Crescendo* and *Diminuendo* had birth."[17]

Regardless of the actual origins, *crescendo* and *diminuendo* were certainly being exploited to the fullest in Mannheim, where Mozart spent five and one-half months. The Mannheim *crescendo* developed into its own "brand," and sometimes was the event itself. *Crescendo* was clearly integrated into the musical texture of compositions by Beethoven and Mozart.

The words *crescendo* and *diminuendo* denote variations of a relatively moderate scale. *Crescendo* was mostly used for ascending lines to increase tension and climactic effects and, conversely, *decrescendo* for descending lines and relaxation. *Crescendo* indicates to the performer where to send the musical direction and expression, more so than today's perception of growth in volume, particularly in Beethoven. With the *crescendo* and *diminuendo* hairpin signs comes the freedom to speed up and slow down, according to *affekt* and "in good taste," as can be seen in Example 6.10.

Music Example 6.10. Beethoven, Piano Sonata, op. 10, no. 2/I, mm. 5–8. (ABRSM). ▶

When a *slur* appears in conjunction with a *crescendo* hairpin sign, it may counter its usual execution, or assist in grouping the musical gestures, as seen in Example 6.11.

Music Example 6.11. Beethoven, Piano Sonata, op. 2, no. 2/II, mm. 27–31. (ABRSM) ▶

INFLUENCES APPLIED

When one performs dynamics from eighteenth-century repertoire on the modern piano, many adjustments are necessary. Dynamic markings provide many clues beyond volume. The performer must determine from the context how and to what extent the dynamic marking(s) will best describe the *affekt* the composer is portraying. Continue to ask, What *affekt* will this create? Am I solely focused on volume or is *affekt* considered? What concept is executed? Am I just playing loudly because there is an *f* in the score or is the composer pointing out something more meaningful for me to express?

Expressing *affekt* is the goal. Dynamics are one of the tools. *Forte* and *piano* are the means to achieve the desired end. When contemplating dynamics, consider that *forte* is loud *and* heavy/wide/broad/angry/anxious/big/strong; *piano* is soft *and* light/sweet/pleading/sorrowful/melancholy. Achieving these descriptors involves more than volume. Heavy and light refer more to the sustaining or detaching of a tone rather than to the loudness or softness. With heavy execution, it is appropriate to hold the tone nearly until the very end of the prescribed duration of the rhythm, but with light execution, it is stylistic to release the key somewhat sooner. Listen carefully on the modern piano to make artistic adjustments. The modern piano requires time for the tone to develop. Therefore, cutting the sound off too quickly will result in a choppy, undesirable effect.

When contemplating extreme *f* or *p*, remember that these markings come out of and in relation to the Baroque tradition and the volume capabilities available on the fortepiano. Making appropriate adjustments on the modern piano will be of great assistance in bringing authenticity to the performance.

A simple exercise will clarify these concepts. Take Example 6.12 to the piano. Using the piano's full capabilities, play the example with a modern concept of *forte* and *piano*. The *forte* notes will be overpowering, stealing sound from the first note of each succeeding note marked *piano* and clipping off before the tone gains full development of sound. Now, play it again. But this time play *as if* you were playing a fortepiano. Think in terms of *affekt* rather than sheer volume, heavy/dark and light/suspenseful. You get the idea. Naturally, adjustments must be made with regard to the instrument and hall, but the musical message is expressed much more effectively when the dynamic markings lead to performances beyond loud and soft.

There are several important considerations to continually keep in mind.

- What is the intended *affekt*?
- How was it probably performed on the period instrument?
- With the direction given by the composer, how can that intention be best realized on this instrument?

Again, take a piece never before played. In a step-by-step fashion, work through the dynamic markings provided. Follow the historical

Music Example 6.12. Mozart, Piano Sonata, K. 332/I, mm. 55–65. Copyright (2005) G. Henle Verlag, Munich.

information now available from the previous section. Enjoy a new artistic "palette," now replete with new subtlety and nuance.

THE LESSON

Play and study Example 6.13 with the following points in mind.

Music Example 6.13. Mozart, London Notebook, KV 15oo, mm. 1–8. Copyright (1983) G. Henle Verlag, Munich.

1. There are many possible choices surrounding dynamics.
    a. Mm. 1–2 *forte* (heavy), 3–4 *piano* (light). Introduce the term *Sturm und Drang.*
    b. Play terraced dynamics to achieve *crescendo* in mm. 5–6.
    c. Introduce the term "terraced dynamics."
2. Using the same strategy as in chapter 5, play the first note of each measure, listening to each downbeat gaining volume as well as *agogic* length.
3. Peak at ms. 7 (a high note on a downbeat).
4. Resolve the phrase with a small *dim.* to ms. 8.

Use the quick reference guide on the companion website to summarize. ▶

CHAPTER 7

✑

Accents and Other Expression Marks

In eighteenth-century music, many accentuation directions are contained within the notation itself. Most of the period literature contains no specific instructions in the form of accents and expression marks. Contextual clues to accentuation are found in *affekt*, structural foundation, harmonic function, interactions between melody and harmony, and rhythmic structure. Accentuation marks written in the score were saved for truly "special" moments.

Notation is an ever-changing language. In the eighteenth century, as each particular symbol was chosen, it may have been assigned a different meaning, depending on the composer. And those meanings may have very well changed over the course of his lifetime. It is beyond the scope of this book to clearly delineate each sign and its specific corresponding meaning to each composer. But there are some fundamental guidelines that are useful.

ACCENTS: EXPRESSIVE INDICATORS

All of the following symbols are signs for accenting or bringing attention to a musical moment in the Classical Era style. Notice that the symbol *f* is considered an accent mark in addition to a dynamic indication.

- *sf, fz, fp, sfp, ffp, f*, staccato, stroke, wedge
- > was used occasionally before 1800

Rosenblum provides information on specific composers.

- Haydn used *fz* or *f*.
- Clementi used *fz* or *sf*. In his early works, he used *f* and *fp*; in his later works he used >.
- Mozart used *fp*, *sf*, *sfp*, *f*, and *mfp*.
- Beethoven used all of the preceding markings except *fz*.
  ○ *sf* was used most frequently in every dynamic context.
  ○ > was used in *pp* and *p* settings and on syncopes.
  ○ *rinforzando* was used as well[1].

Türk defines *rinforzando (rinf.)* as "reinforced."[2] It may be found in two settings. It may indicate a forceful *crescendo* on two to four notes, as in Example 7.1.

Music Example 7.1. Beethoven, Piano Sonata, op. 10, no. 1/II, mm. 39–42. (ABSRM) ▶

Or, as in ms. 15 of Example 7.2 (page 133), it may indicate an additional emphasis on a single note or chord.[3]

Execution is timed within the context of the section at hand. The goal is to reinforce or bring attention to the sound, to make it stronger.

Accentuation Tools

The instrument. The fortepiano itself is one tool for accentuation. Van Oort elaborates on the mechanics of the instrument that facilitate a quick, clear, and "reinforced" accent. "The fortepiano has an inherited quality from the clavichord: in a *sfz*, the pitch goes up almost imperceptibly, so that the note is not just louder but also higher,"[4] creating a biting character and more tension. Due to the quick decay of the fortepiano, accents

Music Example 7.2. Beethoven, Piano Sonata, op. 10, no. 2/I, mm. 13–18. (ABSRM) ▶

are created by length in addition to volume—longer, not just louder—to emphasize a given note.

Dynamics. Dynamics serve as an accentuation tool. Performers with "good taste" determine which dynamics will be used and which will be saved for a special musical event. Furthermore, special attention is given if an accent coincides with dissonances, syncopation, non-harmonic tones, a long note, a particularly high note, a particularly low note, or a large leap.

Time and line direction. Moving *toward* a point, a technique that Türk calls "quickening,"[5] or reflecting *on*/moving *away* from a point, which he calls "hesitating,"[6] impacts the timing of an accent. *Rubato* may be employed to steal time from, or give time to, the line as the *affekt* commands. The trick is in the correct timing, becoming more urgent if one moves the tempo forward:

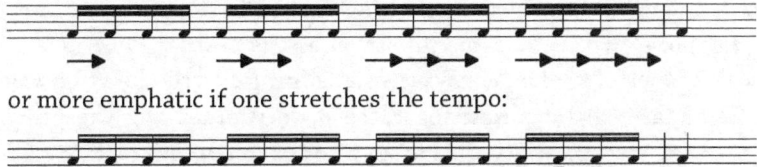

or more emphatic if one stretches the tempo:

All of this tempo fluctuation is decided after the *affekt* is determined.

An emphasized note may be accentuated through *stretching* the tone (*agogics*), which takes time. In Examples 7.3 and 7.4 (see page 134), *agogics* are an appropriate means to execute *fp* and *sf*.

Articulating. Articulating a musical point is accomplished by separating notes in time, either stealing time from the first note or taking time between important parts. By way of its natural rhythmic timing, syncopation is a form of separating by articulation and is always a clue from the composer that "this is important."

Music Example 7.3. Beethoven, Piano Sonata, op. 2, no. 2/I, mm. 55–61. (ABSRM) ▶

Music Example 7.4. Beethoven, Piano Sonata, op. 2, no. 2/I, mm. 254–257. (ABSRM) ▶

Volume and time. The combined use of time and volume together is saved for a special climax.

Rhetorical accents. Rhetorical gestures (repeated motives) *require* the performer do something differently. We have all endured lectures wherein the speaker may have the most interesting content in the world but presents every phrase with the same inflection as the past. Yawn! Any artful "speaker" (performer) *never* says the same thing exactly the same way twice. Good taste dictates noticing these opportunities and executing them in a way to bring variety and vibrancy to the composer's message. Of course, the first step is to determine the *affekt*. With the repeat of a motive comes a change, such as restating the gesture loudly, more urgently, and emphatically; or restating it softly, more reflectively, and with a relaxation in time. When coupled with sequences or changes in texture, this tool proves extremely effective in promoting *affekt*.

Harmony. Harmonic structure guides expression. The dominant preparation chord (I_4^6) becomes expressive as a result of its structural importance. It equals arrival. When a composer inserts an accent concurrently to the arrival of I_4^6, special emphasis of this point of arrival is crucial. An "accent" may appear in many guises, such as changes in phrasing, dynamics, or texture. Refer back to chapter 3 for more details.

SPECIFIC EXPRESSION MARKS

In addition to the signs and symbols discussed in the opening section, composers use specific words to indicate expression. Here, it is best to refer to the treatises and more exhaustive in-depth interpretive volumes as new repertoire is encountered. Simply uncovering the convoluted layers of *calando* is proof enough. Many surprises await when specific definitions behind expression marks are unveiled, bringing newly enlightened meaning to the score.

The curious case of *calando*. Today, *calando* (*mancando, morendo, perdendo, smorzando* and other related terms) is usually understood to indicate a decrease in volume and tempo. Not so clear-cut in the eighteenth century. On pages 74-83 in *Performance Practices in Classic Piano Music,* Rosenblum devotes this entire section to sort things out. Rosenblum does a superb job of explaining how *calando* alone had various meanings, depending on which composer employed its use and when it was used during the composer's lifetime. For instance, *calando* may mean *decrescendo* or *diminuendo* without any tempo fluctuation, as Rosenblum believes is the case with Haydn and Mozart. Clementi used *calando* primarily from the late 1780s through 1790, and it is believed to mean an ever so slight slackening in tempo and decrease in volume. Beethoven shifted from using *calando* to indicate softening only in opp. 1 through 57, but used *diminuendo* to indicate the same from op. 57 forward. Beethoven also chose (in some cases) to hyphenate *calando* to possibly mean a further slackening of tempo while concurrently using a non-hyphenated *decrescendo*. This is a mere portion of the information regarding one expressive direction for only three composers! Clearly, it is important to examine specific details surrounding expression marks in each piece to receive informed direction from the notation. For this process, interpretive texts such as Rosenblum's *Performance Practices in Classic Piano Music,* Brown's *Classical and Romantic Performance Practice, 1750–1900,* and Cooper's *Commentaries (Vol. 1–3) to Beethoven: The 35 Piano Sonatas* are invaluable.

FLEXIBILITY OF RHYTHM AND TEMPO

The general rule is to play in steady time. Not metrically, but with a steady tempo and in time. When one is learning to play with good taste, developing a sense of steady beat is essential. This is, in part, why the coming of the metronome was so highly touted. There is the well-known story of how Beethoven (and Salieri) hailed the benefits of this new invention in 1818.

Many modern pianists take the endorsement literally and play music from the Classical Era with painful rigidity and inflexibility. What is missing to the story is the additional insight Beethoven provided in a letter he wrote to Mosel in 1817. Here, Beethoven distinguishes between time or tempo and character (spirit) by analogy: time or tempo "is really more the body," while "words to describe the character of the piece were meant to refer to the spirit."[7] Beethoven is emphasizing the importance of setting an appropriate steady underlying beat while allowing fluctuations for *affekt* within this boundary. More will be said about the metronome in chapter 13.

It was common practice to tastefully perform unnotated, expressive rhythmic alterations. Things such as adding a dot, double dotting, anticipating a rhythm, or delaying a rhythm to highlight expression were all talked about and described in the literature. Recordings from the late nineteenth and early twentieth centuries substantiate this view. (See Peres Da Costa's *Off the Record*.)

Tempo rubato. This tool allows the performer to put the tension in a specific place. It is very different from today's concept of whole *rubato*. Refer to Example 7.5 while reading Türk's explanation.

> The so-called *tempo rubato* or *rubato* (actually *stolen* time) . . . should be left to the sensitivity and insight of the player. . . . Commonly it is understood as a kind of shortening or lengthening of notes, or the displacement (dislocation) of these.[8]

Music Example 7.5. Türk, *Klavierschule*, 363.

In eighteenth-century style, it is customary for accompaniments to be maintained at a steady pace while the melody weaves in and out of the meter. It is the responsibility of the performer to maintain time with the left hand and allow the right hand to "wash over" the bass. Remnants of this practice can be heard in Peres Da Costa's *Off the Record*. The score is a description of a sound, not a rhythmic math problem to be solved. In notation practice it is not unusual for a measure to contain more or fewer notes than mathematically called for. Eighteenth-century musicians were well aware of the imperfection of notational systems to indicate this practice. They attempted, as best they could, to symbolize their intended sound.

For example, a notated *rubato* may be seen in the grouping of notes within the beat:

Bach explains how this is envisioned:

> He who has mastered tempo rubato need not be fettered by the numerals which divides notes into groups of 5, 7, 11 according to his disposition but always with appropriate freedom he may add or omit notes.[9]

Eighteenth-century practice was gradually replaced with measured *rubato* so that both voices waver from the beat and coincide again at the beginning of each measure. By the beginning of the nineteenth century, composers began notating *rubato*. (Visit the companion website, Diagrams 7.1 and 7.2, to view such an attempt made by Chopin in the nineteenth century and by Mark Zaki in the twentieth century. ▶) Eventually, *rubato* came to simply mean elasticity of tempo, and still means so today.

Eighteenth-century *rubato* is used to highlight or enhance the mood and should never undermine the unity of the movement. This is what I think Beethoven meant when he wrote that the "words to describe the character of the piece were meant to refer to the spirit."[10] When used sparingly, at the proper time, with correct spacing between notes, this tool achieves great effect.

Rhetorical rests. This musical punctuation can be found only when rhythmic rather than metrical playing is employed. This tool is highly conducive to *Galant style* and *Sturm und Drang*. This is where projecting *affekt* can be exciting and great fun! Rhetorical rests are the musical punctuation in the midst of the section for effect. Grammatical (usual) rests encompass the period, comma, semicolon, and colon (. , ; :). Rhetorical (unusual) rests include the question, exclamation, parenthesis, and dash (? ! () —). Questions are most readily seen in melodies that cadence with notes ascending by step or leap. An exclamation contains short phrases or brief melodic interjections that usually end with an ascending or descending leap. A musical dash occurs where the resolution of a dissonance is either delayed or left to the bass. Parentheses occur in a dramatic recitative. It is a brief "aside" that interrupts the main line (which is then resumed). Revisit the examples throughout this book to see a preponderance of rhetorical rests.

Fermata. The fermata is considered an expressive embellishment. Application is calculated to generate an effect larger than any unmarked rests or pauses. It is an expression of surprise or astonishment; a feeling whereby the action appears to come to a brief standstill. Used in this way, it may extend tension or sit on a resolution. To enhance the surprise, an artistic performer refrains from extending the tension with any sense of predictable, metrical beat(s). This technique is what makes for a great suspense novel or movie—getting the next piece of information when least expected. Combining a fermata with a V_7 is like the big set-up to a scene change. The fermata is frequently found immediately preceding a return to a theme or a change to a new theme. As the treatises instruct, the length and breadth is determined by the *affekt.*

Accelerando. The use of *accelerando* is intended to heighten the drama in a noticeable way. Türk makes pertinent comments: "In compositions whose character is vehemence, anger, wrath, and fury, one plays the most forceful passages with a somewhat more hastened (*accelerando*) motion. It is also used when individual ideas are repeated more intensely, when gentle feelings are interrupted by a lively passage, or unexpectedly, to arouse a more passionate *affekt.*"[11]

Ritardando. This expression mark was used more frequently than *accelerando. Ritardando* was also meant to heighten the drama in a noticeable way. In extraordinarily tender, longing, melancholy passages, it brings emotions to a peak. Specifically, it may be used (whether or not notated) with written-out ornamentation and transitions in small notes, when approaching fermatas, in transitions approaching important sections, and in passages toward the end of a composition. It is often linked to *espressivo* or *con espressione.*

Sectional tempo change. Bach explains, "With the change of a section, mood, or mode tempo variants are possible."[12] As stated earlier, the change should be nearly imperceptible—almost unnoticeably varied. The point is to tug subtly at the listener's heart.

INFLUENCES APPLIED

By coming closer to understanding the true meanings of many of the signs and symbols from the eighteenth century, we are saved from fanciful misunderstandings based on non-historical interpretations. Many questions may remain, some of which require further digging, some to which there will never be clear answers. Listen to early recordings to develop a feel for possible expressive liberties. At the least, they provide context.

As with all application of eighteenth-century performing practices to modern playing, first ask questions surrounding the structure and intended *affekt*. Once the *affekt* is determined, all points of accent and expression will become clearer. It will be as if the fog lifts and a vibrant image emerges, calling for the appropriate expressive tool.

As suggested in the previous chapters, begin with a new piece and work through each item discussed in the historical information section of this chapter. Begin with strict adherence to the norms of the day. Necessary adjustments will become clear when you listen with a discerning ear. Look for contextual clues in the score in addition to the obvious indications notated by the composer.

In order to make the transition from playing the style in a literal sense to playing stylistically on the modern piano, consider the following helpful suggestions. When using volume to execute accents on the modern piano (for instance, *sf*, >, *fz*), listen carefully to avoid overpowering the sound, a practice that will create an effect the composer did not at all intend. In chapter 1, it was pointed out that the tone on the modern piano blossoms and grows, whereas the fortepiano tone creates a true "attack." Listen and adjust volume and timing. Bilson's advice to "play it *as if* it were a far lighter instrument than it actually is"[13] will go far in the search for an appropriate dynamic level and length on accents.

Be creative. See how many different ways an expression indication may be executed. Experiment with feeling a "biting" fortepiano accent, placing the timing, using *agogic* accents, finding rhetorical answers, and using harmonic structure to hurry or widen the timing. When determining timing, sing the line. This is extremely helpful in finding the right balance between metrical and rhythmic accentuation.

Remember, many expression marks meant something different to each composer. Furthermore, many expression marks meant something different to each composer, depending on when the work was written. As you encounter individual expression marks, it is best to go to primary sources and take a peek at those gems that will make the work sparkle, treating yourself to another "ah-ha" moment.

As always, it all depends on good taste and finesse. When you contemplate use of any expressive tool, the derivations should be few, minimal, and almost imperceptible.

THE LESSON

Play and study Example 7.6 with the following points in mind.

Music Example 7.6. Mozart, London Notebook, KV 15oo, mm. 1–8. Copyright (1983) G. Henle Verlag, Munich.

1. Keep an overall steady beat that is in line with eighteenth-century practice.
2. Take a very slight timing "pause" (articulation to separate ideas) between mm. 2–3, 4–5, and at the repeat sign.

   √ Practice strategy: practice in gestures to feel how the line is punctuated
3. Take a very slight timing "pause" (articulation to separate ideas) before the downbeat of ms. 8.
4. Take a very slight *ritardando* at the end of ms. 7, with terraced *agogic* accents to the appoggiatura at ms. 8.

Use the quick reference guide on the companion website to summarize. ▶

CHAPTER 8

⌒

Articulation and Touch

I f you are like most modern pianists, you have developed a long, sing-ing, melodic phrase line in your playing. The accompanying long, arcing phrase lines are not typically found in eighteenth-century scores. Rather than indicating long lines, eighteenth-century scores almost exclusively notate segments. Melodic shape is determined by structure, meter, har-monic function, gestures, and melodic consonance and dissonance. Eighteenth-century style requires delineation by grouping, separating, and accenting—articulating ideas.

Legato is the "ordinary" way to play today, whereas non-legato is the norm in eighteenth-century style. Non-legato is the naturally occurring sound on the fortepiano. Ongoing discussion among musicians addressed concerns about how best to create a singing line on the articulate fortepi-ano. As late as 1750, Bach and Türk affirmed non-legato as *"gewöhnlich,"* the usual way of playing. Appropriate note length was argued down to one-half or three-quarters the length of a note's written duration. By 1789, Türk leaned toward a more legato (three-quarter value) "ordinary" way but still inserted the typical reminder that it all relies on musical context when one is determining whether to execute a light or heavy (shorter or lon-ger) touch. In a 1796 letter to piano maker Johann Streicher, Beethoven expressed his belief in a legato singing style.[1] As was true in many respects, Beethoven was ahead of his time. His legato was considered remarkable by all who heard him play; Beethoven himself describes an approach with fingers on the keys so that the attack is not heard.[2] Beethoven believed the slur must sound as if it "were stroked with a bow."[3] By 1800, there was a gradual shift in sentiment underway to favor and compose long lyrical melodies. Legato as the norm gradually gained ground as the nineteenth century dawned.

GENERAL UNDERSTANDING

Eighteenth-century fortepiano articulation markings are based on bowing traditions for stringed instruments. Small segments are the cornerstone. They provide guidance for rhythmic groupings and dynamic direction. With these snippets, rhetorical phrases are built to clearly define the larger structure. So ensconced was the correlation between the rhythm of poetry and the rhythm of music that the "chicken-egg" conflict arose, not dissimilar to that struggle so well-known between Impressionistic art and music. Properly executing these markings is what makes the message comprehensible.

If articulation clues are crafted well enough, little further direction is necessary. In Mozart's piano works, dynamic markings are sometimes sparse or nonexistent because the finesse and style are so thoroughly provided in his plentiful articulation indications. Execution decisions for articulating gestures are based on *affekt*.

Generally speaking, articulation is impacted by motivic unity, the size of the melodic intervals, rhythm, and overall *affekt*. Recurring themes use consistent articulation, and contrasting themes use contrasting articulation. Large melodic skips are often detached (imitating dance gestures), for if the leap is connected rather than articulated, the expression is wasted. Specific notes or gestures may be emphasized through rhythmic accentuation, as described in chapter 5. Legato playing is conducive to a lyrical *affekt*, detached playing to a brilliant *affekt*. The next section introduces the giant of Viennese expressivity—"the sigh."

THE SLUR: THE PILLAR OF VIENNESE EXPRESSIVITY—THE "SIGH"

To make music in Mannheim was a coveted opportunity. Mannheim was a cultural center where the latest fashions and amusements took place. The Mannheim school was famous for its innovations in orchestral music. It was also known for a group of melodic clichés or figures, one of which became known as the "Mannheim Sigh," or "Viennese Sigh." It is the backbone of expressive playing in eighteenth-century style. Rosenblum calls it an "incise" and defines it clearly:

> The slur indicates legato playing of relatively short groups of notes or motives within musical phrases … it provides these incises—short, individually accented and separated groups—with an expressive direction created by the manner in which the first and last notes under the slur are played.[4]

It is merely a stepwise appoggiatura figure that became extremely popular throughout all European countries during the Classical Era. It is typically a relatively short motive of two to four notes within musical phrases.

Purpose. This type of slur is a sign of clarity, not a phrase mark. Notes under a slur simply mean "we belong together." The slur creates groups that allow the performer to articulate and set aside important or new ideas. It gives intentional direction of notes—gestures; much like a painter's small brush strokes. Gestures offer direction regarding where the phrase and musical line is going. The slur indication enlivens the music by lightly ending one gesture and clearly articulating the next. The point is to make the music more interesting!

These small gestures provide the variety and character that combine to complete the larger structures of elements like phrases, sentences, and sections, and ultimately project the *affekt*. Haynes explains the magnitude of what the gesture has to offer and how it differs from the phrase:

> Gestures can be situated next to each other, yet have completely different meanings and characters. Nothing can be assumed; each gesture has its own independent tempo, articulation, and dynamic shape, and is often in contrast with what precedes and follows it. This produces a complex line with constant variety and unevenness.[5]

Haynes explains how the gestures come together:

> The phrase creates another order of meaning, communicating something that could not have been expressed except by combining gestures. The phrase, like the sentence in language, has more individual character and makes a more decisive statement than the gesture. A phrase often represents a complete harmonic progression, finishing with a cadence.[6]

Example 8.1 illustrates Haynes' description. Here, three independent gestures combine to communicate the phrase. Many modern players execute one long phrase with a continuous *crescendo* and miss the charm, the *affekt*, and, I think, the point.

Music Example 8.1. Beethoven, Piano Sonata, op. 14, no. 1/I, mm. 1–4. (ABSRM) ▶

Variety. Rosenblum explains how the slur adds variety: "A slur may *emphasize* the meter if on the downbeat, *oppose* the meter to mitigate its effect, but never *replace* the downbeat."[7] In Example 8.2, the slurs that start on the ends of the beats provide the impish excitement. To displace and make them the downbeat is to miss the excitement of the "bad note" altogether.

Music Example 8.2. Haydn, Piano Sonata in C Major, Hob. XVI:50/I, mm. 1–3. Copyright (1993) G. Henle Verlag, Munich. ▶

The possibilities are boundless. The small slur was discussed specifically and extensively by Leopold Mozart in his pedagogical writings. He was emphatic about the effect of the slur on accentuation. In his *Violinschule*, he provides an example of three measures in triple time with thirty-three different possibilities for accentuation. Noting the possibilities available to the performer, he proclaims: "Now this changes indisputably the whole style of performance."[8]

Because the slur is so important to proper expression in the Classical Era style, it is essential to work from a reliable score, a mandate that brings us full circle to the opening chapter, to the correspondence in which Beethoven cautions Holz thus:

For God's sake please impress on Rampel to copy everything exactly as it stands. . . .
The slurs should be exactly as they are now. It is not all the same whether it is a

 or a ....⁹

This stalwart eighteenth-century indicator is actually a quite simple and natural concept. The notational practice imitates bowing practices for stringed instruments. Classical Era stringed instruments use a convex baroque bow that naturally creates a *diminuendo*. Consequently, the first note under a slur is accentuated more strongly because of the natural tendency of the bow with a slackening of volume on the remaining notes. Likewise, in fortepiano music, the first note under a slur is accentuated while the remaining notes under the slur create a *diminuendo*.¹⁰ Because of the rapid decay of the tone on the fortepiano, it *cannot* be achieved with a *crescendo*. This practice is also a natural vocal tendency. Take a moment to verbalize any number of two-syllable words that contain a first-syllable accent to notice the similarities. In music prior to 1800, the slur *always* means to taper from more stress to less (longer to faster, louder to softer). After 1800, the strictness lessens to denote *generally* tapering off from more stress to less.

Eighteenth-century slurs almost *never* continue over the bar line. To do so would most certainly be for special effect. Rosenblum observes that slurs are demonstrated over the bar line only four times in Türk's 408-page *Klavierschule* (1789):¹¹ was *never* meant to be played .

If a slur over the bar line is found in an edition, further investigation is warranted to verify the authenticity. Nineteenth-century editors of Classical repertoire frequently notated slurs to go *over* the bar line to encourage a longer melodic line. Then, as van Oort observed at the Westfield International Fortepiano Academy, "A *staccato* dot at the end of the slur was added to indicate lightness (not *staccato*) by early nineteenth-century editors after the eighteenth-century language was forgotten."¹² Refer back to chapter 1 (companion website, Diagrams 1.4a, 1.5a, and 1.6a ⏵) to see this practice expressed in early twentieth-century scores.

Expressive qualities. Attention to detail regarding the slur is evident in even the simplest literature. Notice Beethoven's explicit expressive directions in Example 8.3.

Music Example 8.3. Beethoven, Six Minuets, WoO 10, no. 2, Trio. Copyright 1990 by
G. Henle Verlag, Munich. ▶

Slurs may facilitate increased intensity or expressivity. In Example 8.3,
the second half of the trio becomes more expressive, in part, due to the
increased complexity in slurring. Executing the slurs as indicated takes
time and adds to the expressivity of the trio. Another excellent example
is found in the all-too-familiar Für Elise (Henle). Or are we as familiar
with it as we think? Open to the Henle (128) edition. Notice that with
each occurrence of the octave jumps on E (mm. 12, 49, 93), Beethoven
indicates more expressivity through the addition of slurs.

Release. At the ends of phrases or periods, the slur indicates a lessening
of intensity to bring the thought to a pause or close. Example 8.4 displays
the common practice. Türk illustrates how the last note should be executed
with a somewhat shorter duration than its actual notated value—notated
in (c) but executed as notated in (d):

Music Example 8.4. Türk, *Klavierschule*, 331.

The further the two notes of the sigh are apart rhythmically, the shorter and lighter the second note becomes. For instance, an eighth note after a half note is lighter than when following a quarter note.

Understood rules. Yes, there are some understood rules here, too—a "shorthand" of sorts. It is customary to indicate only the first few sets of accentuation in prolonged successions of detached or legato notes. Bach writes that succeeding tones "are to be played similarly until another kind of mark intervenes."[13] Example 8.5 begins with two note slurs in ms. 47 that will continue through mm. 48–49 until Beethoven changes articulation in ms. 50.

Music Example 8.5. Beethoven, Bagatelle in G Minor, op. 119, no. 1, mm. 47–52. Copyright (1978) G. Henle Verlag, Munich.

If there are several consistent slur groups in succession, the composer may be indicating a legato line with subtle emphasis and rhythmic energy assigned to the first note of each group, as in the left hand in Example 8.6.

Music Example 8.6. Mozart, Piano Sonata, K. 309/I, mm. 103–106. Copyright (2005) G. Henle Verlag, Munich.

Slurs on trills that have a termination require special consideration. Türk instructs that ". . . the trill is bound more closely to the following note by the termination."[14] Yet, knowing that slur indications come from bowing practices, which require a change in bow direction from the end of the slur to the next note (albeit imperceptible), the resolution will receive some emphasis. In Example 8.7, the last note of the slur will lead directly into the resolution. Whether or not a new articulation will be executed, and the degree of emphasis, depends on the tempo and *affekt*.

Music Example 8.7. Mozart, Piano Sonata, K. 545/I, mm. 1-4. Copyright (2005) G. Henle Verlag, Munich. ▶

A musical line without slurs allows performer input regarding articulation, thus giving way to much freedom in deciding "possibles." It allows *crescendo* as well as any combination of those *thirty-three* possible permutations offered by Leopold Mozart . . . in good taste.

Technical execution. As introduced previously, these small snippets of two- to four-note slurred groups are one of the most reliable "insider looks" at how the Classical Era style was executed. The Viennese sigh, a symbol used so extensively that it was "trademarked," provides clear direction regarding when to attack and when to release. The "sigh" is the basis of good execution and "good taste." Türk counsels, "Good execution, therefore, is the most important, yet at the same time the most difficult aspect of music making."[15] Or, even more directly emphasized by L. Mozart, "Everything depends on good execution."[16]

The sigh is always executed by going from more to less, with the first note of the group receiving a slight *agogic* and dynamic emphasis. (See Quantz's instruction on the companion website, Text 8.1. ▶) Türk describes the execution for pianists:

> For tones which are to be slurred, the finger should be allowed to remain on the key until the duration of the given note is completely past, so that not the slightest separation (rest) results. . . . It should be observed, in addition, that

the note on which the curved line begins should be very gently (and almost imperceptibly) accented.[17]

The gesture simply indicates attack and release. Notes under the slur should be played in a single impulse without making any movement of the hand. Beethoven teaches, "This will be achieved if it [the hand] is always placed firmly on the first of the two slurred notes and is lifted almost vertically as the second note is touched."[18] Notice that it is the hand, *led by the wrist,* that initiates the release. Following this advice will prevent hopping off the key and avoiding a choking, unmusical staccato, or pushing off the key and avoiding that terrible clunker—the undesired accent.

The first note of a slur and the first note after a slur (which may well be a new slur grouping) is articulated through a clean attack (with varying degrees of emphasis), a clean release (with varying degrees of lightness), and a separation of sound (with varying degrees of time) between the two gestures. How new and fresh each impulse is articulated depends on those influencing traits derived from *affekt.*

The complexity of the double-note slur necessitates discussion. Here lurks a nemesis to the uninformed player! Example 8.8 contains several double-note slur indications that create an execution challenge. It is impossible to execute a *legato* on the repeated notes within the slur without pedal. To employ the pedal is certainly a possibility, but not always appropriate, as in this light and lyrical *leggiero* example.

Music Example 8.8. Mozart, Piano Sonata, KV 570/III, mm. 31–32. Copyright (2005) G. Henle Verlag, Munich. ▶

So what is one to do? Eighteenth-century language to the rescue! Note the simple solution provided by Bach in Example 8.9.[19]

Music Example 8.9. Bach, *Versuch*, Figure 168b.

Although execution of the small slur is a simple affair in design, many challenges in the proper timing and combination of layers demand special attention. Those who take care in these small details are on their way to "good taste."

Take a moment to revisit and play the Beethoven trio in Example 8.3. Most modern editions edit the small slurs out of the second half of the trio and opt for the later-used long phrase slur. Following Beethoven's indicated design will quickly and clearly validate the facility and artistry required to stylistically execute even simple textures such as these. This is the Classical Era style at its simplest and at its finest. Enjoy re-experiencing this tune. Embrace your "ah-ha" moment.

USE OF PROLONGED TOUCH (FINGER LEGATO)

Another "understood" performance practice involves creating legato lines through the use of prolonged touch (instead of pedal), known as finger *legato*. Example 8.10 shows a continuous sixteenth-note passage that contains the melody within the passage. In this case, melody notes are assumed to be held longer than the notated value to bring out the melody. Koch warns that the accentuation should be gentle and not so noticeable as to resemble the "gait of a lame person."[20]

Music Example 8.10. Haydn, Piano Sonatina, Hob. XVI:G1/III, mm. 1–8. Copyright (1972) G. Henle Verlag, Munich. ▶

Similarly, holding all notes in harmonic figures (including the Alberti bass) by prolonging chord tones through finger *legato* is common to the style. This approach may or may not be indicated by a slur line. In Example 8.11, the first, second, and third notes of the group hold until the fourth has been played. This technique is more effective when the pedal is *not* in use.

Music Example 8.11. Mozart, Piano Sonata, K. 280/ii, mm. 45–47. Copyright (2005) G. Henle Verlag, Munich. ▶

LONGER LEGATO GROUPS (SLURS) AND PHRASE INDICATIONS

The typical slur is short, containing two to four notes. Slurs of two to four measures in length appear around 1775–1780. The small articulated gestures indicating the strong-to-weak direction become less noticeable as the slurs grow longer, but the implication of attack and release is still generally valid.[21] Beethoven, and later, Clementi, used longer slurs for structural direction rather than gesture articulation. When one examines long slurs, many points factor into determining the high point or climax. Newman provides guidance. "Deciding the penultimate point may be outweighed by some special peak: an extra high, low, loud, soft, or long tone."[22] In Example 8.12 (see page 152), many of those traits work congruently:

- Newman points to a typical pattern: ". . . a phrase reaches the peak of its rise and fall on its last strong beat before its final note"[23]
- The peak of the Classical phrase tends to (can or may) come near the end of the phrase.
- Longer slurs are often followed by shorter slurs to complement or set off a motive.
- Beethoven seems to purposefully remove accents to propel the sweep forward by using one slur for mm. 1–6.
- The slur sweeps horizontally through three-fourths of the phrase, followed by a vertical two-note slur and clean downbeat to articulate the change of key and perfect-authentic cadence.

Very long slurs (those longer than a phrase) were rarely used in the Classical Era. When found, they are used to clarify the unity of an entire

Music Example 8.12. Beethoven, Piano Sonata, op. 10, no. 2/ii, mm. 1–8. (ABSRM)

passage. Appearance of such phrasing should be a warning to check the authenticity of the score.

Rather than using long slurs to indicate phrasing, eighteenth-century notation practice utilizes grouping notes through beaming as one of the "usual" ways to indicate phrase structure. In Example 8.13, beams that could be joined are separated to indicate phrasing.

Music Example 8.13. Beethoven, Bagatelle, op. 119, no. 1, mm. 53–58. Copyright (1978) G. Henle Verlag, Munich.

INFLUENCES APPLIED

I fear I am beating a dead horse here, but it must be reiterated, *particularly* in this chapter: first and foremost, *play from Urtext editions.* It is impossible to uphold any reliable semblance of the composer's intentions regarding articulation without *Urtext* scores.

By applying the tools in this chapter, your playing may become transformed much like mine and countless others' has been. Haynes's inspiring words describe how coming to know this element of playing changed his perspective:

> I originally learned to phrase by long-line, so it has been a revelation to me to recast Rhetorical music into the smaller units in which it seems originally to have been conceived. To phrase by figure/gesture is to go from two to three dimensions, to endow Baroque music with depth and relief, a natural calmness and an assured sense of timing.[24]

For me, the revelation led to an epiphany of sorts. I felt as if I had been playing a game according to the wrong set of rules and wondering why my results were so limited and frustrating. Then someone came along and provided a new set of rules! It was as if the floor beneath me rocked and I lost my bearings. But as I learned the new rules, I leveled out and regained my footing. Even better, I could see more clearly. The new view is amazing!

Adherence to the *intent* behind articulation markings is what brings authenticity to playing. Here more than ever, avoid attempts at purely recreating eighteenth-century execution on the modern piano. Because here more than ever, attempts to do so will dismally fail the style. The fortepiano was built for articulating the small slur. That is why it was branded "The Viennese Sigh"! The modern piano was built for a tone that blossoms and grows. Quickly releasing the tone over and over again will result in a terribly choppy and uncharacteristic sound. The point is not to try to recreate the fortepiano sound on the piano but, through greater understanding create performances ever closer to those that period composers may have approved of on the modern piano.

For emphasizing the relevance of this information, an important application experience is worth conveying. A pedagogical opportunity surrounding the slur and its appropriate execution presented itself when I was assisting a former student. She came to me, struggling with a Beethoven sonata she was studying at university. She was studying with an esteemed professor who is, as I well know, a good musician and educator. But she was stuck and extremely frustrated. The ending of the thematic figure in the Beethoven Piano Sonata, op. 14, no. 1 (Example 8.14) was causing her fits. The problem presented itself at the end of ms. 4 and where it is recast in mm. 130–135 with the addition of a turn after the dotted-quarter-note attack. The student was struggling to get the final E to sound loudly and clearly enough in ms. 4. When the turns were added in mm. 130–135, execution was a disaster. With eighteenth-century language norms as the guide, the culprits were readily exposed.

- By not using the latest scholarship in *Urtext* editions, the slur was extending through the final E.
- Attempting a four-measure crescendo in mm. 1–4 and trying to crescendo through the turns in mm. 130–135.
- Placing the peak on the last note of the phrase.
- Holding the left-hand dotted quarter note literally through beat 3.
- Playing every rhythm mathematically for its full value.

The problems were *easily* solved for the student by accessing the discoveries from this book:

- Switch to the ABRSM edition to unearth the latest scholarship on Beethoven's articulation and a new discovery: the final E of the phrase is a new articulation, a clean, new "stroke."
- Play in gestures.
- Employ terraced dynamics to accomplish the *crescendo*.
- Realize the peak at ms. 3 and the culmination on beat one of ms. 4.
- Play from more to less with each slur.
- Release the left-hand dotted half note as the sixteenth notes begin.

An "ah ha" moment for the taking!

Music Example 8.14. Beethoven, Piano Sonata, op. 14, no. 1/I, mm. 1–4. (ABSRM) ▶

Mastering the execution of the small slur will bringing authenticity to performing and honor composers' intentions. Clear musical sense and understanding will be more easily achieved and projected. Tremendous freedom of expression is afforded (remember the thirty-three possibilities offered by L. Mozart!).

As in the other chapters, begin with each topic presented in the historical section. The concept and *affekt* are the foundation. Determine where the articulation exhibits and promotes those traits. Now play, making strict application as a jumping-off point. Where does it work? Where do adjustments need to be made?

Although fully articulating all short slurs may not be practical on modern pianos, begin with full execution, making adjustments thereafter, striving to achieve the composer's intent of stress and release. The finesse required in articulating this style may necessitate further development of technique in the areas of finger control and supple wrist, as outlined in chapter 4. With due attention to proper technique, execution initially deemed improbable may prove possible and preferred on the modern piano. A choppy release is probably due to lack of enough stress at the beginning of the gesture. For the problem is usually not the problem; the culprit is usually the note(s) or event(s) that lead into the problem. When in doubt, sing the line or even "scat" the line! This guides appropriate grouping, timing, and attack/release.

Initial experiences in applying articulation and touch can be difficult and maddening. It can also be very rewarding. With sheer adherence to these principles, many musical interpretive questions are answered. Amazing insight to the composer's thought process emerges. The style takes on new vibrancy and vitality. This new information from the old language gives us permission to quit playing robotically and avoid "boring scoring."

THE LESSON

Play and study Example 8.15 with the following points in mind.

Music Example 8.15. Mozart, London Notebook, KV 15oo, mm. 1–8. Copyright (1983) G. Henle Verlag, Munich.

1. Play mm. 1–2 detached but heavy (longer note values).
2. Play mm. 3–4 more detached and lighter (shorter note values).
   ✓ Practice strategy: practice each thought in separate gestures with a pause between, creating an *affekt* for each gesture
3. Reinforce Beethoven's previous pedagogical instruction with the slurs in mm.4–6, 8.
   ✓ Practice strategy: practice each slur in slow motion
   ✓ Practice strategy: practice the slurs in succession, developing intensity through length and volume
4. Return to a detached articulation in mm. 7.
5. Articulate each musical gesture between beats 2–3 in ms. 2 and 4 by slight separation.
6. Ms. 7 is the peak of the phrase, ending in the modulation to C major. Therefore, this will be the longest quarter note and loudest dynamic.
7. Determine how the slur at ms. 8 is different from those at mm. 5–6. Determine how it will be executed differently.
8. Refer to chapter 3 to understand the structure of the phrase and how the gestures support the structure.

Use the quick reference guide on the companion website to summarize. ⊙

CHAPTER 9

꘎

Staccato Dots and the Other Usual Suspects

When I was growing up in the Midwestern region of the United States, an important part of the school day involved playing four-square at recess. For those of you who were deprived of this pleasure, let me explain. It involves a bouncy ball and a surface with squares marked in some way. The goal is to advance to the "king" square and remain there as long as possible. Advancing is gained by bouncing the ball into an opponent's square in such a way that the opponent is unable to pass the play to another square. Each player may hit the ball only once and the ball is allowed only one bounce in the square. Failure to do so means you are "out" and must return to the line, waiting for your turn to re-enter the game.

Master four-square players quickly learn that there are many important factors to successful play: ball size, bounceability, material, inflation, and the surface for play. A medium-sized, fully inflated, rubber bouncy ball on a concrete driveway surface provides the best combination for an exciting game of four-square. It is intense! Every bounce of the ball determines who advances toward the "king" square or is "out" and waiting in line. Placing the ball in just the right spot is one important strategy. But choice of attack—a light lob, a heavy bounce, a sharp spike—that is the key! A great player knows just how to strike the ball to get the opponent "out" and advance toward "king."

Staccato, too, is not simply a matter of sharp and crisp or dull and flat, but is a complex combination of intentionality, nuance, and subtlety to create and execute a desired outcome. With a little childlike creativity and willingness to reflect, you too may find a metaphor that describes and impacts your "game" of *staccato*.

PERIOD PRACTICE

To most modern players there are three basic crisp touches: *detaché or portato, staccato,* and *staccatissimo*. Eighteenth-century musicians set forth basic parameters as well. Bach writes the following:

> Attack and touch are one and the same thing. Everything depends on their force and duration. When notes are to be detached from each other strokes or dots are placed above them, as illustrated in Figure 166 [Example 9.1]. Notes are detached with relation to: (1) their notated length; (2) the tempo, fast or slow; and (3) the volume, forte or piano. Such notes are always held for a little less than half of their notated length. In general, detached notes appear mostly in leaping passages and rapid tempos .[1]

Music Example 9.1. Bach, *Versuch,* Figure 166.[7]

By approximately 1750, the dot, stroke, and wedge were all in use and interpreted synonymously amongst German writers.[2] Notice that in Example 9.1, Bach does not differentiate between the two symbols. Different meanings for different symbols came many years later. Dart interprets thus:

> When the wedge-shaped *staccato* sign is used by composers from Couperin to Beethoven, it never has its modern meaning of *staccatissimo*, which it acquired only in the early years of the nineteenth century. It is the exact equivalent of the staccato dot, and it should be played as though it were one.[3]

Yet surely composers intended more than one meaning for *staccato*. Trying to make sense of this *staccato* issue becomes quite sticky. Available information leaves vague answers. On pages 181–189 in *Performance Practices in Classic Piano Music,* Rosenblum digs deeply into the exceptions and "composer specific" issues. From her work, there are some conclusions that can be drawn. For instance, by 1795–1796, articulation was becoming "graded" by some, with the wedge indicating the most separated touch, dots a separated touch, and dots under a slur line the least separated. By 1802, directions were as specific as three-quarter to one-half or one-quarter value. Haydn, Mozart, and Beethoven used strokes much of the time to indicate *staccato*. Haydn and Mozart usually used the dot on repeated note figures and sometimes in passages with short note values or in context with sections requiring light touch to indicate mild separation. Evidence points to Beethoven's intentions to use the signs differently. However, his sloppy handwriting leaves many questions, and no clear conclusions can be made.[4]

The important overriding component that shatters the limits and brings kaleidoscopic choices for individual creativity to the discussion is *affekt* and its many associated components. General parameters are set forth by Bach on page 154 of *Versuch* and the directions provided from Türk in *Klavierschule*. In 1789, Türk explained that the dot and stroke were synonymous, but that the execution of the symbol was determined by several influencing factors, which are put forth in Table 9.1. Following the table, the abstract is taken to the concrete by examining several musical examples.

Table 9.1. MUSICAL INFLUENCES
ON NOTE LENGTH

Musical Variables:		
Affekt	lively	sad
As seen in		
Tempo	fast	slow
Dynamics	*forte*	*piano*
Skips	big	small
Resulting consequence		
Degree of separation	more	less

Staccato. In Examples 9.2 and 9.3, the dots and written direction *staccato sempre* have entirely different meanings and associated lengths based on musical variables. Example 9.2—reflective, slow, and *piano*, with diatonic steps and small skips —results in a subdued, subtle, less crisp *staccato*, while Example 9.3—lively, fast, *fortissimo*, with chromaticism and larger skips —clearly requires a very detached, crisp *staccato*, what today's performer might categorize as *staccatissimo*.

Music Example 9.2. Beethoven, Piano Sonata, op. 2, no. 2/II, m. 1–2. (ABSRM) ▶

Music Example 9.3. Beethoven, Piano Sonata, op. 2, no. 2/III, mm. 57–59. (ABSRM) ▶

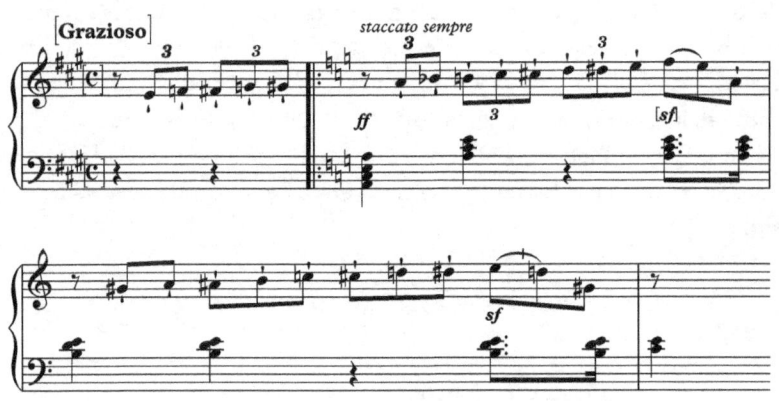

In eighteenth-century music notational language, *staccato* may indicate to play more lightly *or* with accented emphasis, depending on *affekt* and context. Haynes provides enlightening historical context:

> The signs that found their way onto the page often represented the exceptional or unusual. When there is a "forte" marked, it means a musician would normally have played "piano" there. Every sign is thus potentially describing performance practice, but in reverse. Because they were exceptional, markings would have attracted the attention of the eighteenth-century player. When presented with an unexpected articulation, for instance, they would not only have emphasized it (since it was unusual), but, because it was part of the special character of the piece, would have articulated analogous passages in the same way. (The copyist, knowing this, would not have bothered to mark it after the first occurrence.)[5]

For instance, a dot on an anacrusis may actually negate the natural property of its function (which is to serve as a light upbeat) because the dot functions to bring attention to the note, not a superfluous reminder. The anacrusis as light upbeat is an "understood" period performance practice; period composers would not have bothered to indicate the obvious. It was that which was different or out of the ordinary that was notated.

Return to the opening of the third movement of Beethoven Piano Sonata, op. 10, no. 2, Example 9.4. This information substantiates the *requirement* of the absence of a *staccato* marking on the anacrusis to the movement. Here, if a *staccato* appears as a new articulation, it means to make it more important. Placing a *staccato* on the anacrusis to the new movement would, in reality, instruct the performer to accent the upbeat, mitigate the downbeat, and create an effect not at all intended.

Music Example 9.4. Beethoven, Piano Sonata, op. 10, no. 2/III, mm. 1–6. (ABSRM) ▶

Portato. This articulation indicates "these notes are important." *Portato* permits the most connected execution, save legato. It allows for *crescendo* because it is not under a slur and therefore does not require tapering off. Bach explains:

> The notes of Figure 169 [Example 9.5] are played legato, but each tone is notice-ably accented. The term which refers to the performance of notes that are both slurred and dotted is *portato*.[6]

Music Example 9.5. Bach, *Versuch*, Figure 169[8]

From the markings, the performer is expected to exercise educated freedom. Determine the *affekt*. Examine each staccato indication and ponder, what is the composer describing with this *staccato*? How can that intention be best executed? Just as the ball may be bounced to many good effects, so must the performer decide how the *staccato* at hand will best be executed to produce the most convincing *affekt*.

Most often, *staccato* and *portato* are played with the fingers only— germane to the quick action of the fortepiano.

INFLUENCES APPLIED

Uncovering various implications for eighteenth-century staccato opens new possibilities for stylistic, authentic interpretation. Again, begin application with a simple, "never before played" piece. Just as period musicians did, determine the *affekt*. What is the best way to project that *affekt*? Rather than a simple application of *portato, staccato,* and *staccatissimo,* artistic decisions are now called for—what message is the composer providing with the particular marking? How may it best be conveyed? What does each marking mean in this musical context?

Now, move the conceptual decisions to the piano. Determine execution on the basis of attack, weight, length, and release. Executing eighteenth-century staccato on a modern instrument requires careful adjustments to avoid an overpowering or choked sound. Much attention to an appropriate attack and release through careful listening will prove fruitful. At times, a light amount of arm weight is appropriate for a more full sound. Keep the period style in mind to avoid a banging, heavy, hammered sound beyond the intention of the style and capability of period instruments.

Remember, the piano's inherent quality is its capability to create a *legato* line because of the blossoming of the tone. On the fortepiano, an accented legato (as instructed by Bach) tends toward *portato* because of its natural decay. Therefore, when *portato* is encountered on the modern piano, an intentional detaché may be necessary to express the tones according to eighteenth-century norms.

THE LESSON

Play and study Example 9.6 (see page 163) with the following points in mind.

1. There are no staccato indications in this piece. Discuss eighteenth-century style implications.
   a. Lack of staccato marks does not mean the lines are to be played legato, but with varying degrees of detachment

Music Example 9.6. Mozart, London Notebook, KV 15oo, mm. 1–8. Copyright (1983) G. Henle Verlag, Munich.

2. Discuss varying types of touch, based on *affekt*. Consider many possibilities.
3. Explore appropriate execution possibilities to express the previously decided *affekt*.
   a. The quarter notes in mm. 1–2 will be the longest and heaviest—up to three-quarters of a beat
   b. The quarter notes in mm. 3–4 will be of medium length and light weight—one-half of a beat, responding to the opening gesture
   c. The quarter notes in mm. 7-8 will be of medium length and weight, bringing conclusion to the statement

Use the quick reference guide on the companion website to summarize. ⊙

CHAPTER 10

⌒〜⌒

Ornaments

To many musicians, the word "ornament" brings a sense of foreboding and trepidation. Paralysis sets in at the mere thought of deciphering, interpreting, and incorporating the funny little signs and symbols into their playing. Perhaps by stepping back a bit and becoming better acquainted with these clever tools, dread may be replaced with joyful anticipation.

Before getting caught up in an ornamental tornado, look at the word itself. An ornament is simply a decoration; an addition to make something more beautiful, more lovely, more exciting . . . more. Music alone can be seen as ornamental. Imagine watching a movie without the music. The storyline may be compelling enough, but with the addition of music . . . well! You get the point. It does not have to be a complicated affair to embellish the "storyline," and in all actuality, simpler is often better.

BACKGROUND INFORMATION

Ever-changing mobile. The practice of ornamenting melodies has been in existence as long as performers have spontaneously interpreted music, dating back to 400 CE and Gregorian chant. Ornaments were originally improvised (unnotated), gradually became indicated with signs, and eventually were written into the line of the score. One system of performing and indicating ornaments did not replace the other, but emphasis merely shifted until one system gradually faded away as the next took hold. The middle of the eighteenth century through the nineteenth century was a time of transition from the Baroque practice of indicating ornaments by symbol to the Romantic practice of gradually absorbing ornaments into the notation. Compare a cross section of scores to follow this gradual shift in notation practices.

Affekt. In the Classical Era style, the performer's goal is to move the listener, have *something to say*. In order to do so, ornaments must complement the *affekt*. Quantz sheds light on the topic:

> The embellishments or graces which I have described [those which are an energetic, intense *affekt*] serve, in accordance with the temper of the piece, to excite cheer and gaiety, while the simple appoggiaturas, on the contrary, arouse tenderness and melancholy.[1]

Proper execution of ornaments and artistic playing are intimately connected. Bach writes about their interdependence:

> The true art of playing keyboard instruments depends on three factors so closely related that not one of them can, nor indeed dare, exist without the others. They are: Correct fingering, good embellishments, and good performance.[2]

Roles. Embellishments, today called ornaments, serve specific roles. Due to the rapid decay of the fortepiano, ornaments are necessary to extend melodic lines. In his *Versuch*, Bach often speaks of various ornaments that "enliven" the tones. They provide spontaneity, creativity, variety, and enhance expressivity. They allow the performer the opportunity to impart stress and accent to the line. In short, Bach says, "They make music pleasing and awaken our close attention."[3]

How much? This calls for good taste—deciding on which ornaments to use and how frequently to use them. The following vignette makes the point. When my son was in kindergarten, he had a couple of buddies over around the July 4th holiday. One of the boys was telling stories about fireworks. Each story became bigger and more grandiose. Finally, when the embellishing went too far, with a car being lifted six feet off the ground from exploding fireworks, one of the other boys could take it no longer and exclaimed, "Give me a break!" Bach and Quantz make their analogies with food and finery. (Citations on the companion website, Text 10.1. ▶)

On or before the beat? That is the million-dollar question! Historical perspective is interesting but not conclusive. Period literature makes clear that harmony and voice leading are to be taken into consideration when determining the best placement of ornaments. Beyond that, it is a mixed bag of information. It's no wonder ornaments eventually came to be carefully notated into the texture of the score. In the mid-1700s, Bach was a strong proponent of ornaments taking the rhythm from the main note and never occurring before the main note, a choice that means on the beat. Some contemporaries were critical of this view; credibility to grace notes coming before the beat can be found in period flute and violin tutors. This is just one of many questions that surface when contemplating ornamentation. Complete answers to this question, as well as the many exceptions, are beyond the scope of this book. What you will find here are historically defined parameters and general guidelines to get started in performing indicated ornaments. Bach recognized the multitude of exceptions yet the need for a baseline:

> It is difficult to prescribe the correct context for every embellishment, for all composers are free to introduce their favorites where they will. . .Suffice it if we instruct our reader through a few well-established precepts and examples.[4]

ORNAMENTS IN THIS BOOK

Ornaments discussed in this book were selected from beginning keyboard works most frequently encountered during initial exposure to eighteenth-century literature:

- Beethoven: Bagatelles, op. 33, WoO 52, WoO 56, op. 119, op. 126;
  Dances for Piano, 12 Minuets, WoO 7, 12 German Dances, WoO 8,
  6 Minuets, WoO 10, 7 Ländler, WoO 11, 12 German Dances, WoO 13,
  6 Ländler, WoO 15, Allemande, WoO 81, Minuet WoO 82
  6 Ecossaises, WoO 83, Walzer, WoO 84, WoO 85, Ecossaise, WoO 86
  7 ContreDanses, WoO 14;
  Für Elise, WoO 59
- Haydn: Dances, Hob., IX:3, IX:8, IX:11, IX:12, XXXIc:17b;
  Marches, Hob. VIII:1, VIII:2;
  Sonatinas, Hob. XVI:1, 7, 8, 9, 10, G1, 3, 4, Hob. XVII:D1
- Mozart: German Dances, KV509;
  London Notebook (39 works in all);
  Minuets, KV 1, 2, 3, 4, 5, 9a, KV 33B, KV61gII, KV94, KV315g

The sample supplied 250 total works (each dance or movement counting as one work). The appearance of each ornament was tallied to determine frequency and, tangentially, importance. Understanding the embellishments found in these works can help achieve the beginnings of performing eighteenth-century ornaments stylistically:

- Trill: 104 works
- Appoggiatura: 101 works
- Turn: 29 works
- Two-note slide: 10 works
- Three-note slide: 4 works

Total works in survey: 250

BASIC CONVENTIONS

Eighteenth-century scores contain varying combinations of notes and signs to indicate embellishment. Some ornaments are already absorbed into the texture of the music but many are indicated as symbols or small notes in varying rhythms such as an eighth, sixteenth, or thirty-second note(s), with or without a slash. In situations where the ornament consists of small note(s) or multiple flags, neither are indicators of the length of the grace. Quantz describes, "It is of little importance whether they have one or two crooks."[5] Rather, Bach distinguishes that the ornament's length is determined "in proportioned relationship to the length of the principal note, the tempo and the affect of a piece."[6] In Example 10.1, the principal note is long, the tempo is *adagio*, and the *affekt* of F Minor implies sadness, gloom, and despair. Therefore, the trill will unfold accordingly. In Example 10.2 (page 168), the principal note is short, the tempo is *presto*, and the *affekt* of F Major is joyful and clever. The ornaments are executed with a quick snap.

Music Example 10.1. Mozart, Piano Sonata, KV 280/ii, mm. 1–5. Copyright (2005) G. Henle Verlag, Munich. ▶

Music Example 10.2. Mozart, Piano Sonata, KV 280/III, mm. 1–5. Copyright (2005) G. Henle Verlag, Munich. ▶

Bach further explains that "ornaments are to be played in the context of the immediate key."[7] Example 10.3 illustrates how contextual direction may be indicated. Regardless, it is understood to play "in the key" whether or not so indicated by the composer.

Music Example 10.3. Haydn, Twelve Minuets, Hob. IX:11, no. 1, mm. 13–16. Copyright (1996) G. Henle Verlag, Munich. ▶

The *general* rule is to begin ornaments on the beat with the upper auxiliary. But there are many specific points to consider when determining how best to execute an ornament. Tempo, *affekt,* desired emphasis on a dissonance (which may require some harmonic analysis), the instrument on which the work will be played, the performer's ability, and the hall in which the work will be performed factor into embellishing decisions.

If there is a special notation, it is most likely pointing to the exception rather than the rule. (See Haynes's remarks in chapter 9.) For instance, in Example 10.4 (see page 169), the trill in reality begins before the beat and is anticipated on the main note. Mozart is notating something "other than" the ordinary, as is common period practice.

Before digging into specific ornaments, a few more general comments. Bach offers golden nuggets of advice that simplifies work, illuminates

Music Example 10.4. Mozart, Piano Sonata, K. 309/I, mm. 65–67. Copyright (2005)
G. Henle Verlag, Munich. ▶

answers, and perhaps brings some of the joyful anticipation hinted at in
the opening paragraph. Play each excerpt without any ornamentation
first to clarify melodic direction and appropriate voice leading, making
appropriate choices more obvious. Then, incorporate ornaments according
to common practice. The ear must be trained through constant listening
to good music in order to apply ornamentation artistically. Continually
listen to recordings by those artists recommended in chapter 1. Seek out
recordings that have been vetted by informed reviewers such as Clive
Brown, who reviews for Oxford's *Early Music* journal. Seek out live performances of esteemed historically informed performancing artists.

SPECIFIC ORNAMENTS

Trill. Bach calls this the most important ornament. Trills, he says, "enliven
melodies and are therefore indispensable:"[8]

> The short trill is the least dispensable, the most attractive, but at the same
> time the most difficult embellishment. . . . It must literally crackle. It adds life
> and brilliance to a performance.[9]

A small note before a trill generally indicates the starting note only and
not its length. Türk describes its execution. "With respect to the strength
and weakness of trills, this must in general be judged by the character
of the composition and especially by each musical thought which is to
be expressed."[10] Historical literature provides considerable guidance.
The trill varies according to its function within *context*. The speed of the
oscillations adjusts to the tempo and expression of the passage. It typically lasts for the full value of the main note. To execute a long trill, the
performer may start somewhat slowly and accelerate. At the Westfield
International Fortepiano Academy, van Oort offered further advice to
facilitate execution: Always count trills, taking out beat pulses to speed
up the trill.[11]

The predominant view is that the starting note of the trill is the upper auxiliary (u.a.). There are many understood exceptions to the u.a. trill:

- When motivic unity must be preserved
- When trills are approached by stepwise motion (ascending and descending) and an appoggiatura would interrupt the smoothness and clarity of the line
- When the main note is the dissonance and an u.a. would create a consonance
- When an u.a. might prove less appropriate for musical reasons such as parallel fifths, parallel octaves, or after a rest
- When the key of the piece is to be established in the opening notes of a section or piece

According to Bach, the best fingering combinations for the right hand are *2-3* or *3-4*; for the left hand *1-2* or *2-3*.[12] Using the thumb on a black key may be the best choice. Do not automatically dismiss this option.

The suffix is frequently written out in the form of a turn ending, as in Example 10.5. If a termination is not indicated, the performer is expected to add one where it would fit to effect a smooth transition from the trill to the melodic line.

Music Example 10.5. Beethoven, Bagatelle, op. 119, no. 3, mm. 17–24. Copyright (1978) G. Henle Verlag, Munich. ▶

Appoggiatura. Period musicians believed this ornament was one of the "must haves." In his *Klavierschule*, Türk devotes an entire chapter, divided into four parts, to this ornament. He explains that this ornament comes from *appoggiato*, which means "actually: leaning, supported, and in music; sustained."[13] It serves as the basis for other harmonically oriented ornaments such as the trill and the turn, both of which grow out of or are an extension of the *appoggiatura*. Bach explains many of the melodic functions of the *appoggiatura* and then emphasizes that it "enhance[s] harmony as well as melody."[14] And in doing so it provides an accented dissonance—the spice! Quantz underscores the importance of *appoggiaturas*:

> *Appoggiaturas* are both ornamental and essential. Without appoggiaturas a melody would often sound very meager and plain. . . . Hence, dissonance must be used from time to time to rouse the ear. And in this connection *appoggiaturas* can be of considerable assistance, since they are transformed into dissonances, such as fourths and sevenths, if they stand before thirds or sixths reckoned from the bass, and are then properly resolved by the following notes [by "the following notes" Quantz is simply referring to those notes that would typically follow based on period performance norms].[15]

Why are *appoggiaturas* notated as little notes? Quantz answers this question as well: "To avoid confusion with ordinary notes, they are marked with very small notes, and they receive their value from the notes before which they stand."[16] Understanding the true meaning of *appoggiatura* brings an "ah-ha" to those who wonder why "runs" of sixteenth notes are written as a little-note *appoggiatura* rather than normally notated rhythms; it is the composer's wish that the first note of the group receive special attention. In Example 10.6, the *appoggiatura* should be *leaned into* rather than played straight through. *Agogic* rhythmic treatment is also appropriate, as outlined in chapter 5.

Music Example 10.6. Mozart, Piano Sonata, KV 311/I, mm. 1–4. Copyright (2005) G. Henle Verlag, Munich. ⏵

The *appoggiatura* is never approached in a legato fashion. There is always space in time directly before the *appoggiatura*, called an articulated silence. Both Bach and Türk report that the *appoggiatura* itself "is always louder than and it must be slurred *to* the following note, whether a slur marking is present or not."[17]

Short appoggiatura. The function of the short *appoggiatura* is rhythmic accentuation and harmonic color. *Affekt* determines its length and whether the *appoggiatura* or the main note is accented. This little embellishment takes a very small, scarcely noticeable part of the value of the main note. In Example 10.7, it is a quick little snap played on the beat.

Music Example 10.7. Mozart, Allegro, KV 3, mm. 25–30. Copyright (1983) G. Henle Verlag, Munich. ▶

Long appoggiatura. The long *appoggiatura* serves to connect and complete harmony at phrase divisions or at cadences. Context determines its length. Bach and Türk both provide common practice parameters. Bach explains that the usual rule of duration depends on the length of the main note. An *appoggiatura* on a main note that is a half note may take a full quarter-note value and an *appoggiatura* on a main note that is a dotted half note may take a half note from the main note. *Affekt* is a determining factor in the choice.[18]

Important exception: Example 10.8 is an excellent illustration of what Haynes calls "describing performance practice, but in reverse."[19] Mozart notates an ornament to begin before the beat and on the main note. Although the upper auxiliary *appoggiatura* begins the trill on F, the anticipation E♭ gives the impression of an ornament beginning on the main note, before the beat. Visit Example 10.4 to see another instance of "performance practice in reverse."

Music Example 10.8. Mozart Piano Sonata, K 457/I, mm. 1–4. Copyright (2005) G. Henle Verlag, Munich. ▶

Turn. According to Bach, the turn is "an easy embellishment which makes melodies both attractive and brilliant."[20] The turn is quite a utilitarian ornament! It occurs on any beat, above long and moderately short notes, on ascending and descending notes, in skips and in stepwise progressions, on repeated notes, on unprepared notes, and on or after *appoggiaturas*. The interval between the outer notes is most often a minor third.

The execution and timing depend largely on the *affekt* of the piece. The rhythmic arrangement varies, depending on context. If there is enough time, the turn should be on the beat and allow a pause on the main note, like in Example 10.9. In short notes or in fast tempi, the main note may be incorporated into the turn and the turn is often incorporated into the line. The internal rhythmic arrangement of the turn is remarkably changeable. Turns between notes or over a dot are delayed until shortly before the following note, again, depending on context.

Music Example 10.9. Beethoven, Bagatelle, op. 119, no. 1, mm. 9–12. Copyright (1978) G. Henle Verlag, Munich. ▶

Bach further explains, "When the turn alone is used, its symbol may appear either directly over a note or after it, somewhat to the right."[21] There are many problems with sloppy notation practices left behind by period composers and copyists. For example, in Beethoven's Piano Sonata in A Major, op. 2, no. 2, a variety of turn placements occur throughout the work, leaving an unanswered question: Was it intentional or simply a consequence of sloppiness?

Because the turn is utilitarian and nothing more than a very short trill with only one rotation, developing facility is of utmost importance. In Example 10.10, Türk provides an excellent exercise to develop skill in performing the turn.

Music Example 10.10. Türk, *Klavierschule*, 273.

Slide. The slide consists of two or three anticipatory small notes played before the main note. The slide is preferred on strong beats, is acceptable on weak beats, but is not used before a completely unimportant beat. The notes of the slide are always stepwise to the main note and slurred to the note. The slide with two tones is always used to fill in a leap and is always played rapidly.[22]

Period debate and discussion abounds regarding ornaments on or before the beat, the slide being a case in point. All notated examples of the slide in Bach's *Versuch* and Türk's *Klavierschule* demonstrate the slide occurring on the beat. Quantz complicates matters in his *Versuch* by describing slides (both ascending and descending) that fill in leaps of the fourth. The slide may begin before the beat and take its time from the preceding note(s). Quantz does acknowledge that this is a departure from regular practice.[23] In his *Violinschule*, L. Mozart illustrates passing *appoggiaturas*, all clearly notated before the beat. This information suggests that both realizations coexist in this style. The overriding guideline is *affekt and good taste*.

In Example 10.11, common practice suggests the slide on the beat. However, the performer must decide which execution enhances the desired *affekt*. Remember, one purpose of ornaments is to heighten interest through the use of dissonance. Here, the slide and the principal note are consonant with the bass note and is, therefore, not a determining factor. If the intention is to bring attention to the downbeat, make ms. 11 a strong measure, and create a sparkling high point with the F, the slide should come before the downbeat. If, however, the desired effect is to create anticipatory space with the quarter rest on ms. 10, delay the F, and save the rhythmic strong point for the high C at ms. 13 that leads to the aesthetic high point D in ms. 14, the slide should come on the beat. These are the types of thoughtful considerations that enter into decisions of execution.

Music Example 10.11. Mozart, Minuet, K. 315g/V, mm. 9–12. Copyright (1983) G. Henle Verlag, Munich. ▶

The slide with three tones is an exact inversion of the turn and may be notated in a variety of ways, as Bach illustrates in Example 10.12.

Music Example 10.12. Bach, *Versuch*, Figure 157.[26]

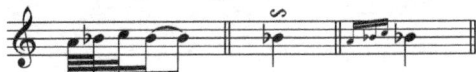

The three-note slide is most often found over a repeated note. The *affekt* and tempo of the movement determine the slide's pace and the execution follows suit accordingly. In Example 10.13, the slide is used in a moderate tempo, in A Minor, and on a main and important beat. An appropriate *affekt* is grief and sorrow, which calls for a slow, heavy execution of the slide.

Music Example 10.13. Mozart, Rondo in A Minor, KV 511, mm. 1–3. Copyright (2005) G. Henle Verlag, Munich. ▶

INFLUENCES APPLIED

Begin developing facility in playing ornaments as soon as possible, just as scales should be prepared before encountering them in the repertoire. Bach recommends developing facility early on.

> Practice embellishments until they can be performed skillfully with proper facility. Since this is an assignment on which a lifetime may well be spent (embellishments demand in part more technique and dexterity than runs) the student should not be detained after his ability, depending on his aptness and age, is great enough to stand him in modest stead.[24]

Determine *affekt*. As ornaments are encountered in the score, first learn the passage without ornaments. This approach makes appropriate voice leading easier to hear.

Solid information from period sources is essential. Yet, as the use of a specific ornament is contemplated, several points should be considered. In this style, there is no standardized notational system for ornaments. From the brief discussion of differing opinions comes the realization that there is no singular correct choice for executing ornaments. Informed interpretation today acknowledges that choice depends on historical context, sensitivity to *affekt*, musical components within the piece, current tastes, and performer ability. (See the extended discussion on the companion website, Text 10.2. ▶)

To develop authentic and genuine performances, decide if the ornament creates the desired sound or *affekt*. Determine if the ornament will work on the available instrument. Determine if the physical capability to execute the ornament musically exists. Ornaments indicated in the score are the composer's *suggestion* for ways to enliven the message. Bach assures that ornaments are not required. "Ornaments that lose their charm through poor execution are better omitted entirely."[25] It is better to play with good execution and *affekt* than to create awkward bumps in the road.

Contemplate creative ways in which new (unnotated) embellishing ideas may be incorporated; look to repeated passages, repeated sections, or the uninteresting, predictable parts in the score. Ornamentation should make the work better—choose carefully so as not to ruin the dish with too many spices.

After careful consideration and incorporation of these ideas, many more questions will come to mind. For a full discussion beyond the scope of this book, refer to the numerous treatises available on eighteenth-century ornamentation.

THE LESSON

Play and study Example 10.14 with the following points in mind.

Music Example 10.14. Mozart, London Notebook, KV 15oo, mm. 1–8. Copyright (1983) G. Henle Verlag, Munich.

1. Consider the indicated *appoggiatura* found in regular note values at mm. 5–6.
   a. Preceded with an articulated rest
   b. Emphasis on the F♯ slurred to the G
   c. The G receives less than the full quarter-note value, releasing lightly with the wrist

2. Consider the indicated *appoggiatura* notated with a small note value at ms. 8.

  a. Although not indicated with the ♮, the small note is understood to be played in context and will be performed a B♮.
  b. The B♮ *appoggiatura* becomes a quarter note or nearly a half note, slurred to the C, releasing as Türk instructs in Example 10.15.

Music Example 10.15. Türk, *Klavierschule*, 331.

3. Consider some of the ornamental options available on the repeat.
  a. A two-note slide in the right hand to fill in the fourth in ms. 1 or 2
  b. An *appoggiatura* in the right hand in ms. 4
  c. Extending the *appoggiatura* at ms. 8 to become a trill
  d. Filling in the skips in the left hand at ms. 7
  e. A turn on the final beat of ms. 7
4. Work through and listen to each possibility to determine viability on the basis of harmonic structure and good taste.
5. Limit choices to embellish the line with tasteful spices—less is more!
6. Incorporate only ornaments that can be played well.

Use the quick reference guide on the companion website to summarize. ▶

CHAPTER 11

✧

Repeats

Decoration is "for variety in often-repeated and similar passages."
—L. Mozart, *Violinschule*

O ne inimitable quality of the performing arts is that they are temporal—never the same twice. As material is repeated, with or without
variants, it is always changing because *time* has transpired from the first
statement. Allowing time to act *upon* the gesture ensures that some type
of change has taken place when the gesture returns. In the performing
arts, the artist doesn't use the gesture to create personal expression, but
rather the gesture, as it evolves through time and the influence of *affekt*,
uses the artist to express the art. The true beauty lies in the unrepeatable
moments experienced as our art is expressed.

HISTORICAL BACKGROUND

The easiest way to recognize that a gesture may be repeated in music
notation is through repeat signs. Two questions often arise when
eighteenth-century repeat signs are encountered: when do I repeat and
what do I do on the repeat? To respond in a historically informed context,
we must look at common period practices, see how practices have changed,
and look at tasteful, plausible choices for performing today. For as Haynes
observes, "Where seventeenth- and eighteenth-century musicians had a
casual view of written music, and no doubt 'improved' pieces regularly, a

modern performer usually feels a definite constraint about altering any-thing."[1] Read on and begin to ease the constraint!

In Baroque music, the return to the opening section is unaltered . . . on paper. It is an understood responsibility of the performer when playing in this style to tastefully embellish the repeat. The interest comes from the embellishing. This practice continues into the Classical Era. In small forms such as minuets and trios, it is quite clear that repeats are to be per-formed with expressive embellishment of some sort, including the *da capo* of the scherzo or minuet. "*Senza replica*" is notated to indicate the section not be repeated.

Variants are viewed as a necessity to avoid monotonous playing and an opportunity to demonstrate refinement, finesse, and good taste. L. Mozart explains that decoration is "for variety in often-repeated and similar pas-sages."[2] In his dissertation, *Free Variation of Repeated Passages in Mozart's Keyboard Music,* Andrew Willis discusses the pitfalls involved if variants on repeats are avoided or ignored:

> A musician of Mozart's day who repeated material verbatim might have risked being judged inartistic, if not downright incompetent. A musician of our day who wishes to perform Mozart's music in a manner consistent with the aes-thetic concerns of Mozart's time must likewise develop the skill to vary repeated material or risk missing an important implication of the musical style.[3]

This style is malleable and the *expectation* is to "compose as you go." Gjerdingen explains, "Today we tend to equate 'compose' with 'invent,' yet the older, more literal meaning of 'put together' (com + posare) may provide a better image of galant practice."[4] The *New Oxford American Dictionary* says the same. "ORIGIN late Middle English (in the general sense 'put together, construct')."[5] To perform in eighteenth-century style, we are expected to embellish repeats. It was (and is now!) a sign of possessing artistic social grace.

Embellishing repeats is yet another tool available for expressing *affekt*. It is another "understood" principle that the composer's version is presented unembellished first so the listener will know what is the composer's work and what is the performer's work. The performer then incorporates personal embellishments to further express *affekt*. Türk and Bach advise and warn that "they [performer-generated embellish-ments] must be of significance and at least as good as the given melody;"[6] they "must always be at least as good as, if not better than, the original [statement]."[7]

The concept of repeating sections has gone out of vogue with most modern players, perhaps because many performances suffer a verbatim nothing-new-to-say mentality. Musicologist Barry Cooper urges us to rethink this position:

> In a long movement with many repeated sections . . . there is a temptation to omit some or all of the repeats. This temptation should be resisted. Repeats form an integral part . . . right up to the finale of Beethoven's very last sonata (op. 111), and to omit them suggests an impatience to get the music finished as quickly as possible, instead of enjoying it for as long as possible.[8]

Furthermore, failing to perform repeats alters compositional structure. And, structure is fundamental to eighteenth-century style. One look at balance when the performer is contemplating omitting repeats will impact decisions. Any surprises such as deceptive cadences that occur further into the piece will lose their impact if the previous material is cut in half. So, perhaps the question isn't whether or not to repeat, but what is available for use on repeats that will help make the music our own as it did for performers in the Classical Era?

Since there are no extant recordings, the next-best solution is to rely on what was written about the practice. For this, treatises provide much information. General observations begin the discussion.

- Any repeat, whether a simple gesture, a phrase, or an entire section, should have a purpose.
- The performer should be able to explain the intended *affekt* sought, *why* a repeat was chosen—such as a change in dynamics for intensity or shift in register for expressive design—and how it is accomplished in the embellishment.
- Once determinations are made, the question simply boils down to "how is this executed? What is done at the keyboard to make the intention clear to the audience?"

REPEATS IN FIRST MOVEMENTS OF SONATAS

The Classical Era saw a blossoming of the middle class and growth in the number of amateur musicians, resulting in a surge in the popularity of secular music. This growing popularity and availability of the piano provided the perfect setting for increased output in writing and performing sonatas. Sonata-allegro form flourished in the keyboard music of the Classical Era.

Historically, repeated sections were signified in a number of ways. According to Quantz, a piece may be divided by a simple double bar line. In this instance the performer is instructed to play to the end, *da capo*, and repeat the first section. Repeat signs are followed in the customary fashion. Sometimes the word *bis* is found above notes to also indicate a repeat.[9] (See more from Quantz on the companion website, Text 11.1.⏵)

It seems there were as many opinions as there were writers about what to do when there are two dots on each side of a double bar. Three general schools of thought emerged. The group led by Türk believed that every marked repeat should be followed. Clementi recommended a balanced approach. If the second half of a movement was excessively long, it was advised to forgo the repeat. As sonata-allegro form took hold and the function of the structure shifted, thoughts regarding strict adherence to the traditional repeat signs shifted as well. In the first movements of sonatas, Grétry philosophically argued that taking repeats was an antiquated extension of old forms and beliefs and was incompatible with rhetoric: "A sonata is a discourse. What would we think of a man who, cutting his discourse in two, repeated each half?"[10]

His point is well taken. Sonata-allegro form moves from a somewhat static event in Baroque dance music (see chapter 3), wherein the embellishment itself serves the purpose of interest on the repeat to the new Classical event, wherein the structure itself does the work that was previously assigned to ornaments.[11] The tension created in the journey of moving *into* the non-tonic key, traversing through several modulations, and dramatically reinstating themes in the recapitulation now draws the listener's attention. If this is the case, a repeat of the exposition may not be necessary.

Haydn and Mozart used double repeat signs in almost all (one exception each) opening sonata allegro movements.[12] Knowing Beethoven's great interest in prosody, we can hardly wonder that balance was of utmost importance. The evidence supports that decisions surrounding the inclusion of repeat signs were intentional rather than out of habit or customary practice.

Choosing to observe repeat signs in sonata-allegro movements is a complicated affair when it involves embellishments. Rosen argues that ornamentation on the repeat of the exposition presents confusion on two fronts. The first point of confusion is that if there are embellishments during the repeat of the exposition, the material being manipulated here (in the exposition) will reappear in a less-ornamented fashion in the recapitulation and thus confuse the placement of the dramatic climax. The other issue is that if embellishments continue into the recapitulation, they will obscure and minimize the structural changes (and corresponding expressive significance) *already* made by the composer in the recapitulation.[13] In addition, there is a concern about elaborations already present in the composition itself prior to performer-generated embellishments. The answer is embedded in the Classical Era approach to performing. Decisions must be well thought out and made intentionally. The performer must take great care in making embellishment decisions to build *to* the climax.

THEME AND VARIATIONS

Clearly, another form that begs for discussion is theme and variation. Repeat signs are frequently involved, and the concepts previously outlined apply. Variation repeats definitely warrant embellishment of some sort. It was common practice to choose which variations would be repeated and was a certain guarantee that not everything be repeated, as that would be in poor taste.

There are some simple observations that provide guidance in plotting out *affekt* when you are working through any set: the "triplets variation" functions to smooth out the *affekt*, the minor variation is always "troubled," and the variation before the slow variation is usually orchestral.

GUIDELINES

The concerns surrounding repeating entire sections aside, it was a customary practice to create variants on a repeated phrase, or segment. Just as it is in good taste to vary inflection, tone, and volume when entering into discource, so it is in eighteenth-century musical style. And there were many well-known possibilities that were utilized to design personal musical discourse in the Classical Era. Even as the Romantic Era compositional practice of incorporating embellishments into the fabric of the score took hold, the art of individually expressed embellishments continued well into the twentieth century. Any belief that the composer's notes are hallowed scripture limits the intended beauty of eighteenth-century style.

A simple checklist from Willis's *Free Variation of Repeated Passages in Mozart's Keyboard Music* provides advice and admonitions from his study of the scores and period treatises:

- Ornamentation must never clash with the expressive character of the piece.
- Ornamentation must not serve to *merely* show off the performer.

- Ornamentation must augment the interest of the original version.
- Ornamentation is more suitable when the original version is plain or ordinary, less suitable when the original is ornate or distinctive.
- Ornamentation must display harmonic acumen so that, as Türk instructs, "each variation must be based upon the given harmony."[14]
- Ornamentation must display impeccable taste.
- Ornamentation is suitable for the repetition of previously heard material.[15]

Variations are most often progressive in nature, from the simplest to the most complex. Play through any Classical Era repertoire for clear models. An excellent starting place is any set of variations or second movement of a piano sonata, such as Haydn's Piano Sonata in C Major, Hob. XVI:50/ii.

Much of today's conception of expressing variations is limited to dynamic contrasts between *forte* and *piano*—woefully, by depressing or releasing the *una corde* pedal. It is one of the simplest and most overused methods employed by modern musicians. A close second is the trill. Yet there is *so much more!* Why be limited to the use of two tools in building an artistic mansion? In looking back, this is where modern players are offered some of the newest, most "innovative" ideas. Gjerdingen provides historical perspective: "Though the skill and invention of those composers remains impressive however one might try to explain their abilities, there are obvious advantages that a stockpile of 'interchangeable parts' would give to the rapid, secure crafting of complex compositions."[16] A "stockpile" is now available, at your fingertips. Table 11.1 (see page 184) lists simple variants found in eighteenth-century repertoire that add to the charm, grace, and invention when material is repeated. As the arrow indicates, the options may be applied in either direction, Option 1↔Option 2.

To further expand a working base, three resources are recommended. Being a great pedagogue, Bach left not only instruction through his *Versuch*, but also wrote *Sechs Sonaten für Clavier mit veränderten Reprisen: 1760*. This collection contains realized examples of appropriate embellishments within the musical context of actual repertoire. Another nearly exhaustive resource is Quantz's *Versuch*, wherein he methodically works out fourteen examples of fragments with multiple variants. Andrew Willis in his 1994 dissertation, *Free Variation of Repeated Passages in Mozart's Keyboard Music*, meticulously works through the notated variations found in the works of Mozart. Spend some time with these sources. The possibilities are limitless!

Table 11.1. EMBELLISHING OPTIONS

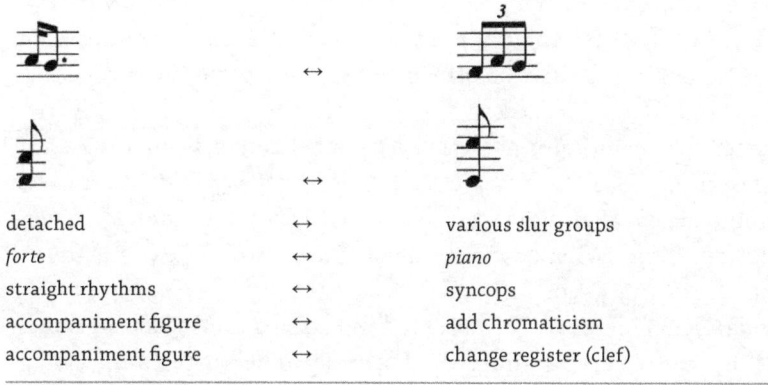

detached	↔	various slur groups
forte	↔	piano
straight rhythms	↔	syncops
accompaniment figure	↔	add chromaticism
accompaniment figure	↔	change register (clef)

In his *Versuch*, Bach points out exceptions: "Yet, not everything should be varied."[17] Türk similarly warns about tasteful choices when choosing variations:

> Those passages which in themselves are already of striking beauty or liveliness, as well as compositions in which sadness, seriousness, noble simplicity, solemn and lofty greatness, pride, and the like are predominant characteristics should be completely spared from variations and elaborations, or these should be used very sparingly and with suitable discrimination.[18]

Good decision making about when, what, and how to embellish develops through continued study of the repertoire, practicing various options, and listening to good performances.

INFLUENCES APPLIED

Through the early 1800s, it was assumed the performer would create variants when material repeated. The pianist's role shifted in the modern era to a literalist philosophy: perform only what is on the page, what others had created. Today, the pendulum may possibly swing back toward center in a new way. We may intermingle the old (period notation, instruments, and performance practices) with the new to create authenticity. To no longer play the same material over and over, hoping for more musical results. To be rid of "boring scoring." To take a chance, to be original, to create individual art rather than duplicate what has already been done! What an exciting opportunity!

Visit the companion website to hear Audio Examples 11.1a-11.2c where variations are modeled for Beethoven's Minuet in G Major, Trio, WoO 10, no. 2 ⓑ and Seven Variations on "God save the King," WoO 78, Variation V ⓑ. Continue to listen to renowned fortepianists such as those listed in chapter 1. Look for creative solutions and stylistic patterns as you study scores.

When first attempting to use the tool of embellishing, begin with a simple dance from Mozart's *London Notebook* or Beethoven's *German Dances*. Determine the *affekt* of the work by using tools provided in previous chapters. Ask questions: What does the embellishment do *for* the work? Does it add interest or vitality, or enliven the passage?

Decide when repeats will be observed. Whether adopting a traditionalist attitude and observing all repeats faithfully or bearing in mind changing taste through the eras, keep in mind "balance, proportion, and length" to come to a tasteful rendition of the work.

Experiment with many of the various options provided in Table 11.1. Refer to chapter 10 for additional choices. Judicious, tasteful choices will inspire creativity, infuse originality, and result in individuality. Go to the *uninteresting* parts to add an embellishment. Care needs be taken in making choices so that choices add *to* rather than detract *from* the *affekt*. Quantz provides sage words of wisdom: "There is more art in saying much with little, than little with much."[19] It is exciting to use this new set of tools, and it is tempting to embrace embellishing to the full, adding all sorts of goodies! Don't become that kindergartner who gets to decorate his own cookie and uses an over-abundance of frosting and every sprinkle, nut, and candy topping on the table. Three questions will prudently guide decisions: "What can I do, when should I do it, and how often?" Exaggerate when experimenting. This action alone will frequently eliminate bad choices.

Willingness to create genuine performances in this style requires simply diving in. As with anything new, the first go-round will be time consuming, rough, and perhaps not particularly pleasing. But with time, solutions will come and enjoyment will grow. It is an immensely pleasing experience to be acted *upon* by the gesture and the *affekt* as a vehicle to express art.

Making note of variations in the score for many festivals and competitions will be honored when accompanied by the following direction for the adjudicator: "All variants realized on repeats are in accordance with historically informed eighteenth-century performance practice."

THE LESSON

Play and study Example 11.1 with the following points in mind.

Music Example 11.1. Mozart, London Notebook, KV 15oo, mm. 1–8. Copyright (1983) G. Henle Verlag, Munich.

1. Play with no embellishments during the first statement.
2. Explore many possibilities on the repeat.
   a. Dynamic contrast
   b. Filling in right-hand thirds in mm. 4–6, incorporating chromaticism if possible
   c. Filling in left-hand thirds in ms. 7
   d. Adjusting rhythms
   e. Reversing direction of the thirds in mm. 4–6
   f. Turning single lines into thirds in mm. 1 and 2 while reducing the thirds in mm. 3 and 4 to single notes
3. Choosing only one or two variants creates good taste.
4. Gradually increase complexity as embellishments are applied.

Use the quick reference guide on the companion website to summarize. ▶

CHAPTER 12

✧

Damper Pedal

The damper pedal in the Classical Era style is a horse of a different color. Syncopated pedaling is not described until the latter half of the nineteenth century. Again, it has not "always been that way!" In the Classical Era style, rhythmic pedal is the norm: the pedal is activated and released with the notes and not overlapped. This type of pedaling enhances the attack of the downbeat or specific note(s), a technique that is appropriate to the style. This style of pedaling may have been necessary also, in part, due to the slow damper response found in many of the period fortepianos.

Use of the pedal is not the norm, but a deliberate and planned decision for a specific *timbre* or to enhance *affekt*. The sparsity of indications in the score supports this claim. Haydn indicated pedal only twice, during long special-effect sections where he specifically intended mixed harmonies. Mozart left no pedal indications, and his use of pedal was scarcely noted in others' reports of his playing. Beethoven indicated pedal more but was criticized by his contemporaries for doing so.

The Viennese five-octave fortepiano damper pedal was a knee-operated lever rather than a foot-operated device. This less efficient pedal by knee versus foot was simply because pedal wasn't used much in writing for the Viennese fortepiano.

PURPOSE OF THE DAMPER PEDAL

Sound quality. Dampers are activated as a way to improve legato as a sound *quality*. Rarely are dampers activated to merely produce a long legato line.

Most melodic ranges are well within an octave and should be connected with fingers rather than relying on the pedal. In Example 12.1, pedal use is appropriate from mm. 274 through 278 to intentionally warm the sound quality and intensify the diminished seventh chord at the cadence.

Music Example 12.1. Beethoven, Piano Sonata op. 2, no. 2/I, mm. 274–278. (ABRSM) ⏵

Sustaining the bass. The pedal may be used to sustain the bass. In sections where the chords and harmony change infrequently, such as pedal points (again, in Example 12.1), the damper pedal may be activated and maintained throughout a section. Slurs under or over a long singular harmony may indicate activating the pedal.

Shift of affekt. The damper pedal may help generate a shift in mood within a movement like in Example 12.2. Activating dampers here provides an excellent opportunity to contrast the *affekt* from the intense opening to this rich second theme. Adding pedal also enhances the legato sound quality, brings out an important theme, and substantiates the structure.

Rich sonorities. The damper pedal furthers rich sonorities indicated by slurs (Example 12.2).

Music Example 12.2. Beethoven, Piano Sonata, op. 10, no. 1/i, mm. 37–44. (ABSRM) ⏵

Implementing dynamic contrasts. In Example 12.3, Mozart uses *forte* as a form of accentuation rather than a dynamic direction. Incorporating the damper pedal supports the intended purpose. It is appropriate practice to use pedal with *forte* or *sforzando* to facilitate accentuation.

Music Example 12.3. Mozart, Piano Sonata, K. 332/I, mm. 60–65. Copyright (2005) G. Henle Verlag, Munich.

In Example 12.4, pedal may be used in a number of ways, depending on the intended *affekt*. It may highlight the surprise *forte* in mm. 76 and 77, the mysterious harmonic effect at mm. 78–79, or warm the sound on the two note slurs in mm. 76, 77, 80, and 81.

Music Example 12.4. Mozart, Piano Sonata, K. 280/I, mm. 76–81. Copyright (2005) G. Henle Verlag, Munich.

Tenderness and gentleness in *pianissimo* passages may be enhanced with the damper pedal.

Intentional blurring for effect. Because of the quick decay and thinner overtones on the fortepiano, long pedals were possible and used to the composer's advantage. In such instances, it was conceived as a means of changing *timbre* (much like changing registers on the harpsichord) and *not* a means to a legato melody line. Although it is quite common to refer to Beethoven's famous *Moonlight* sonata or the "ghostly" sections of the *Tempest* sonata to demonstrate the practice of raised dampers throughout to create a collective or composite sound in long stretches, I particularly enjoy the effect created in Example 12.5, Haydn Piano Sonata in C Major, Hob. XVI:50. Knowing of the fortepiano's quick decay, Haydn seized the opportunity to indicate raised dampers throughout the section while at the same time subtly articulate the main theme. The cumulative effect is stunning!

Music Example 12.5. Haydn, Piano Sonata, Hob. XVI:50/I, mm. 120–124. Copyright (1993) G. Henle Verlag, Munich. ▶

THE MODERATOR

The moderator is another tool available to bring special effect to the sound quality in eighteenth-century music. For a complete discourse on the subject, visit Michael Cole's *The Pianoforte in the Classical Era*. The moderator can be described in a simple sense.

- A ribbon of woven silk is introduced between the hammer and the string.
- The ribbon slides forward from the hitchpin block.

- A rod passes through a hole drilled through the yoke for the performer's access.[1]
- The mechanism is hand-activated by a lever (up until circa 1790) that is placed directly above the middle of the keyboard.[2]
- Activation and release requires taking the hand from the keys to move the lever.[3]

The moderator was found on Walter pianos (which Mozart owned). According to Cole, the moderator was created in response to the harder, bigger sound of the Walter compared to the Stein. The moderator did not appear on the Stein or Stein/Streicher pianos until after 1800.[4]

Listen to Examples 12.5b2 and 12.6b on the companion website ⊙ to hear the unique sound quality achieved with the moderator activated. With judicious adjustments, these same brilliant effects can be expressed on the modern piano.

Music Example 12.6. Beethoven, Piano Sonata op. 27, no. 2/i, mm. 1–5. (ABRSM) ⊙

INFLUENCES APPLIED

Although playing period instruments to learn the sound quality is the best way to answer the following application questions, decisions can still be made *as if* the instrument were available. When considering pedal, first look to the *affekt*. What will use of the pedal describe? Does the decision to use pedal enhance structure, articulate formal function, bring attention to a specific voice, or purposely create an effect? What adjustments can be made on the modern piano to achieve the desired effect?

The modern piano contains more overtones and thus requires considerable adjusting and intent listening when the performer is making pedaling decisions. Rhythmic pedal should be experimented with to maintain Classical Era–style clarity. Use of partial pedal—one-half to one-quarter pedal—helps keep overtones cleared out. Frequent pedal changes keep the lower strings lighter.

Audio Examples 12.5c and 12.6c ▶ on the companion website present reconciled versions to demonstrate how the open-pedal effect can be realized on the modern piano. In Audio Example 12.5c I use very light pedal. I glean articulation clues from the harmonic function in the bass (highlighting the 7-6 suspensions) and the slurs in the soprano to provide pedal choices. For the *Moonlight* sonata, Dr. Ann Chang, Artist-in-Residence, Associate Professor (Piano) at the University of Nebraska and Artistic Director of the Lied Center for Performing Arts, recommends pedaling lightly and changing pedal anywhere *but* on the downbeat. In Audio Example 12.6c the pedal is depressed as lightly as possible. I listen as the sound accumulates. When a pedal change is necessary, I follow Dr. Chang's recommendation. I find the later in the triplet figure I change the pedal, the better the effect.

Remain ever-mindful and faithful to the Classical Era style. Listen carefully to ensure articulation is not obscured or covered. Clarity of line and harmony supersedes long pedal. On 2-5-1 cadential bass lines, keep things clean to separate the notes and clarify the harmonic function. Pedal should not be used on the modern piano to thicken intentionally slender sounds. However, thin textured writing might require an ever so slight touch of pedal to warm the sound. Pedal may also be called for to highlight a specific note, the peak of a phrase, or to allow the tone to blossom on attack. Failure to do so may result in a choked, incoherent tone. Prudent and economical use will go a long way in catching the listener's attention. Reserve the pedal for special occasions.

THE LESSON

Pedal is neither indicated nor appropriate in this piece. Discuss the *affekt* of the piece and why this is the case. Listen to recordings that use pedal to begin developing the sound concept.

Use the quick reference guide on the companion website to summarize. ▶

CHAPTER 13

ᴄᴠᴐ

Indicated Tempo

Tempo marks have frequently designated aspects of composition other than its speed.
An 18th-century *adagio* frequently indicated an appropriate means of expression.[1]

—*The Harvard Dictionary of Music*

BACKGROUND

An appropriate performance tempo is essential to produce the desired *affekt*. Although this point seems self-evident, eighteenth-century pedagogues had strong enough conviction about the influence of tempo on *affekt* to specifically address the topic. Briefly, Türk states, "More careful composers are accustomed to indicate the character of a composition as well as its tempo."[2] Again, *affekt* comes first.

The Harvard Dictionary of Music provides historical context that again negates the myth "but it's always been that way!"

> Prior to 1600, tempo marks were practically unknown, since the pace of a composition was expressed in the notation itself, the note values then used having absolute durations that were variable only within small limits. By 1611 Banchieri (1568–1634) prescribes *adagio, allegro, veloce, presto, più presto,* and *prestissimo* in his *Organo suonarino* (1611).[3]

It is in this arena that eighteenth-century repertoire finds itself. Tempo meanings are expressed by mixing the old (the interaction of the time signature, note values, and period dances) with the new (specific terms to indicate intention). Although inherent tempo parameters provided guidance, composers were ever striving to specify their intentions more clearly. Indicating a specific tempo marking alone, however, did not solve the problem. There were (and still are) several mitigating and influencing factors to contend with to arrive at L. Mozart's goal: "time . . . the soul of music."[4]

Tempo interpretations varied from one region or country to another. Underlying *affekt* associated with the tempo was also an influencing factor. What's more, each composer's individual taste impacted tempo marking choice. And, the interpretations changed over time. A cross section of three music dictionaries spanning just ninety years is presented in Table 13.1 (page 196). An examination of four frequently used eighteenth-century terms illustrates the point.

Alla breve. The associated meaning of *alla breve* changed over time. Notice that in 1740, Brossard makes no reference to the speed of *alla breve*. Fifty years later, speed is definitely indicated, and by 1827, its use is considered nearly obsolete.

Cut time was discussed extensively amongst period musicians. Beliefs were all over the map in search of one true, treasured definition. Some felt cut time was a bit faster; some felt it twice as fast. There were even mathematical calculations offered up to determine an "appropriate" pace. The larger point here seems to be *affekt*. With the use of cut time comes a shift in accents, which consequently affects forward propulsion and, tangentially, tempo. In Example 13.1, the *affekt* of the sonata changes significantly if it is played in common time rather than cut time. The forward propulsion of the line to the A♭ in ms. 2 and the B♭ in ms. 4 is most effectively achieved through Beethoven's direction to play in cut time. Examine other examples such as Beethoven Piano Sonatas op. 10, no. 3 and op. 27, no. 2 to further study this concept.

Music Example 13.1. Beethoven, Piano Sonata, op. 2, no. 1/i, mm. 1–4. (ABSRM) ▶

The changing allegro. In 1740, *allegro* was specifically defined to be "without hurry" and focused on *affekt*. Quantz supports this observation in his *Versuch*:

Table 13.1 TERMINOLOGY SURVEY FROM PERIOD MUSIC DICTIONARIES

	Brossard[27] 1740	Rousseau[28] 1779	Busby[29] 1827
Alla breve	Name of music consisting of two semi-breves or four minims.	A kind of measure of two times, very quick. No longer in use in Italy, and only in church-music.	A certain species of quick common-time, consisting of two breves, or measures, in a bar. Was formerly in very general use in ecclesiastical music, but is now obsolete in Italy, and nearly so in every other part of Europe.
Allegro	Brisk, lively, gay and pleasant, yet without hurry and precipitation, and quicker than any tempo except *presto*.	The second fastest of the five principal degrees of movement. Allegro signifies lively, and it is also the indication of a lively movement, the most so of any after *presto*. But, we must not think, on that account, that this movement is proper for gay subjects only; it is often applicable to transports of passion, distraction, or despair, which partake nothing less than of gaiety.	Gay, quick. A term expressive of the third degree of musical rapidity. Generally applied to lively movements, but sometimes, in conjunction with another word, placed at the beginning of compositions intended to rouse and stimulate the more violent passions: as *Allegro Agitato, Allegro Furioso*. . . .
Assai	Often joined with *allegro, adagio, presto.* Much (or) motions of a piece be kept in middle degree of quickness or slowness; enough, but not too much of either.	Found joined to the word which denotes the movement of an air: wherefore *presto assai; largo assai* signifies very quick, very slow.	Usually joined to words allusive to the time of any composition, and increases its power; as *Adagio*, slow; *Adagio Assai*, more slow, or very slow; *Allegro Assai*, more quick, or very quick.
Minuet	Extremely quick and short steps	[No entry]	A movement of three crotchets or three quavers in a bar; of a slow and graceful motion, and always beginning with the beating note. There are other minuets of a time somewhat quicker, and which were formerly much used as concluding movements of overtures, sonatas, &c.

The principal character of the Allegro is one of gaiety and liveliness, just as
that of the Adagio, on the contrary, is one of tenderness and melancholy. The
word *Allegro* has a very broad meaning in the designation of musical pieces,
and in this sense applies to many kinds of quick pieces, such as Allegro, Allegro
assai, Allegro di molto. . . .[5]

By 1827, *allegro* had picked up momentum as well as expanding the
scope of the term's definition. Türk's definition in the 1789 *Klavierschule*
instructs, "Swiftly, that is, not quite as quickly as *presto*."[6] By the 1802 edition he clarifies, "A far more moderate tempo generally taken for granted
for an *allegro* composed fifty years or more ago than for a more recent
composition with the same heading."[7] In Chapter 5, revisit the discussion about the change *allegro* underwent in the Clementi Piano Sonatina,
op. 36, no. 1. Cooper contends, too, that eighteenth-century *allegro* may
not have been as fast as it was envisioned, even one generation later:

While playing the second movement of Beethoven's Piano Sonata in D, WoO
47, No. 3, the detailed slur and staccato patterns become virtually impossible
at this speed [set by Czerny]. Here it is difficult to take the crotchet at more
than 80 and 72 respectively without the music sounding a desperate scramble.[8]

Assai is another example of the slippery slope of tempo-related definitions. Not only does the terminology shift over time, any given term may
have more than one meaning. For example, Türk provides different definitions within *Klavierschule*. Early on, *assai* is defined: "quite a bit, rather,
or very" when connected to a tempo. Later in the same book, he defines
it: "enough" when connected to a dynamic marking.[9]

The final example of the precarious footing of indicated tempi definitions is the *minuet*. If a composer is using the Italian *minuet* as a basis, a
lively, quick, $\frac{3}{8}$ is most likely indicated. The more moderate, noble tempo
in $\frac{3}{4}$ is derived from the French *minuet*. Newman compares the two: "Two
types of *minuet* of distinctly different character and tempo were still being
danced and performed in the Classical Era."[10] Determining an appropriate
tempo requires examining the indicated tempo marking, the time signature, predominant note values, the individual composer, and the date of
the composition.

Inherent tempo. As explained extensively in Chapter 5, each time signature has its own manner of execution and inherent movement. Knowledge
and application of inherent tempo traits predate the indicated labels written at the beginning of a piece or section and must be considered when
determining tempo.

To briefly summarize, the larger the note represented by the denominator, the heavier the execution and slower the tempo. For example, $\frac{4}{2}$, $\frac{3}{2}$, or $\frac{2}{2}$ are likely to move more heavily and more slowly than $\frac{4}{4}$, $\frac{3}{4}$, or $\frac{2}{4}$. Within any meter, the subdivisions of structural note values indicated slower movement (i.e., quarter notes implied a faster tempo than sixteenths). Türk provides an example: "An *allegro* with some thirty-second notes intermingled, should not be played as fast as when its most rapid passages consist of only eighth notes."[11]

Interactions. In Sulzer's *Allgemeine Theorie II*, Schulz provides direction in his *Takt* regarding the interaction of indicated tempo and execution (determined by chosen note values): "If a piece should have a light execution but at the same time a slow tempo, the composer will select a meter of short or shorter values and will make use of *andante, largo,* or *adagio*."[12] Example 13.2 is an excellent illustration of this theory in practice.

Music Example 13.2. Mozart, Piano Sonata, K. 309/II, mm. 1–4. Copyright (2005) G. Henle Verlag, Munich. [▶]

Schulz explains further: "And conversely, if a piece should have a heavy rendition and at the same time a fast tempo, the composer will select a heavy meter and indicate *vivace, allegro,* or *presto*."[13] Example 13.3 provides the opposing theory in practice.

Music Example 13.3. Beethoven, Piano Sonata, op. 14, no. 1/I, mm. 1–4. (ABSRM) [▶]

Table 13.2 helps clarify the relationship between indicated tempo markings and compositional traits. Whether the tempo marking dictates the trait(s) or vice versa is irrelevant. It is understanding the relationship that is important.

Table 13.2. INFLUENCING TEMPO INTERACTIONS

Typically Found in Faster Tempo	Typically Found in Slower Tempo
Slow harmonic rhythm	Quick harmonic rhythm
Simple texture	Thick texture
Simple articulation	Complex/varied articulation
Little ornamentation	Highly ornamented

From period documents it appears the purpose of an indicated tempo was to further corroborate directions already supplied through elements implied by meter, note values, and understood dance tempi. Bach supplies the clues:

> The pace of a composition, which is usually indicated by several well-known Italian expressions, is based on its general content as well as on the fastest notes and passages contained in it. Due consideration of these factors will prevent an allegro from being rushed and an adagio from being dragged.[14]

Bach merely points to the common practice of using "well-known Italian terms" as an additional aide in determining an appropriate "pace."[15] There is no list to which he refers. There *is*, however, throughout the course of his book, exhaustive discussion on how to interpret the written notation to come to an informed conclusion regarding *affekt* and appropriate tempo.

Türk provides concrete definitions. Indicated tempo definitions have been synthesized from *Klavierschule*[16] and formatted in Table 13.3 to clarify some of those "well-known Italian terms."

Table 13.3. ENCAPSULATED INDICATED TEMPO DEFINITIONS

Largo	slow, broad, extended, solemn slowness, spacious, expansive
Larghetto	smoothly flowing quality, calm, agreeable sentiments
Adagio	slow
Grave	seriously, more or less slow
Andante	(going), signifies a serene and measured pace, and is the mean between fast and slow
Comodo	easy-going, leisurely, not fast
Moderato	moderately
Maestoso	majestically, lofty, slower rather than faster
Allegretto	a little fast, or cheerful
Allegro	quick, swiftly
Presto	fast, rapidly

The overriding factor to be considered when settling on any tempo choice is provided by Quantz. His advice should be heeded:

> The tempo must be set in accordance with the most difficult passage-work. For, everything that is hurriedly played causes your listeners anxiety rather than satisfaction. Your principal goal must always be the expression of the sentiment, not quick playing.[17]

Brown's *Classical and Romantic Performing Practice 1750–1900* is an excellent source for further discussion of indicated tempo and their associated meanings.

THE METRONOME

The Classical Style projects meaning through *affekt* rather than a mechanized tempo. Yet making an appropriate tempo choice and harnessing wide tempo swings were of grave concern. With the ever-blossoming ranks of amateur musicians in the Classical Era, clear tempo indications became even more important to the composer; tempo choices could make or break the piece.

Prior to the invention and use of the metronome, composers looked for ways to indicate appropriate tempo parameters. For instance, in Türk's *Klavierschule,* use of a pocket watch to time the length of a work's performance and therefore determine the tempo was suggested. With this method comes problems. The entire work must be performed to determine whether the pacing is accurate. If it was not, the entire work must be re-performed, in the hopes that the adjustment is correct. And could the tempo be remembered tomorrow?!

In his *Versuch*, Quantz goes to great lengths to scientifically determine tempo in relation to the human pulse, note values, and indicated tempo markings. Over the course of eight pages, he takes into consideration various combinations of meters, note values, dance tempi, physical health, demeanor, and passion to provide guidance in calculating tempo.

Needless to say, the invention of the metronome was welcomed by many, including Beethoven. Although it is commonly known as Mälzel's metronome, *The Harvard Dictionary of Music* clarifies that it was actually invented circa 1812 by Dietrich Nikolaus Winkel of Amsterdam. Johannes N. Mälzel copied the device, "adding a scale of tempo divisions, and patented it as a 'metronome.'"[18] It is believed Beethoven was the first composer to use Mälzel's metronome. In 1817, he published metronomic indications for all the movements of his (then) eight symphonies.[19]

The benefit of the metronome is the entirely mechanical ability to mark time with absolute equality. The detriment is the entirely mechanical ability to mark time with absolute equality. If you are old enough to remember the first automated voices on answering machines, you might remember how the syllables were utterly equally mechanized—monotone at its finest! It sounded terribly unnatural and was actually quite difficult to understand. This was not the purpose of the metronome.

Our world is full of predictable patterns that are metronomic on the grand scale with variable changing rhythms of ebb and flow. The natural shifting of the length of days in the seasons, the changing tide tables, the change of one's heartbeat—all represent a mechanized predictability within flexibility of patterns and passions in time. *This* is what Beethoven endorsed. In the Vienna publication, *Allgemeine musikalische Zeitung*, February 14, 1818, Beethoven and Salieri co-signed an endorsement, hailing the benefits of this new tool—an "indispensable aid":[20]

> Mälzel's metronome is here! The usefulness of his invention will be proved more and more; moreover all the composers of Germany, England, France have adopted it; we think it necessary on the strength of our conviction to recommend it also to all novices and students, whether in song, the pianoforte or any other instrument, as a useful, indeed indispensable aid. Through its use they will discover the easiest way to grasp note values and to learn to practice. . . . [that] his feeling for the beat will so quickly be guided and corrected that such things will give him scarcely any more difficulty. We believe that this universally useful invention of Mälzel's must also be promoted on this account.[21]

Over the years, this endorsement has been misconstrued into "turn on the metronome and go!" What is usually ignored are Beethoven's reservations, expressed in the months leading up to this endorsement. In the instructive notes, Beethoven pointed out the limitations on the holograph of his song "Nord oder Süd":

> [The metronome marking should be] 100 according to Mälzel, but this can apply only to the first measures, because feeling also has its tempo; this is, however, not completely expressed in this figure (namely, 100).[22]

Beethoven hailed the arrival of this new tool, yet was aware of its place. So pleased was he that he used it extensively in preparation for an upcoming performance of the Ninth Symphony, providing tempi indications for the performers—fifteen in all! (To read Beethoven's comments, see the companion website, Text 13.1. ▶)

The advent of the metronome was considered a fabulous tool. It provided composers an opportunity never before available: to pinpoint the exact tempo at any given point. But it was *never* intended to pinpoint the speed of an entire section or piece, or to set a single tempo marking in stone for all time. For that would defeat the most important goal of the Classical Era style—to say something and move the listener through *affekt*. Brahms affirmed his agreement on this point years later in a letter to Clara Schumann:

> To give metronome marks immediately seems to me not possible. In any case you must allow the work to lie for at least a year, and examine it periodically. You will then write in new numbers each time and finally have the best solution.[23]

Composers were simply pleased to have a means to better convey the intended *affekt* of the music, an *affekt* that could be attained only at an indicated tempo. Sadly, the metronome has the ability to turn music making into a monotonous sewing machine. Brahms says it best in correspondence to George Henschel, where he sternly objects to rigid adherence to the metronome:

> I think here as well as with other music the metronome is of no value. Those [metronome indications] which can be found in my works—good friends have talked me into putting there, for I myself have never believed that my blood and a mechanical instrument go well together. The so-called "elastic tempo" is moreover not a new invention. "Con discrezione" should be added to that as to many other things.[24]

It is important to recognize that interpretations change with time and may be misunderstood, as is pointed out in *The Harvard Dictionary of Music*: "Unfortunately, the tempi indicated in his [Beethoven's] 'Hammerklavier' Sonata and Ninth Symphony are almost impossibly fast."[25] Classical Era instruments are different from modern instruments in many ways, including a lighter action that allows for greater playing speed. Also, Beethoven was known to be virtuosic and played very fast, or perhaps this was Beethoven's reaction to playing he heard only in his mind as his hearing deteriorated. It may simply be a matter of "in vogue" tastes changing over time. This is all information for wisdom that provides the freedom to make informed decisions.

The Classical Era style projects the composer's musical concept through *affekt*. The indicated metronome marking is one more tool to help the performer understand the composer's intention. When it is all said and done, if the following question can be answered, the performer will have arrived at an appropriate tempo: what is the general intent, the spirit, at the core of the indicated tempo?

INFLUENCES APPLIED

Eighteenth-century piano music was composed with specifically intended *affekt* that required appropriate *tempi*. The score provides many clues to determine acceptable parameters. Visit credible sources; the insight provided will greatly inform concept development. Determine the *affekt* of the piece. Examine inherent tempo clues as they interact with any written indication at the beginning of a section, movement, or piece. Reconcile and merge inherent and indicated tempo directions. Determine how the clues apply to the particular piece at hand.

Determine what tempo choices are possible as a translated style with the capabilities of the piano at hand. Determine what tempo is appropriate in the hall in which the music will be played. The capability of the performer will also be an influencing factor. Remember Quantz's advice to set the tempo by the most difficult passage work and to choose a tempo to enhance expressing the *affekt*.[26] Choosing a tempo that may be executed *well* to convey the desired *affekt* is always preferred.

Use the metronome as a tool to aid in getting at the *affekt*. Look for plausible parameters. There is no absolute right or wrong. The final goal is to play the style on the modern piano at a tempo that strives for truth. The overriding concern should not be about speed, but rather capturing the *essence* of the directions left nearly 300 years ago; communicating the composer's intent with realistic, tasteful playing while developing a personal, authentic, genuine, and artistic performance.

THE LESSON

Play and study Example 13.4 with the following points in mind.

Music Example 13.4. Mozart, London Notebook, KV 1500, mm. 1–8. Copyright (1983) G. Henle Verlag, Munich.

1. There is no indicated tempo.
2. Follow inherent tempo indicators to guide decisions.
   a. ¾ triple meter—more moderate tempo derived from the French minuet
   b. Quarter and eighth notes—execution on the heavier side

Use the quick reference guide on the companion website to summarize. ▶

CHAPTER 14

⌒∿⌒

Final Words

Having unearthed countless eighteenth-century period practice gems, we have now discovered its gestalt. Through examination of historical documents and exploration of the fortepiano, through the search for that which was authentic in the eighteenth century (both notated and unnotated), and the pursuit for means to apply it to modern playing, we have discovered a treasure that is far greater than the sum of these parts: authenticity in our own time.

We have dug up and exposed the transitory nature of this music notational practice: a subjective written language whose meanings change from piece to piece, place to place, person to person, and generation to generation. We have discovered that the eighteenth-century written symbol is *not* doctrine carved in stone with a singular correct answer, but is a description of a sound aesthetic. In spite of its ambiguities, we have come to better understand the language as preserved through primary source literature, scholarly interpretations, and *Urtext* editions.

One final exercise is now suggested to promote reading proficiency. Türk, being the consummate pedagogue, composed *Twelve Pieces for Instruction* at the conclusion of his *Klavierschule*. Take this opportunity to try your hand at applying the principles learned in this book. Play the pieces using your newfound interpretive tools. Quiz yourself. Check your answers against Türk's referenced key. Enjoy your progress as you come closer to truly comprehending, bringing back to life, and making your own this once-forgotten language.

Eighteenth-century music notational language: complete yet imprecise. A complete, objective system with subjective meanings whose main goal is to have *something to say*—to project *affekt*. The discoveries made bring answers. Yet continue digging. Ask questions:

- What did the composer *say*?
- What did the composer *mean*?
- What clues did the composer leave?
- What educated, tasteful, thought-out choices are available?
- Which interpretation works best?
- Am I being flexible enough to believe in more than one interpretation (more than one right answer)?
- What will I say and mean in *my* interpretation?

In faithfully respecting the tradition, we may now do much more. We may express this style on today's instrument. We are called to confront "the way it's always been done" and dare to truly be transformed by our *Discoveries*. Peres Da Costa challenges us to be courageous and bold:

> Indeed, it may be argued that it cannot be achieved at all. However, a willingness to push the boundaries of accepted taste, coupled with guidance from historical sources, will undoubtedly lead to fresh, insightful, and inspired interpretations of music of the old masters.[1]

We must make conscious decisions. Decide how the information discovered may be applied to develop a style that is truly an authentic, genuine, creative, and personal interpretation. Decide which influences will be applied. Listen with a discerning ear. Continuously respond with hands and feet to the feedback from the notation, the instrument, and the ear. This is how determinations are made about what should or should not be translated on the modern piano. Do not be discouraged. Learning to "speak" this new language requires willingness and patience. Over time, decisions will come more readily and more easily.

An exciting possibility: new musical moments from the full continuum of time. Music exists in the universe to be met midstream, captured, and made our own, as well notated by W. A. Mozart in Example 14.1.

Music Example 14.1. Riemann, 1912.[2]

Seize the opportunity to use these tools to get at an eighteenth-century musical sound aesthetic. Enjoy each gem—your own personal treasure trove; your *Discoveries from the Fortepiano* to perform on the modern piano!

Use the companion website quick reference guide to summarize. ⏵

NOTES

CHAPTER 1

1. *BBC News* website (news.bbc.co.uk/2/hi/health/3858087.stm, 2012).
2. *Live Science* website (http://www.livescience.com/203-maggots-leeches-medicine.html, 2012).
3. Thurston Dart, *The Interpretation of Music* (New York: Harper & Row, 1963), 76–77.
4. Ibid., 167.
5. *US History* website (www.ushistory.org/documents/pledge.htm, 2012).
6. *United States Mint* website (www.usmint.gov/about_the_mint/fun_facts/?action+fun_facts5, 2012).
7. C. P. E. Bach, *Essay on the True Art of Playing Keyboard Instruments*, (Leipzig: Schwickert, 1753, 1762), translated by William J. Mitchell. (W. W. Norton and Company, Inc., 1949, renewed © 1976 by Alice L. Mitchell.), 29.
8. Barry Cooper, ed., *The Thirty-five Piano Sonatas of Beethoven*, Vol. I (Associated Board of the Royal Schools of Music, 2007), 17.
9. *New Oxford American Dictionary*, 3rd ed. (Oxford University Press, 2010), 108.
10. Sadie, Stanley, ed. *The New Grove Dictionary of Music and Musicians*, 2nd ed., vol. 26 (Oxford University Press, 2004), 163–64.
11. Bruce Haynes, *The End of Early Music* (New York: Oxford University Press, 2007), 10. By permission of Oxford University Press, USA.
12. Richard Taruskin, ed., *Text and Act: Essays on Music Performance* (Oxford University Press, 1995), 79.
13. Johann Mattheson, *Der Vollkommene Capellmeister* (Hamburg, 1739), as translated by Robin Stowell in *The Early Violin and Viola*, (Cambridge, 2001), as found in Haynes, *The End of Early Music*, 24. By permission of Oxford University Press, USA.
14. Bart van Oort, "To Speak or Sing" (lecture presented, The Geske Lectures, Hixson-Lied College of Fine and Performing Arts, the University of Nebraska–Lincoln, 2007), 6–7.
15. Haynes, *The End of Early Music*, 152. By permission of Oxford University Press, USA.
16. Dart, *The Interpretation of Music*, 29–30.
17. Harold Schonberg, *The Great Pianists from Mozart to the Present* (Simon and Schuster, 1963), 35.
18. Theodor von Frimmel, *Beethoven-Studien*, 2 volumes (Munich: Müller, 1905, 1906), as translated by William S. Newman in *Beethoven on Beethoven: Playing His Piano Music His Way* (W. W. Norton and Company, Inc., 1988), 50.

19. Sandra Rosenblum, *Performance Practices in Classic Piano Music* (Indiana University Press), 1988, 34.

20. Newman, *Beethoven on Beethoven: Playing His Piano Music His Way,* 29.

21. Leopold Mozart, *A Treatise on the Fundamental Principles of Violin Playing* (Augsburg, 1756, 1787), as translated by Editha Knocker (London, Oxford University Press, 1948), 255–256.

22. Daniel Gottlob Türk, *Klavierschule* (1789, Leipzig and Halle), as translated by Raymond H. Haggh (University of Nebraska Press, 1982), 6, with permission from the author's daughter, Barbara Haggh-Huglo.

23. *New Oxford American Dictionary*, 981.

24. Sadie, *The New Grove Dictionary of Music and Musicians*, vol. 26, 163.

25. Sadie, *The New Grove Dictionary of Music and Musicians*, vol. 2, 387, 391.

26. Ibid., 388.

27. Michael Cole, *The Pianoforte in the Classical Era* (Oxford University Press, 1998), 150. By permission of Oxford University Press.

28. Sadie, *The New Grove Dictionary of Music and Musicians*, vol. 13, 628.

29. Ibid., 710–711.

30. Sadie, *The New Grove Dictionary of Music and Musicians*, vol. 17, 270.

31. Sadie, *The New Grove Dictionary of Music and Musicians*, vol. 20, 657–658.

32. Cole, *The Pianoforte in the Classical Era,* 150. By permission of Oxford University Press, USA.

33. Sadie, *The New Grove Dictionary of Music and Musicians*, vol. 25, 907–908.

34. Dart, *The Interpretation of Music,* 37.

35. Cole, *The Pianoforte in the Classical Era,* 198. By permission of Oxford University Press, USA.

36. Rosenblum, *Performance Practices in Classic Piano Music,* 6.

37. James Parakilas, *Piano Roles* (Yale University Press, 2001), 17–18.

38. Katalin Komlós, "After Mozart: The Viennese Piano Scene in the 1790's," paper presented at Early Music Days, Esterhazy Castle, June 28, 2013, 1.

39. Bach, *Essay,* 36.

40. J. A. Hiller, *Wöchentliche Nachrichten und Anmerkungen die Musik betreffend* (Leipzig, 1769), as translated by Cole in *The Pianoforte in the Classical Era,* 335. By permission of Oxford University Press.

41. Bach, *Essay,* 172.

42. Ibid., 172, 369.

43. Cole, *The Pianoforte in the Classical Era,* 2. By permission of Oxford University Press.

44. Ibid., 178.

45. Schonberg, *The Great Pianists from Mozart to the Present,* 25.

46. Rosenblum, *Performance Practices in Classic Piano Music,* 49–50.

47. Cole, *The Pianoforte in the Classical Era,* 188. By permission of Oxford University Press.

48. Rosenblum, *Performance Practices in Classic Piano Music,* 38.

49. Haynes, *The End of Early Music,* 48. By permission of Oxford University Press, USA.

50. van Oort, "To Speak or Sing," 13–14.

51. Haynes, *The End of Early Music,* 103. By permission of Oxford University Press, USA.

52. van Oort, "To Speak or Sing," 7–8.

53. Türk, *Klavierschule,* 338.

54. Ibid., 329.
55. Dart, *The Interpretation of Music*, 12.
56. Haynes, *The End of Early Music*, 103. By permission of Oxford University Press, USA.
57. Türk, *Klavierschule*, 323.
58. Haynes, *The End of Early Music*, 105. By permission of Oxford University Press, USA.
59. Neal Peres Da Costa, *Off the Record* (Oxford University Press, 2012) , xxiii.
60. Ibid., xvi.
61. van Oort, "To Speak or Sing," 7–8.
62. Dart, *The Interpretation of Music*, 13–14.
63. Emily Anderson, trans. and ed., *The Letters of Beethoven, 3 volumes* (London: Macmillan, 1961), as discovered in Rosenblum, *Performance Practices in Classic Piano Music*, 17.
64. Schulz, "Symphonie," in Sulzer, Johann Georg *[Allgemeine] Theorie II* (1771–1774), as translated by Rosenblum, *Performance Practices in Classic Piano Music*, 16.
65. Dart, *The Interpretation of Music*, 15.
66. Cooper, *The Thirty-five Piano Sonatas of Beethoven*, Vol. 1, 10.
67. Malcolm Bilson, "Pianos in Mozart's Time (Revisited)" (*Piano Quarterly*, 96: 29–31, Summer 1974), 31.
68. Newman, *Beethoven on Beethoven: Playing His Piano Music His Way*, 47.
69. Ibid.
70. van Oort, "To Speak or Sing," 8.
71. Dart, *The Interpretation of Music*, 167–168.
72. Andrew Willis, *Free Variation of Repeated Passages in Mozart's Keyboard Music*, (DMA Dissertation, Cornell University Press, 1994), 1.
73. Dart, *The Interpretation of Music*, 13.
74. Newman, *Beethoven on Beethoven: Playing His Piano Music His Way*, 17.
75. Ibid., 30.
76. Reader's Digest Association, *The Reader's Digest Great Encyclopedic Dictionary Including Funk & Wagnalls Standard College Dictionary* (Reader's Digest Association, Inc., 1966), 553, 724.
77. *New Oxford American Dictionary*, 719, 932.

CHAPTER 2

1. Türk, *Klavierschule*, 337.
2. Bach, *Essay,* 148.
3. C. F. Pohl, "Jahresberichten des Wiever Conservatoriums" (1869–1870), later with commentary by George Schünemann, *Gesellschaft der Musikfreunde in Wien* (Beethoven-Jahrbuch, 1939), as discovered in Paul Badura-Skoda, ed., *Carl Czerny on the Proper Performance of All Beethoven's Works for Piano "Reminiscences of Beethoven"* and chapter II and III from vol. IV of the *"Complete Theoretical and Practical Piano Forte School Op. 50"* (European Music Distribution Corporation, 1970), 5.
4. Franz Wegeler, and Ferdinand Ries, *Beethoven Remembered: The Biographical Notes of Franz Wegeler and Ferdinand Ries*, as discovered in O. G. Sonneck, ed., *Beethoven: Impressions by His Contemporaries*, 52.
5. Haynes, *The End of Early Music*, 8. By permission of Oxford University Press, USA.
6. Ibid.,135.

7. Heinrich Christoph Koch, *Introductory Essay on Composition, Vol. II, Part I* (1787), as translated by Nancy Kavoleff Baker in Nancy K. Baker and Thomas Christensen, eds., *Aesthetics and the Art of Musical Composition in the German Enlightenment* (Cambridge University Press. 1995), 155–156.

8. *New Oxford American Dictionary*, 26.

9. Don Michael Randel, ed., *The Harvard Dictionary of Music*, 4th ed. (Harvard University Press, 2003) , 17.

10. Ibid., 341.

11. Ibid., 290-91.

12. Willi Apel, ed., *The Harvard Dictionary of Music*, 2nd rev. and enlarged ed. (Harvard University Press, 1969), 296, 288.

13. Don Michael Randel, ed., *The Harvard Dictionary of Music*, 846.

14. Quantz, *On Playing the Flute*, 116.

15. Türk, *Klavierschule*, 337.

16. Ibid.

17. Malcolm Bilson and Bart van Oort, The Art of the Fortepiano (lectures and master classes, Middelburg, The Netherlands, 2008).

18. J. L. Akrill, ed., *The New Aristotle* (Princeton University Press, 1987), 320.

19. Johann Georg Sulzer, *General Theory of the Fine Arts, Part I, Chapter III: Musical Issues,* translated by Thomas Christensen in Baker and Christensen, *Aesthetics and the Art of Musical Composition in the German Enlightenment*, 103.

20. Türk, *Klavierschule*, 391, 393–396.

21. Johann Phillipp Kirnberger, *The Art of Strict Musical Composition* (Berlin, 1771), translated by David Beach and Jurgen Thym, New Haven and London: Yale University Press, 1982, 400.

22. Ibid.

23. Türk, *Klavierschule*, 349.

24. Kirnberger, *The Art of Strict Musical Composition*, 400.

25. Ibid., 377.

26. Türk, *Klavierschule*, 348.

27. Johann George Sulzer, "Ausdruck," *[Allgemeine]Theorie der Schönen Künste*, translated by Beach and Thym in Kirnberger, *The Art of Strict Musical Composition*, 377.

28. Kirnberger, *The Art of Strict Musical Composition*, 382.

29. Türk, *Klavierschule*, 111.

30. Ibid., 391, 393–396.

31. Kirnberger, *The Art of Strict Musical Composition*, 328.

32. Ibid., 323–24.

33. Ibid., 337.

34. Haynes, *The End of Early Music*, 55. By permission of Oxford University Press, USA.

35. Kirnberger, *The Art of Strict Musical Composition*, 340.

36. Ibid., 340–41.

37. Rita Steblin, *A History of Key Characteristics in the Eighteenth and Early Nineteenth Centuries* (UMI Research Press, 1983), 50.

38. Charles Rosen, *The Classical Style: Haydn, Mozart, Beethoven* (New York: W. W. Norton and Company, 1972), 28.

39. Türk, *Klavierschule*, 337.

40. Georg Joseph Vogler, *Betrachtungen der Mannheimer Tonschule*, 3 vols. (Mannheim, Germany, 1778-1781), Facsimile reprinting, 4 vols. (Hildesheim,

Germany, and New York: Georg Olms, 1974), as translated by Steblin in *A History of Key Characteristics in Eighteenth and Early Nineteenth Centuries*, 222.

41. J. J. H. Ribock, "Über Musik; an Flötenlieber Insonderheit," Cramer's *Magazin der Musik*, as translated by Steblin in *A History of Key Characteristics in Eighteenth and Early Nineteenth Centuries*, 228.

42. C. F. D. Schubart, *Ideen zu einer Ästhetik der Tonkunst*, edited by Ludwig Schubart (Vienna: Degen, 1806), reprint, edited by P. A. Merbach (Leipzig: Wolkenwanderer-Verlag, 1924), as translated by Steblin in *A History of Key Characteristics in Eighteenth and Early Nineteenth Centuries*, 228.

43. Ibid., 232.

44. William Gardiner, ed., *The Life of Haydn, by Marie Henri Beyle [L. A. C. Bombet]*, as translated by Rev. C. Berry (London), reprint (Boston: J. H. Wilkins & R. B. Carter, 1839), as discovered in Steblin, *A History of Key Characteristics in Eighteenth and Early Nineteenth Centuries*, 232.

45. Vogler, *Betrachtungen der Mannheimer Tonschule*, 3 vols., as translated by Steblin in *A History of Key Characteristics in Eighteenth and Early Nineteenth Centuries*, 238.

46. Anonymous, "That Keys Influence Musical Thinking," *The Spectator*, as translated by Steblin in *A History of Key Characteristics in Eighteenth and Early Nineteenth Centuries*, 243.

47. Schubart, *Ideen zu einer Ästhetik der Tonkunst*, as translated by Steblin in *A History of Key Characteristics in Eighteenth and Early Nineteenth Centuries*, 245.

48. Ribock, "Über Musik; an Flötenlieber Insonderheit," as translated by Steblin in *A History of Key Characteristics in Eighteenth and Early Nineteenth Centuries*, 245.

49. E. T. A. Hoffmann, Review of *Christus am Ölberg*, by Ludwig van Beethoven, *Allegmeine Musikalische Zeitung* (Leipzig), as discovered in Steblin, *A History of Key Characteristics in Eighteenth and Early Nineteenth Centuries*, 250.

50. Schubart, *Ideen zu einer Ästhetik der Tonkunst*, as translated by Steblin in *A History of Key Characteristics in Eighteenth and Early Nineteenth Centuries*, 252.

51. Ribock, "Über Musik; an Flötenlieber Insonderheit," as translated by Steblin in *A History of Key Characteristics in Eighteenth and Early Nineteenth Centuries*, 252.

52. Ibid., 257.

53. Johann Mattheson, *Das Neu-eröffnete Orchestre*, as translated by Steblin in *A History of Key Characteristics in Eighteenth and Early Nineteenth Centuries*, 265.

54. Quantz, *On Playing the Flute*, 164.

55. Schubart, *Ideen zu einer Ästhetik der Tonkunst*, as translated by Steblin in *A History of Key Characteristics in Eighteenth and Early Nineteenth Centuries*, 272.

56. Vogler, "Ausdruck, (musikalisch)," *Deutsche Encyclopädie, oder Allgemeines Real-Wörterbuch aller Künste und Wissenschaften*, as translated by Steblin in *A History of Key Characteristics in Eighteenth and Early Nineteenth Centuries*, 274.

57. Ribock, "Über Musik; an Flötenlieber Insonderheit," as translated by Steblin in *A History of Key Characteristics in Eighteenth and Early Nineteenth Centuries*, 274.

58. Schubart, *Ideen zu einer Ästhetik der Tonkunst*, as translated by Steblin in *A History of Key Characteristics in Eighteenth and Early Nineteenth Centuries*, 278.

59. Ribock, "Über Musik; an Flötenlieber Insonderheit," as translated by Steblin in *A History of Key Characteristics in Eighteenth and Early Nineteenth Centuries*, 278.

60. Schubart, *Ideen zu einer Ästhetik der Tonkunst*, as translated by Steblin in *A History of Key Characteristics in Eighteenth and Early Nineteenth Centuries*, 281.

61. Vogler, "Ausdruck, (musikalisch)," *Deutsche Encyclopädie, oder Allgemeines Real-Wörterbuch aller Künste und Wissenschaften*, as translated by Steblin in *A History of Key Characteristics in Eighteenth and Early Nineteenth Centuries*, 281.

62. Justin Heinrich Knecht, *Gemeinnützliches Elementarwerk der Harmonie und des Generalbasses*, vol. I (Augsburg, Germany: Julius Wilhelm Hamm), as translated by Steblin in *A History of Key Characteristics in Eighteenth and Early Nineteenth Centuries*, 281.

63. Schubart, *Ideen zu einer Ästhetik der Tonkunst*, as translated by Steblin in *A History of Key Characteristics in Eighteenth and Early Nineteenth Centuries*, 286.

64. Ribock,"Über Musik; an Flötenlieber Insonderheit," as translated by Steblin in *A History of Key Characteristics in Eighteenth and Early Nineteenth Centuries*, 289.

65. Quantz, *On Playing the Flute*, 164.

66. Schubart, *Ideen zu einer Ästhetik der Tonkunst*, as translated by Steblin in *A History of Key Characteristics in Eighteenth and Early Nineteenth Centuries*, 296.

67. Ribock,"Über Musik; an Flötenlieber Insonderheit," as translated by Steblin in *A History of Key Characteristics in Eighteenth and Early Nineteenth Centuries*, 296.

68. Schubart, *Ideen zu einer Ästhetik der Tonkunst*, as translated by Steblin in *A History of Key Characteristics in Eighteenth and Early Nineteenth Centuries*, 301.

69. Schubart, *Ideen zu einer Ästhetik der Tonkunst*, as translated by Steblin in *A History of Key Characteristics in Eighteenth and Early Nineteenth Centuries*, 303.

70. Ribock, "Über Musik; an Flötenlieber Insonderheit," as translated by Steblin in *A History of Key Characteristics in Eighteenth and Early Nineteenth Centuries*, 306.

71. Johann Mattheson, *Das Neu-eröffnete Orchestre*, Hamburg: der Autor und Benjamin Schiller Wittwe (der Autor, 1720), as translated by Steblin in *A History of Key Characteristics in Eighteenth and Early Nineteenth Centuries*, 51–52.

72. Kirnberger, *The Art of Strict Musical Composition*, 353–54.

73. Bach, *Essay*, 163.

74. Kirnberger, *The Art of Strict Musical Composition*, 353.

75. Ibid., 373, 374.

76. Bach, *Essay*, 163.

77. Kirnberger, *The Art of Strict Musical Composition*, 374.

78. Türk, *Klavierschule*, 321.

79. Bilson and van Oort, The Art of the Fortepiano, 2008.

80. Tilman Showroneck, *Beethoven the Pianist* (New York: Cambridge University Press, 2010), 120–121.

81. Quantz, *On Playing the Flute*, 87.

82. Ibid., 127.

83. Ibid., 118.

84. Newman, *Beethoven on Beethoven: Playing His Piano Music His Way*, 122.

CHAPTER 3

1. Robert O. Gjerdingen, *Music in the Galant Style* (New York: Oxford University Press, 2007), 10–15.

2. Ibid., 4.

3. Bach, *Essay*, 163.

4. Gjerdingen, *Music in the Galant Style*, 77–88.

5. Türk, *Klavierschule*, 323.

6. Willis, *Free Variation of Repeated Passages in Mozart's Keyboard Music*, 12.

7. Haynes, *The End of Early Music*, 36. By permission of Oxford University Press, USA.

8. Ibid.

9. Newman, *Beethoven on Beethoven: Playing His Piano Music His Way*, 184-85.

10. Bart van Oort, Westfield International Fortepiano Academy (lectures and master classes, Cornell University, Ithaca, NY, August 7–13, 2011).

11. Türk, *Klavierschule*, 352.

12. Apel, *The Harvard Dictionary of Music*, 26.

13. Randel, *The Harvard Dictionary of Music*, 31.

14. Apel, *Harvard Dictionary of Music*, 26.

15. Peres Da Costa, *Off the Record*, 46.

16. Ibid., 43–44.

17. Bach, *Essay*, 159–60.

18. Türk, *Klavierschule*, 269.

19. Bach, *Essay*, 159-60.

20. Türk, *Klavierschule*, 282–83.

21. Bilson, "Early Music Days," 2013.

22. Ibid.

23. Bilson and van Oort, "The Art of the Fortepiano."

24. Bart van Oort, Fortepiano at Villa Bossi (lectures and master classes, Associazione Musicale, Villa Bossi, Italy, June 23–27, 2010).

CHAPTER 4

1. Türk, *Klavierschule*, 18.

2. Ibid., 321.

3. Quantz, *On Playing the Flute*, 120.

4. Bach, *Essay*, 30.

5. Ibid.

6. Badura-Skoda, ed., *Carl Czerny on the Proper Performance of All Beethoven's Works for Piano*, 15.

7. Türk, *Klavierschule*, 30.

8. Carl Czerny, *Letter to a Young Lady on the Art of Playing the Pianoforte* (Boston: Oliver Ditson & Co.,1871), as translated by James Alexander Hamilton (Kessinger Publishing, LLC, 2009), 5–6.

9. Badura-Skoda, ed., *Carl Czerny on the Proper Performance of All Beethoven's Works for Piano*, 5.

10. van Oort, Westfield International Fortepiano Academy.

11. Bach, *Essay*, 42–43.

12. Badura-Skoda, ed., *Carl Czerny in the Proper Performance of All Beethoven's Works for Piano*, 16.

13. Elliot Forbes ed., *Thayer's Life of Beethoven* (Princeton: Princeton University Press, 1970), as discovered in Newman, *Beethoven on Beethoven: Playing His Piano Music His Way*, 278.

14. Anonymous review, *Harmonicon VII [October 1829]: A Letter to a Young Piano Forte Player*, Printed for the Benefit of the Spanish Refugees (London: Hailes, 1829), as discovered in Rosenblum, *Performance Practices in Classic Piano Music*, 195.

15. Bach, *Essay*, 41.

16. Ibid., 49.

17. Ibid., 12.

18. Ibid., 38.

19. Muzio Clementi, *Introduction to the Art of Playing on the Piano Forte* (London: Clementi, Banger, Hyde, Collard & David, 1801), reprinted (Da Capo Press, 1974), 14.
20. Newman, *Beethoven on Beethoven: Playing His Piano Music His Way*, 286.
21. Ibid.
22. Türk, *Klavierschule*, 130.
23. Bilson and van Oort, The Art of the Fortepiano.
24. Jophann Baptist Cramer, *21 Etüden für Klavier: Nach dem Handexemplar Beethovens aus dem Besitz Anton Schindlers*, ed. Hans Kann (Vienna: Universal, 1974), as translated by Rosenblum in *Performance Practices in Classic Piano Music*, 200.
25. Anonymous review, *Harmonicon VII [October 1829]: A Letter to a Young Piano Forte Player*, as discovered in Rosenblum, *Performance Practices in Classic Piano Music*, 195.
26. Bilson and van Oort, The Art of the Fortepiano.
27. Ibid.
28. Rosenblum, *Performance Practices in Classic Piano Music*, 191.
29. van Oort, Westfield International Fortepiano Academy.
30. Clementi, *Introduction to the Art of Playing on the Piano Forte*, 14.

CHAPTER 5

1. van Oort, "To Speak or Sing," 16.
2. Howard Ferguson, *Keyboard Interpretation from the 14th to the 19th Century*, (New York: Oxford University Press, 1987), 85.
3. Ibid.
4. Kirnberger, *The Art of Strict Musical Composition*, 375–376.
5. Ibid., 377.
6. Ibid., 376.
7. Ernst-Günther Heinemann, ed., *Sechs Sonatinen by Clementi, op. 36* (G. Henle Verlag, Munich, 2011), Preface.
8. Türk, *Klavierschule*, 349.
9. L. Mozart, *A Treatise on the Fundamental Principles of Violin Playing*, 219.
10. Ibid.
11. Quantz, *On Playing the Flute*, 123.
12. Türk, *Klavierschule*, 325.
13. Ibid.
14. Ibid., 326.
15. Clive Brown, *Classical and Romantic Performance Practice, 1750–1900* (New York: Oxford University Press, 1999), 16.
16. Ibid., 14.
17. *New Oxford American Dictionary*, 1497.
18. Haynes, *The End of Early Music*, 8. By permission of Oxford University Press, USA.
19. Ibid., 48. By permission of Oxford University Press, USA.
20. Türk, *Klavierschule*, 334.
21. van Oort, "To Speak or Sing," 9.
22. Heinrich Christoph Koch, *Musikalisches Lexikon, Article: 'Accent'* (Frankfurt, Germany), as translated by Clive Brown in *Classical and Romantic Performance Practice, 1750–1900*, 29.
23. Haynes, *The End of Early Music*, 91. By permission of Oxford University Press, USA.

24. Kirnberger, *The Art of Strict Musical Composition*, 409.

25. Randel, *The Harvard Dictionary of Music*, 947.

26. Charles Rosen, *The Classical Style: Haydn, Mozart, Beethoven* (W. W. Norton and Company: New York, 1972), 57.

27. Kirnberger, *The Art of Strict Musical Composition*, 408.

28. William E. Caplin, *The Classical Form: A Theory of Formal Function for the Instrumental Music of Haydn, Mozart, and Beethoven* (New York: Oxford University Press, 1998), 59.

29. Ibid., 65.

30. van Oort, Westfield International Fortepiano Academy.

31. Türk, *Klavierschule*, 345.

32. Quantz, *On Playing the Flute*, 133.

33. Bach, *Essay*, 153.

34. Türk, *Klavierschule*, 79.

35. Dart, *The Interpretation of Music*, 13–14.

36. L. Mozart, *A Treatise on the Fundamental Principles of Violin Playing*, 41–42.

37. Quantz, *On Playing the Flute*, 133.

38. L. Mozart, *A Treatise on the Fundamental Principles of Violin Playing*, 41.

39. Tilman Skowroneck, *Beethoven the Pianist* (New York: Cambridge University Press, 120–121.

40. Howard Mayer Brown and Stanley Sadie, *Performance Practice: Music after 1600* (New York: W. W. Norton and Company, 1989), 231.

41. Bilson and van Oort, The Art of the Fortepiano.

CHAPTER 6

1. Apel, *Harvard Dictionary of Music*, 303.

2. Audun Ravnan, A Statistical Study of Dynamic Indications in the Piano Sonatas by Haydn, Mozart, and Beethoven (unpublished paper), as discovered in Rosenblum, *Performance Practices in Classic Piano Music*, 60.

3. Ibid.

4. Ibid.

5. Rosenblum, *Performance Practices in Classic Piano Music*, 60–61.

6. Bach, *Essay*, 162.

7. Türk, *Klavierschule*, 112–13.

8. Rosenblum, *Performance Practices in Classic Piano Music*, 58.

9. Bach, *Essay*, 163.

10. Quantz, *On Playing the Flute*, 165.

11. Türk, *Klavierschule*, 111.

12. Bach, *Essay*, 163.

13. C. F. D. Schubart, *Ideen zu einer Ästhetik der Tonkunst* (Vienna, 1806, written 1784–5), as translated by Eugene K. Wolf in Neal Zaslaw, ed., *The Classical Era from the 1740s to the End of the 18th Century* (Englewood Cliffs, NJ: Prentice Hall, 1989), 228.

14. Apel, *Harvard Dictionary of Music*, 303.

15. Rosenblum, *Performance Practices in Classic Piano Music*, 69.

16. Ibid., 70.

17. P. A. Scholes, ed., *Dr. Burney's Musical Tours in Europe* (Oxford University Press), as discovered in Zaslaw, *The Classical Era from the 1740s to the End of the 18th Century,* 230.

CHAPTER 7

1. Rosenblum, *Performance Practices in Classic Piano Music*, 86–87.
2. Türk, *Klavierschule*, 112.
3. Ibid., 119.
4. van Oort, "To Speak or Sing," 15.
5. Türk, *Klavierschule*, 359.
6. Ibid.
7. Hugo Riemann, ed., Alexander Wheelock Thayer, *Ludwig van Beethovens Leben*, 5 vols., trans. by Hermann Dieters [Leipzig: Breitkopf and Härtel, 1907], as discovered in George Barth, *The Pianist as Orator: Beethoven and the Transformation of Keyboard Style* (Ithaca: Cornell University Press, 1992), 10.
8. Türk, *Klavierschule*, 363.
9. Bach, *Essay*, 162.
10. Reimann, ed. Alexander Wheelock Thayer, *Ludwig van Beethovens Leben*, 5 vols., tran. Hermann Dieters, ed. Hugo Riemann [Leipzig: Breitkopf and Härtel, 1907], as discovered in Barth, *The Pianist as Orator: Beethoven and the Transformation of Keyboard Style* (Ithaca: Cornell University Press, 1992), 10.
11. Türk, *Klavierschule*, 360.
12. Bach, *Essay*, 161.
13. Bilson, "Pianos in Mozart's Time (Revisited)," 31.

CHAPTER 8

1. Schonberg, *The Great Pianists from Mozart to the Present*, 87.
2. Rosenblum, *Performance Practices in Classic Piano Music*, 152.
3. Theodor von Frimmel, *Beethoven-Studien*, 2 vols. (Munich, Müller, 1906, 1906), II. This sketch was sold at the Liepmannssohn auction in May 1904, as translated by Rosenblum in *Performance Practices in Classic Piano Music*, 152.
4. Rosenblum, *Performance Practices in Classic Piano Music*, 158.
5. Haynes, *The End of Early Music*, 193. By permission of Oxford University Press, USA.
6. Ibid., 195. By permission of Oxford University Press, USA.
7. Rosenblum, *Performance Practices in Classic Piano Music*, 160.
8. L. Mozart, *A Treatise on the Fundamental Principles of Violin Playing*, 123–24.
9. Emily Anderson, trans. and ed., *The Letters of Beethoven*, 3 volumes, London: Macmillan, discovered in Rosenblum, *Performance Practices in Classic Piano Music*, 17.
10. Rosenblum, *Performance Practices in Classic Piano Music*, 174.
11. Ibid., 158–59.
12. van Oort, Westfield International Fortepiano Academy.
13. Bach, *Essay*, 154–155.
14. Türk, *Klavierschule*, 251–252.
15. Ibid., 331.
16. L. Mozart, *A Treatise on the Fundamental Principles of Violin Playing*, 215.
17. Türk, *Klavierschule*, 344.
18. Johann Baptist Cramer, *21 Etüden für Klavier: Nach dem Handexemplar Beethovens aud dem Besitz*, as translated by Rosenblum, *Performance Practices in Classic Piano Music*, 200.
19. Bach, *Essay*, 156.

20. Heinrich Christoph Koch, *Musikalisches Lexikon* (Frankfurt: Hermann dem jüngern, 1802; facs., Hildesheim, Germany: Olms, 1964) col. 1598, as translated by Sandra Rosenblum in *Performance Practices in Classic Piano Music*, 156.

21. Rosenblum, *Performance Practices in Classic Piano Music*, 156.

22. Newman, *Beethoven on Beethoven: Playing His Piano Music His Way*, 185.

23. Ibid.

24. Haynes, *The End of Early Music*, 194. By permission of Oxford University Press, USA.

CHAPTER 9

1. Bach, *Essay*, 154.

2. Rosenblum, *Performance Practices in Classic Piano Music*, 183.

3. Dart, *The Interpretation of Music*, 101.

4. Rosenblum, *Performance Practices in Classic Piano Music*, 183–87.

5. Haynes, *The End of Early Music*, 106. By permission of Oxford University Press, USA.

6. Bach, *Essay*, 156.

7. Ibid., 154.

8. Ibid., 156.

CHAPTER 10

1. Quantz, *On Playing the Flute*, 98.

2. Bach, *Essay*, 30.

3. Ibid., 79.

4. Ibid., 82.

5. Quantz, *On Playing the Flute*, 91.

6. Bach, *Essay*, 83.

7. Ibid.

8. Bach, *Essay*, 99.

9. Ibid., 110–111.

10. Türk, *Klavierschule*, 247.

11. van Oort, Westfield International Fortepiano Academy.

12. Bach, *Essay*, 102.

13. Türk, *Klavierschule*, 111.

14. Bach, *Essay*, 87.

15. Quantz, *On Playing the Flute*, 91.

16. Ibid.

17. Bach, *Essay*, 87; Türk, *Klavierschule*, 209.

18. Bach, *Essay*, 90.

19. Haynes, *The End of Early Music*, 106. By permission of Oxford University Press, USA.

20. Bach, *Essay*, 112.

21. Ibid.

22. Ibid., 136–137.

23. Quantz, *On Playing the Flute*, 160.

24. Bach, *Essay*, 38–39.

25. Ibid., 86.

26. Bach, *Essay*, 137.

CHAPTER 11

1. Haynes, *The End of Early Music*, 207. By permission of Oxford University Press, USA.
2. L. Mozart, *A Treatise on the Fundamental Principles of Violin Playing*, 180.
3. Willis, *Free Variations of Repeated Passages in Mozart's Keyboard Music*, 32.
4. Gjerdingen, *Music in the Galant Style*, 51.
5. *New Oxford American Dictionary*, 356.
6. Türk, *Klavierschule*, 312.
7. Bach, *Essay*, 165–166.
8. Cooper, *The Thirty-five Piano Sonatas of Beethoven*, vol. 1, 14.
9. Quantz, *On Playing the Flute*, 69–70.
10. André Ernest Modeste Grétry, *Mémoires, ou essai sur la musique* (1789), as translated by Rita Benton in *Nicolas Joseph Hüllmandel and French Instrumental Music in the Second Half of the Eighteenth Century* (Unpublished Ph. D. dissertation, State University of Iowa, 1961), as discovered in William Newman, *The Sonata in the Classic Era*, 3rd. ed. (W. W. Norton and Company, Inc., 1983), 654.
11. Rosen, *The Classical Style: Haydn, Mozart, Beethoven*, 100–101.
12. Rosenblum, *Performing Practices in Classic Piano Music*, 72.
13. Rosen, *The Classical Style: Haydn, Mozart, Beethoven*, 101.
14. Türk, *Klavierschule*, 313.
15. Willis, *Free Variations of Repeated Passages in Mozart's Keyboard Music*, 34–37.
16. Gjerdingen, *Music in the Galant Style*, 51.
17. Bach, *Essay*, 165.
18. Türk, *Klavierschule*, 313.
19. Quantz, *On Playing the Flute*, 120.

CHAPTER 12

1. Cole, *The Pianoforte in the Classical Era*, 166. By permission of Oxford University Press, USA.
2. Ibid., 211.
3. Ibid., 166.
4. Ibid., 225.

CHAPTER 13

1. Randel, *The Harvard Dictionary of Music*, 643, 647.
2. Türk, *Klavierschule*, 111.
3. Apel, *Harvard Dictionary of Music*, 837.
4. L. Mozart, *A Treatise on the Fundamental Principles of Violin Playing*, 30.
5. Quantz, *On Playing the Flute*, 129.
6. Türk, *Klavierschule*, 105.
7. Daniel Gottlob Türk, *Klavierschule, oder Anweisung zum Klavierspielen für Lehrer und Lernende* (Leipzig and Halle: Scwickert; Hemmerde und Schwetschke, 1802), as translated in Rosenblum, *Performance Practices in Classic Piano Music*, 318–319.
8. Cooper, *The Thirty-five Piano Sonatas of Beethoven*, vol. 1, 14.
9. Türk, *Klavierschule*, 106, 113.
10. Newman, *Beethoven on Beethoven: Playing His Piano Music His Way*, 108.
11. Türk, *Klavierschule*, 107.

12. Schulz, "Takt," in Sulzer, *Allgemeine Theorie II*, as translated by Susan Rosenblum in *Performance Practices in Classic Piano Music*, 307.
13. Ibid.
14. Bach, *Essay*, 151.
15. Ibid.
16. Türk, *Klavierschule*, 105.
17. Quantz, *On Playing the Flute*, 130–31.
18. Randel, *The Harvard Dictionary of Music*, 507.
19. Apel, *Harvard Dictionary of Music*, 524.
20. Emerich Kastner, ed., *Ludwig van Beethoven's sämtliche Briefe* (Tutzing: Hans Schneider, 1975), as discovered in Barth, *The Pianist as Orator*, 49–50.
21. Ibid.
22. Hugo Riemann, ed., Alexander Wheelock Thayer, *Ludwig van Beethovens Leben*, trans. by Hermann Dieters [Leipzig: Breitkopf and Härtel, 1907], as discovered in George Barth, *The Pianist as Orator: Beethoven and the Transformation of Keyboard Style* (Cornell University Press, 1992), 51.
23. Letter from Brahms to Clara Schumann, Feb. 1878, as translated in *The New Grove Dictionary of Music and Musicians*, 2nd ed., vol. 25, 274–275.
24. Location of original letter unknown (Maggs Brothers, http://www.maggs.com, catalogue 504, item 835, Summer 1928), as discovered in George S. Bozarth, *Johannes Brahms and George Henschel: An Enduring Friendship* (Harmonie Park Press, 2008), 132.
25. Apel, *The Harvard Dictionary of Music*, 524.
26. Quantz, *On Playing the Flute*, 130–131.
27. *UNL Libraries* website. Sébastien de Brossard, *A musical dictionary; being a collection of terms and characters, as well ancient as modern; including the historical, theoretical, and practical parts of music: As also, an Explanation of some Parts of the Doctrine of the Ancient; Interspersed With Remarks on their Method and Practice, and curious Observations on the Phoenomena of Sound Mathematically considered, As it's Relations and Proportions constitute Intervals, And those again Concords and Discords. The whole carefully abstracted from the best authors in Greek, Latin, Italian, French, and English Languages. By James Grassineau*, (Gent: London, 1740), <http://0-find.galegroup.com.library.unl.edu/ecco/infomark.do?&source=gale&prodId=ECCO&userGrouuserG=linc74325&tabID=T001&docId=CW106300946&type=multipage&contentSet=ECCOAECCOArt&version=1.0&docLevel+FASCIMILE>, May 31, 2013, 6, 13, 131.
28. J. J. Rousseau, *A Complete Dictionary of Music* (1779), as translated by William Waring (AMS Press Inc. 1975), 2nd ed., 20, 24.
29. Thomas Busby, *Complete Dictionary of Music* (London, England, 1827), as transferred by University Microfilms International (Ann Arbor, Michigan, 1979), Section D, E, P.

CHAPTER 14

1. Peres Da Costa, *Off the Record*, 310.
2. Hugo Riemann, *Handbuch der Phrasierung, Max Hessels Illustrierte Handbücher, Band 16, Fünfte Auflage* (Berlin: Max Hesses Verlag, 1912).

BIBLIOGRAPHY

Akrill, J. L., ed. 1987. *The New Aristotle Reader*. Multiple translations. Princeton, NJ: Princeton University Press.

Apel, Willi, ed. 1969. *Harvard Dictionary of Music*. 2nd rev. and enlarged ed. Belknap Press of Harvard University Press.

Bach, C. P. E. 1949. *Essay on the True Art of Playing Keyboard Instruments*. (1753.) Translated and edited by William J. Mitchell. New York: W. W. Norton.

Bach, C. P. E. circa 1992. *Sechs Sonaten fürs Clavier mit veränderten Reprisen: 1760*. Présentation par Philippe Lescat. Fac-similé Jean-Marc Fuzeau Series. Fac-similé rélisée de l'exemplaire Rés. FM 127718 conservé à la Bibliothèque Municipale de LYON (France). Courlay, France: J. M. Fuzeau.

Badura-Skoda, Paul, ed. 1970. *Carl Czerny on the Proper Performance of All Beethoven's Works for the Piano "Reminiscences of Beethoven" and chapters II and III from Volume IV of the "Complete Theoretical and Practical Piano Forte School Op. 500."* New York: European American Music Distribution Corporation.

Baker, Nancy K., and Thomas Christensen, eds. 1995. *Aesthetics and the Art of Musical Composition in the German Enlightenment*. New York: Cambridge University Press.

Barth, George. 1992. *The Pianist as Orator: Beethoven and the Transformation of Keyboard Style*. Ithaca, NY: Cornell University Press.

BBC News. Accessed December 24, 2012. news.bbc.co.uk/2/hi/health/3858087.stm.

Beethoven, Ludwig van. *Beethoven's Letters with Explanatory Notes by Dr. A. C. Kalischer*. 1972. Translated by J. S. Shedlock. New York: Dover Publications.

Bichakjian, Bernard. 2002. *Language in a Darwinian Perspective*. Bochum Publications in Evolutionary Cultural Semiotics. New Series, Vol. 3. Frankfurt: Peter Lang Publishing.

Bie, Oscar. 1966. *A History of the Pianoforte and Pianoforte Players*. Translated by E. E. Kellett and E. W. Naylor. New York: Da Capo Press.

Bilson, Malcom. 1974. "Pianos in Mozart's Time (Revisited)." *Piano Quarterly*. 86: 29–31.

Bilson, Malcom. 1983. "Beethoven and the Piano." *Clavier*. Vol. 22, no. 8, 18–21.

Bilson, Malcolm, dir. 2011. *Performing the Score*. Performed by Malcolm Bilson and invited period expert artists. Ithaca, NY: Cornell Technologies Educational Center. DVD.

Bilson, Malcolm. 2013. Early Music Days, lectures and master classes, Fertöd, Hungary, June 22–29, 2013.

Bilson, Malcolm, and Bart van Oort. 2008. The Art of the Fortepiano. Lectures and master classes, Middelburg, The Netherlands, July 5–12, 2008.

BioTherapeutics, Education and Research Foundation. Accessed December 24, 2012. www.bterfoundation.org/node/19#HistoryofMaggotTherapy.

Booth, Dan, dir. 2005. *Knowing the Score.* Performed by Malcolm Bilson. Ithaca, NY: Cornell Technologies Educational Center. DVD.

Bostrom, Marvin John. 1960. *Keyboard Instruction Books of the Eighteenth Century.* Ann Arbor: University of Michigan.

Bozarth, George S. 2008. *Johannes Brahms and George Henschel: An Enduring Friendship.* Sterling Heights, MI: Harmonie Park Press.

Breitman, David. 2011. Westfield International Fortepiano Academy Lectures and master classes, Cornell University. Ithaca, NY, August 7–13, 2011.

Brown, Clive. 1999. *Classical and Romantic Performance Practice, 1750–1900.* New York: Oxford University Press.

Brown, Howard Mayer, and Stanley Sadie. 1989. *Performance Practice: Music after 1600.* The Norton/Grove Handbooks in Music. New York: W. W. Norton.

Busby, Thomas. 1827. *Complete Dictionary of Music.* (London: 1979.) Ann Arbor, Michigan: University Microfilms International.

Caplin, William E. 1998. *Classical Form: A Theory of Formal Function for the Instrumental Music of Haydn, Mozart, and Beethoven.* New York: Oxford University Press.

Christina Bratterud. Accessed January 23, 2013. http://www.fortepiano.no/page3/page12/page3.html.

Clementi, Muzio. 1974. *Introduction to the Art of Playing on the Piano Forte.* (London. 1801. Clementi, Banger, Hyde, Collard & David.) New York: Da Capo Press.

Cole, Michael. 1998. *The Pianoforte in the Classical Era.* Oxford: Clarendon Press.

Cooper, Barry, ed. 2007. *The Thirty-five Piano Sonatas by Beethoven.* 3 vols. London: Associated Board of the Royal Schools of Music.

Czerny, Carl. 2009. *Letters to a Young Lady on the Art of Playing the Pianoforte.* Boston: Oliver Ditson & Co. 1871. Translated by James Alexander Hamilton. Kessinger Publishing, LLC.

Dart, Thurston. 1963. *The Interpretation of Music.* Harper Colophon Series. New York: Harper & Row.

Deacon, Terrence W. 1997. *The Symbolic Species. The Co-Evolution of Language and the Brain.* New York: W. W. Norton.

Early Music. Accessed November 27, 2014. http://www.earlymusic.pl/chopinproject/interview_2.htm.

Ferguson, Howard. 1987. *Keyboard Interpretation from the 14th to the 19th Century.* New York: Oxford University Press.

Gjerdingen, Robert O. 2007. *Music in the Galant Style.* New York: Oxford University Press.

Grand Piano Solutions: Four Phases of Tone. Accessed June 15, 2011. http://grand-pianosolutions.com/four-phases-of-tone.html.

Haynes, Bruce. 2007. *The End of Early Music: A Period Performer's History of Music for the Twenty-First Century.* New York: Oxford University Press.

Heinemann, Ernst-Günter, ed. 2011. *Sechs Sonatinen by Clementi, Op. 36.* Munich: G. Henle Verlag.

Kirby, F. E. 1966. *A Short History of Keyboard Music.* The Free Press.

Kirnberger, Johann Philipp. 1982. *The Art of Strict Musical Composition.* (Berlin: 1771.) Translated by David Beach and Jurgen Thym. New Haven, CT and London: Yale University Press.

Komlós, Katalin. "After Mozart: The Viennese Piano Scene in the 1790's." Paper presented at Early Music Days, Esterhazy Castle, Fertőd, Hungary, June 28, 2013.

Litz, Robert J., and Jeremy Tusz, dirs. 2009. *The Virtual Haydn: Complete Works for Solo Keyboard.* Performed by Tom Beghin. Naxos. Blue-ray Audio and Blu-ray DVD.

Live Science. Accessed December 26, 2012. http://www.livescience.com/203-maggots-leeches-medicine.html.

Ludwig van Beethoven. Accessed March 1, 2011. http://www.lvbeethoven.com/VotreLVB/VosImages/TrudeliesLeonhardt_3Viennoise_En.gif.

Michael Cole. Accessed March 1, 2011. www.squarepianos.com/fortepiano.htm.

Mozart, Leopold. 1948. *A Treatise on the Fundamental Principles of Violin Playing.* (Augsburg, 1756, 1787.) Translated by Editha Knocker. London: Oxford University Press.

Neue Mozart Ausgabe. Accessed December 21, 2013. http://dme.mozarteum.at/DME/main/index.php?l=.

New Oxford American Dictionary. 2010. 3rd ed. New York: Oxford University Press.

Newman, William S. 1983. *The Sonata in the Classic Era.* 3rd ed. New York: W. W. Norton.

Newman, William S. 1988. *Beethoven on Beethoven: Playing His Piano Music His Way.* New York: W. W. Norton.

Parakilas, James, Edwin M. Good, Cynthia Adams Hoover, et. al. 2001. *Piano Roles: Three Hundred Years of Life with the Piano.* New Haven, CT: Yale University Press.

Pauly, Reinhard G. 1973. *Music in the Classic Period.* 2nd ed. Englewood Cliffs, NJ: Prentice Hall.

Peres da Costa, Neal. 2012. *Off the Record.* New York: Oxford University Press.

Quantz, Johann J. 1985. *On Playing the Flute.* 2nd ed. (1752.) Translated with notes and an introduction by Edward R. Reilly. New York: Schirmer Books.

Randel, Don Michael, ed. 2003. *The Harvard Dictionary of Music.* 4th ed. Belknap Press of Harvard University Press.

Reader's Digest Association. 1966. *The Reader's Digest Great Encyclopedic Dictionary Including Funk & Wagnalls Standard College Dictionary.* Pleasantville, NY: Reader's Digest Association.

Reilly, Edward R. 1971. *Quantz and His Versuch: Three Studies.* New York: American Musicological Society.

Riemann, Hugo. 1912. *Handbuch der Phrasierung: Max Hessels Illustrierte Handbücher.* Band 16, Fünfte Auflage. Berlin: Max Hesses Verlag.

Rosen, Charles. 1972. *The Classical Style: Haydn, Mozart, Beethoven.* New York: W. W. Norton.

Rosenblum, Sandra. 1988. *Performance Practices in Classic Piano Music.* Bloomington: Indiana University Press.

Rousseau, J. J. 1975. *A Complete Dictionary of Music.* (1779.) 2nd ed. Translated by William Waring. New York: AMS Press.

Sadie, Stanley, ed. 2004. *The New Grove Dictionary of Music and Musicians.* 29 volumes with index. 2nd ed. Oxford University Press.

Sadie, Stanley. 1984. *The New Grove Mozart.* New York: W. W. Norton.

Schonberg, Harold C. 1963. *The Great Pianists from Mozart to the Present.* New York: Simon and Schuster.

Skowroneck, Tilman. 2010. *Beethoven the Pianist.* New York: Cambridge University Press.

Sonnek, O. G., ed. 1956. *Beethoven: Impressions by His Contemporaries.* New York: Dover Publications.

Steblin, Rita. 1983. *A History of Key Characteristics in the Eighteenth and Early Nineteenth Centuries.* Ann Arbor, MI: UMI Research Press.

Steinway & Sons. Accessed November 27, 2013. http://www.steinway.com/pianos/steinway/grand/model-d/.

Stickney Piano Service. Accessed June 26, 2014. www.stickneypiano.com/diagrams.html.

Strunk, Oliver, ed.1965. *The Classic Era: Source Readings in Music History*. New York: W. W. Norton.

Taruskin, Richard, ed. 1995. *Text and Act: Essays on Music Performance*. New York: Oxford University Press.

Türk, Daniel Gottlob. 1982. *Klavierschule*. (1789.) Translated by Raymond H. Haggh. Lincoln, NE: University of Nebraska Press.

United States Mint. Accessed December 26, 2012. In God We Trust www.usmint.gov/about_the_mint/fun_facts/?action=fun_facts5.

Richards, Robert J. "The Linguistic Creation of Man: Charles Darwin, August Schleicher, Ernst Haeckel, and the Missing Link in Nineteenth-Century Evolutionary Theory." University of Chicago. Accessed June 26, 2014. home.uchicago.edu/rjr6/articles/Schleicher--final.doc.

UNL Libraries. May 31, 2013. *Brossard, Sébastien de. A musical dictionary; being a collection of terms and characters, as well ancient as modern; including the historical, theoretical, and practical parts of music: As also, an Explanation of some Parts of the Doctrine of the Antient; Interspersed With Remarks on their Method and Practice, and curious Observations on the Phoenomena of Sound Mathematically considered, As it's Relations and Proportions constitute Intervals, And those again Concords and Discords. The whole carefully abstracted from the best authors in Greek, Latin, Italian, French, and English Languages. By James Grassineau, Gent. London, 1740.* <http://0-find.galegroup.com.library.unl.edu/ecco/infomark.do?&source=gale&prodId=ECCO&userGroupName=linc74325&tabID=T001&docId=CW106300946&type=multipage&contentSet=ECCOArticles&version=1.0&docLevel+FASCIMILE>.

US History. Accessed December 26, 2012. www.ushistory.org/documents/pledge.htm.

van Oort, Bart. 2010. Fortepiano at Villa Bossi. Lectures and master classes, Associazione Musicale Villa Bossi, Italy, June 23–27, 2010.

van Oort, Bart. "To Speak or to Sing." 2007. Lecture, Norman and Jane Geske Lectureship in the History of the Arts series, Hixson-Lied College of Fine and Performing Arts, University of Nebraska–Lincoln, November 2007.

van Oort, Bart. 2011. Westfield International Fortepiano Academy. Lectures and master classes, Cornell University, Ithaca, NY, August 7–13, 2011.

Walden, Daniel K. S. 2010. "PianoFortePiano: Exploring the Use of Historical Keyboards as a Heuristic Guide to Performance on the Modern Piano." MTNA e-Journal 2(2): 10–21: http://mtnaejournal.org/publication/?i=61278.

Willis, Andrew. 1994. *Free Variation of Repeated Passages in Mozart's Keyboard Music*. DMA Dissertation. Ithaca, NY: Cornell University Press.

Zaslaw, Neal, ed. 1989. *The Classical Era from the 1740s to the End of the 18th century*. Englewood Cliffs, NJ: Prentice Hall.

Zuckerkandl, Victor. 1956. *Sound and Symbol: Music and the External World*. Translated by Willard R. Trask. Bollingen Series XLIV. New York: Pantheon Books.

PERMISSIONS

Gratitude to the authors and publishers who granted me permission to use their material in this book. The information gathered during my research was essential to understanding, interpreting, and presenting the resulting ideas set forth in *Discoveries*.

From *Essay on the True Art of Playing Keyboard Instruments,* by C. P. E. Bach, translated by William J. Mitchell. Copyright 1949 by W. W. Norton & Company, Inc., renewed © 1976 by Alice L. Mitchell. Used by permission of W. W. Norton & Company, Inc.

Reprinted by permission of the publisher from THE HARVARD DICTIONARY OF MUSIC, Fourth Edition, edited by Don Michael Randel, pp. 17, 31, 290-291, 341, 643, 846, 947, Cambridge, Mass.: The Belknap Press of Harvard University Press, Copyright © 1986, 2003 by the President and Fellows of Harvard College.

William S. Newman, *Beethoven on Beethoven: Playing His Piano Music His Way.* Copyright 1988, by William S. Newman. All rights reserved. Published simultaneously in Canada by Penguin Books Canada Ltd., 2801 John Street, Markham, Ontario L3R 1B4. Printed in the United States of America First Edition W. W. Norton & Company, Inc., 500 Fifth Avenue, New York, N.Y. 10110.

Daniel Gottlob Türk, *Klavierschule* (1789, Leipzig and Halle), as translated by Raymond H. Haggh (University of Nebraska Press, 1982), 337. Permission by the author's daughter, Barbara Haggh-Huglo.

© 2007 by The Associated Board of the Royal Schools of Music Reprinted from Beethoven: The 35 Piano Sonatas, edited by Barry Cooper Reproduced by kind permission. All rights reserved

INDEX

Note: Page numbers followed by *d, t,* and * denote diagrams, tables, and examples, respectively.